TERRITORIES

Hudson Bay

P9-BIM-692

Churchill

Churchill River

• Tadoule Lake

• Lynn Lake

Bird

River

Gillam

Nelson River

Thompson •

MANITOBA

Grass River
Provincial Park

Flin Flon •

Ponton

River

Cumberland
House

The Pas

Saskatchewan

Grand Rapids

Lake
Winnipeg

Telfort

Tisdale

Lake

Winnipegosis

Dauphin •

Riding Mountain
National Park

Narcisse

ONTARIO

Qu'Appelle River

Lake
Manitoba

Gimli

Fort
Alexander
Reserve

REGINA

Whitewood

Assiniboine

Selkirk

Delta Beach

WINNIPEG

Langbank

River

Brandon

Portage la Prairie

Shilo

Steinbach

Forget

Souris

Treesbank

Cardinal

St.-Pierre Jolys

Grunthal

Estevan

Glenboro

St. Malo

Big Muddy
Lake

Winkler

Red River

Souris R.

Scale:

KILOMETRES

0   50   100   150   200

0   50   100

MILES

Beyond Forget

Beyond Forget

Rediscovering the Prairies

Mark Abley

Douglas & McIntyre
Vancouver/Toronto

Douglas & McIntyre Ltd.
1615 Venables Street
Vancouver, British Columbia V5L 2H1

Published in the United States of America by
Sierra Club Books, San Francisco

Canadian Cataloguing in Publication Data

Abley, Mark, 1955–
   Beyond forget

   Includes index.
   ISBN 0-88894-520-5

   1. Prairie Provinces – Description and
travel – 1981–   *   2. Abley, Mark, 1955–
I. Title.
FC3234.2.A25 1986   917.12′043   C86-091464-X
F1060.92.A25 1986

Design by Verna Wong
Map by Angus Weller
Typeset by The Typeworks
Printed and bound in Canada by Gagné Printing Ltd.

For my father and mother

Acknowledgements

I wish to thank the Explorations Program of the Canada Council and its officer for the prairies, Richard Holden. Without an Explorations grant, I could never have travelled so far or so long. My thanks to Terrence Heath, Michael Ondaatje and Anne Szumigalski, whose letters of support enabled me to receive the grant.

I was given far more help, encouragement and good advice for this book than I deserved. Many of the helpers appear in these pages (sometimes under assumed names) and I thank them all warmly. My apologies if I have bruised their feelings. Among those westerners who are neither named nor described, I would like to thank Mazo and Ron Black, Donna Bland, Larry Bruder, Sharon Butala, Jyotsna and Larry Custead, Ed Dyck, Helen Findlay, Doris and Douglas Ford, Caroline Heath (who first suggested that I should write a book of travel), Anne Kitchen, Ron Marken, Ted McLachlan, Muriel McLeod, Ann Saville, Esther Warkov and Brenda Zeman.

In eastern Canada I received assistance and useful suggestions from Anne Collins, Gary and Jan Geddes, Adrian King-Edwards,

Megan McLeod, Donald Winkler and Nellie Reiss of the Lawrence Lande Foundation at McGill University. I was fortunate to write much of the book in the serene apartment of Claude Fortin. For answering specific inquiries, I am grateful to Louis Chagnon, Hugh Dempsey, George Kernaghan, Walter Kupsch and Barbara Montalbetti. And for supporting the typescript in the marketplace, my gratitude goes to Lee Davis Creal of the Lucinda Vardey Agency.

I want to give particular thanks to three people. To my wife Ann, my first reader, I owe a willingness to endure the months of absence, sweet support in the months of writing, and much practical advice. To a former teacher, Frank Roy, I owe my knowledge of the birds of the west and something of my love for its language. And to my friend Tom Murison, more than anyone else, I owe my belated recognition of the value and integrity of prairie culture. If each of them finds something in this book to treasure, I will be content.

The mistakes in *Beyond Forget* are my own. Its ideas, on the other hand, come from many sources. I have drawn inspiration from these works in particular: *Canadian Literary Landmarks* by John Robert Colombo; *The Canadian Prairies: A History* by Gerald Friesen; *Saskatchewan* by Edward McCourt; *Grass Roots* by Heather Robertson; *Visions of the New Jerusalem,* edited by Benjamin Smillie; *Travels in Saskatchewan and the Rocky Mountains* by the Earl of Southesk; and *Wolf Willow* by Wallace Stegner. In Chapter IX I am indebted to *Criddle-de-diddle-ensis* by Alma Criddle; in Chapter XV to *Wilderness Man* by Lovat Dickson, *Long Lance* by Donald Smith and *FPG: The European Years* by Douglas O. Spettigue. The italicized passages in the final chapter come from the Book of Joshua.

The man who finds his homeland sweet is still a tender beginner; he to whom every soil is as his native one is already strong; but he is perfect to whom the entire world is as a foreign land.

— Hugh of St. Victor

The only precious thing is a place to leave.

— Terrence Heath

· I ·

Home was a yellow bungalow with chokecherry trees and rhubarb bushes, and a round hole in the fence where a pair of wrens, every year, would try and fail to raise a brood under the interested gaze of our cats. Home was a hundred yards from the South Saskatchewan River: late at night I would turn and listen to the drifting gulls or the wail of an ambulance as it hurtled victims down the riverside road to the hospital nearby. Home was a haven against the drifts and the dust. It was a house lined with classical records and books about the Church of England, where two newspapers arrived in the mail each week: the London *Observer* and the Swindon *Football Pink*.

I read them both. Stretched out on the carpet beside *Encyclopaedia Britannica,* I could almost forget that home stood in Saskatoon, at the heart of the Canadian prairies, and that ten thousand miles of forest and ocean divided me from the Mermaid Theatre and the County Ground. It wasn't only England that captured my imagination: I devoured books set in the Adirondacks and the Apennines, Toronto and Shanghai. But somehow, I never read the west. I didn't grow up absurd, but I grew up lost. It never occurred to me

1

that the streets of my tranquil city might be as rich and complex as a foreign avenue. Even when I had begun to roam the world, I failed to make the connections in front of my eyes. A winding river parts Saskatoon, with a stone university rising from one bank and the business district nestled beyond the other; it took me a few trips to France before I saw that Paris shares the form.

At twenty, I left for good. I was confident, ambitious; I wanted to test myself against a larger world than the prairies seemed to offer. The desire is widespread, even ordinary. A local theatre company once created a revue entitled *If You're So Good, What Are You Doing in Saskatoon?* It was an immodest hit. The play touched a nerve of arrogance and fear, inferiority and pride, for the prairies are full of talented people not quite believing in themselves. Easy — too easy — to dismiss their world as a backwater. Many of its settlers saw the Canadian west as a breadbasket for the planet; others hoped it might provide a new Jerusalem. Nobody seems sure how to see it now.

Since 1975 I've lived in two eastern provinces and three English counties, and in all of them the west has nagged me like an unfinished dream. In a thatched village or a brick terrace, images of Saskatchewan would rise unbidden to my mind. One night in Montreal, I decided to complete the dream. I wanted to explore a province, a region, a pattern of culture that I had rejected with such ignorance and ease. I wanted to discover what my home had been a refuge *from*.

Which is one way to explain why I should be sitting on a patch of brown grass above the old river, a week after Easter, watching a gopher watching me. I had been away from the west long enough for anything to come as a novelty. His dark eyes, rimmed with white, skittered from the high silhouette of churches and apartments to the cabbage-size lumps of scruff ice floating downstream; and back to me. To a gopher, all kinds of shapes and movements mean danger. He climbed onto his thin hind legs to get a better view of his perils.

I began to read a salmon-pink leaflet that I had plucked off the sidewalk outside a forbidding office tower. The provincial government once decided to honour a couple of pioneers by the names of

2

Stone and Sturdy; accordingly, the Sturdy-Stone Building arose in concrete. Someone had been sprinkling pamphlets there, and by the waters of the South Saskatchewan I learned *Why Souls Go To Hell*: disobedience, abominations, whoremongers, murderers, the Devil and His Works, Hell Itself, and the all-embracing Night Season ("a time of ignorance and unbelief").

Damnation flourishes in the west. It even emerges in the bright, flamboyant mural that the prairie painter William Kurelek made for the chapel of St. Thomas More College a mile across the river. Kurelek's intellectual theme is the union of man with God. But visually, his mural renders the history and landscape that have generated prairie civilization. The focal point is a fierce Christ who stands, as the painter said, "dead centre between the wild West and the ordered West." Christ's head pokes over the smooth horizon along with a trio of grain elevators that loom like orange crosses above a fragile town. The shining crowd approaching him includes navvies from Ireland, cooks from China, nuns from Quebec, Hutterites, Jews, a Cockney with a flag, and an assortment of other human flotsam. High above their heads, at the painting's summit, white birds drift around the sun.

Yet Kurelek's Christ is enigmatic. His outstretched hand suggests a warning to this piebald multitude. On both sides of the mural the earth has cracked apart to expose a horde of arms, shaking their fists at the Lord. Blind to the faceless damned, a labourer and a capitalist turn away in derision. At the far left, a bolt of lightning impales an ebony cloud. The thunder is advancing on the crowd.

Kurelek could see that by the 1970s the fabric of prairie settlement was coming under deep stress, and in spite of his faith he seemed unsure that civilization would survive the coming storm. In the mural, even the college's patron, stern Sir Thomas More, may be suffering an attack of doubt. While his arm points up towards Christ, his eyes remain fixed on a family of gophers, oblivious in their sunlit grass to the human commotion overhead. "It's not for me to judge," Kurelek said, "who the lost really are."

When I stirred a cramped foot, the gopher dived for cover. I had a pretty good idea of how he felt. With a driver's licence only five months old and next to no experience at the wheel, I was proposing

3

to explore the west alone in a rented car. Buses and trains were too limiting, bicycles and feet too slow to consume these immense distances. I had no itinerary, only a desire to measure myself against the contours of three big provinces. Sometimes I too felt a longing to hide in a private darkness.

Lacking a convenient burrow, I wandered across the park to a pedestrian tunnel that undercuts the traffic of University Bridge. The city faded in a haze of grey. Inside the tunnel I read a message on the stone wall. Its black capital letters had been inscribed days or years ago by some precise hand:

OVER ITS WHITE BONES WHEN THEY ARE BARE
THE WIND SHALL BLOW FOR EVER MORE

I left the tunnel as an orange canoe slipped below the bridge, its boatmen labouring against the current, forcing the bow into the breeze a few yards from a passing ice-floe. In the distance, seven hunched figures were fishing at a weir. A crow lazed on the ice, gaining a free, slow ride in the direction of Hudson Bay.

The canoe shone against the dark water, a slim trap for the sun. A siren grew in my ears like a memory; startled, the crow took wing. Everything was on the move.

4

Poring over an atlas of Saskatchewan years ago, I discovered a place called Forget. I wanted to go at once, but the lack of a vehicle made the trip impossible. The town was evidently tiny, and I didn't feel inclined to ask at the Saskatoon Bus Depot for a return ticket to Forget. With a car (a sleek beige Dodge), I could fulfil the old wish.

A middle-aged man in a plaid shirt tapped on its window. I was sitting in a parking lot, fingering the highway map: a roundabout journey to Forget seemed apt.

"How many cylinders has she got?"

I didn't have a clue. I opened up the engine, and together we peered in.

"How many miles will she do to the gallon?"

I didn't know that one either. He walked away bemused.

I chose an easy route to begin, driving southeast along a wide road under a wider sky. On the green boards the names were British: Bladworth and Chamberlain, Aylesbury and Craik. I could have turned off across a sunken valley to Imperial, Holdfast or Penzance. As the last pockets of snow disappeared from the roadside ditches, a shy exhilaration settled over me. Departure is the mother of hope.

The land belies the Englishness of its names. Lacking the intricacy of footpaths and hedgerows, its fields stretch out for miles. Western horizons can seem both infinitely remote and close at hand, for the absence of haze in the atmosphere illuminates the sky with a sharp, dry light. Whether the light encourages reason or madness is another question. The highway swerved away from the invisible path of Tom Sukanen, a settler who gave up on Canada during the drought of the 1930s and used his scrap of land to build a ship. Its name was *Sontianen:* dung beetle. He probably aimed to sail it down the Saskatchewan River, through Hudson Bay, across the North Atlantic and up into the Baltic Sea: a Finnish Odysseus regaining his evergreen birthright after decades of exile. Living on

5

gophers and raw horseflesh, scrounging the district's wood and metal, Sukanen completed his task, after a fashion. But his starved animals were too weak to drag the vessel sixteen miles to the riverbank, and the voyage foundered before the ship touched water. His neighbours saw to it that Sukanen was committed to the provincial asylum. After years in captivity, he died.

"What we mourn for the dead," John Berger once wrote, "is the loss of their hopes."

South of Saskatoon the undulating land begins to smoothen out, and the aspen groves ("bluffs" in the local parlance) grow few and far between. The prairies, in short, become nearly as flat as outsiders expect. Most of western Canada is *not* flat and treeless; yet generations of travellers, looking glumly out through glass on the Trans-Canada Highway or the Winnipeg-Vancouver train, have assumed their southerly route to be typical of the entire region. They fail to grasp that the route was chosen precisely because of its flatness: road and track could be laid down fast without any sleight of engineering. In the 832 miles from Winnipeg to Calgary, the Canadian Pacific Railway needed to construct only two large bridges. Scenery was the last thing on the builders' minds.

Instead of skimming the ochre tableland of the Regina Plains, I turned east along some old roads to Fort Qu'Appelle. Local radio kept me company. Though a newscast told me nothing about peace or rumours of war, I learned that three new pesticides soon would poison the market and that a Harlem Globetrotter had been born again. I flicked the dial and bumped into "Chapel Time," broadcast twice a day from the town of Melville. It is not, as I first imagined, a moment for uplift or chastisement; it merely gives the tidings from a funeral parlour.

The road slumped into the Qu'Appelle, a wide valley that a melting glacier gouged out of the plain. The river in the valley's crease is incongruously narrow; grasses and stubble extend for a mile on each flank of the water before, abruptly, the land rises to the rim of the plain. That morning the valley had an air of wasted expectation, as though some promised call to greatness had failed to materialize. I switched off the engine and the radio. Far across the river, a meadowlark delivered his liquid, full-throated song. I was the only traffic. A cricket tried to fill the silence.

The car climbed back onto the plain, passing gullies red with dogwood bushes and a slough with forty-three wild swans. A disc jockey I heard on an empty road invited the world to a fund-raising dance to keep his town's stampede alive. A long herd of Herefords munched at me with interest. The Dodge and the day billowed onwards; I felt at ease with them both.

I turned south to cross the Trans-Canada by the town of Whitewood. Nothing visible in the present community—painted wood, some concrete, a splash of neon—hints at its remarkable past, when the rolling, fertile bushland of the region, crowded with animals to shoot, was a haunt of European gentry. The brass band of Whitewood once contained four French counts. Like most settlers, they ran into financial trouble; unlike most settlers, they scraped together the funds to return home.

Southeast of Whitewood, a Devonian gentleman named Edward Pierce tried to recreate bucolic England in a village he christened Cannington Manor. Its residents farmed, made cheese and milled; their Snowdrop Flour won the grand prize of a competition held at the Chicago World's Fair in 1893. They also engaged in steeplechases, cricket matches and performances of Shakespeare. It was a touching, absurd dream; but the prairies abjured its rough magic. After Pierce's death, Cannington Manor fell on hard times. The railway shunned the village, and it died. Pierce had held the place together by a force of will that was equalled only by his snobbery. When a girl from Manitoba was rash enough to call herself Canadian, Pierce asked her, "If a man was born in a stable, would he be a horse?"

In a local bank I met suspicion.

"What does that mean?"

The teller was pointing to the red inscription on the cover of my bankbook: *compte d'épargne à intérêt quotidien.*

"It means 'daily interest savings.' I live in Montreal."

"Oh."

I expected her to welcome me to Saskatchewan. She didn't.

·III·

Ten miles south of Whitewood I passed an abandoned frame house, guarded by a shelterbelt of yellow poplars. Such images are common in Saskatchewan, where the landscape reiterates a history of work and loss. In some parts of the prairies, just as in the west of Ireland, crumbling houses outnumber the flourishing homes. The growth in the size of properties—and the indebtedness of farmers—has accompanied a piecemeal emptying of the countryside. Throughout the Canadian west, the family farm is a declining species.

To call this process a social failure is, perhaps, to romanticize a rural way of life that can be cruel and exhausting. No farmer can reject solitude, labour and risk. By now the grandchildren of the men and women who broke the land and built the little towns are often ensconced in the suburbs of Regina or Vancouver, and to the great majority of them these peeling, leaning houses are nothing more than relics of the hard passage to a safe prosperity. But depopulation gives the country a sombre, beaten look. It also lays the towns and villages under siege. If the pioneers could have glimpsed the standard of comfort that most of their descendants enjoy, no doubt they would have been delighted. Had they also seen the fate of their homes, land and communities, many would have felt dismay.

On the prairies, history is rarely incorporated into the life of the present. Instead, it lies at an angle across it. All you have to do to enter the past is to step out of your car, scramble under a barbed-wire fence, and disturb the sleep of insects in an empty building.

The walls of the wooden house had been white; the window frames, a dark green. I pushed its back door open and strolled into a silent, anonymous history. Every room bore evidence of a defunct care. Floral wallpaper still drooped above the mattresses in the bedrooms, and glass remained intact in most of the windows. The kitchen held a stove and an Empire bread oven, in addition to a wringer washer. I opened a dusty trunk in the living room to find the novels of "Mrs. Humphry Ward" and a certain *Heralds of*

8

Empire, published in Toronto in 1913 and dedicated "to the New World Nobility." A long sofa by the trunk still had some promise in its cushions. In the loft, an iron bedstead flanked a pile of magazines: *True Confessions, Our Little Messenger,* a *Maclean's* from 1958. In those days it cost fifteen cents.

The afternoon had clouded over. As I walked past a rusted clutter of machinery and a family of tottering sheds, a cool drizzle began to fall. A few hundred yards away, across a field of rich, deserted earth, stood a grove of pine trees, unusual in this district. I picked my way along the border of the field to investigate.

The pines concealed a garden of graves and a small church made of a pliable, brindled stone. Its anonymous builder was talented at masonry: his square tower looked strong enough to last a millennium. The impression of prairie Romanesque was spoilt only slightly by a thin wooden door that resembled the backside of a barber's shop. I thought the door would be locked. I was wrong.

But the church too seemed frozen in another time. It smelled of disuse. I walked around it shivering, half-expecting to find a black-and-white photograph of a king, and wondering why the building stood a mile from the closest village. A gesture of faith, or a blunder? Unused for months or decades, a pot-bellied Coleman stove overshadowed the stone font. White light, streaming in through the plain windows, brightened the six pews. Under the back pew a framed, signed oil painting of the church was lying face down on the floor.

I picked it up and looked for somewhere to hang it. On the north wall, a charter from May 1939 declared that the parish of St. Paul's, Langbank, Saskatchewan, housed a chapter of the Anglican Young People's Association. My eyebrows rose: difficult enough to imagine a bevy of young people here, let alone Anglican ones. How many of them had died in Normandy or Sicily, the New World's nobility enriching the Old World's soil?

The church's herald of joy had been a harmonium. It boasted eleven stops: the Dulciana, the Vox Humana, the Vox Angelica . . . A black spider was drowsing on the title page of the hymnal: *The Book of Common Praise,* an edition of 1909. A high board listed the hymns from the last service, whenever that was. Out of curiosity

9

I leafed through the *Common Praise,* and saw that the congregation had sung:

> The Church has waited long
>   Her coming Lord to see;
> And still in loneliness she waits,
>   A friendless stranger she.
>   Age after age has gone,
>   Sun after sun has set,
> And still in weeds of widowhood,
>   She weeps a mourner yet.

As I left, I tugged the rope in the porch. Nothing. I pulled harder; and a thin, rheumatic squeal rang dutifully, misleadingly, out beyond the graves, the highway and the pines to fade among the empty fields.

·IV·

It had no doctor's office, no grocery, no gas station. It had, in fact, no shops of any kind, for the hardware store facing the railway was boarded up long ago. It retained a pale brick church with a metal spire, but the church was locked; and the tall building opposite, where a colony of nuns used to reside, lay tilted open to the elements, lacking windows and part of the roof. I drove up and down six gravel roads, and I'd seen it all. The only thing left to do was to park on the widest street, climb

10

onto a high cement sidewalk, and stroll into the town's last business: the beverage room of the Forget Hotel.

It was empty, of course. Or rather: amid the pinball machines, the pool table and the juke boxes, no human being was in evidence. I sat down and waited. Like most Saskatchewan pubs, the room was windowless. Above the bar hung thirty-three dollar bills, each of them signed by a different hand. I counted the money twice, and I stared at a woven picture on the wall, which showed dogs standing on their hind legs and playing a game of pool. Their tongues were hanging out. The bulldog was preparing to shoot.

"What'll you have?"

I jumped a few inches off the black chair. The bartender, a boy of about nineteen, had come up behind me without a sound, padding across the carpet in sneakers. His fluffy brown hair surmounted an attempt at a fluffy moustache.

"A Boh, please."

I wanted to see if Bohemian, a Saskatchewan lager, tasted as good in Forget as in memory. It was the beer I had ordered when I first entered a bar at fifteen, nervous in spite of a borrowed driver's licence. Only when we had left the bar and I felt totally relaxed did I discover that the owner of the licence was also underage.

"Do you live in Forget all year round?" I asked.

He made a small grimace.

"No, I live in Regina. It's my sister and brother-in-law that own this hotel. She's gone to the store up in Stoughton, and I'm just keeping the bar open till she gets back . . ."

The beer was tedious and gaseous: another triumph for memory.

". . . And by the way, it's not For-*get*. It's *Four*-jay."

"Sorry, I didn't realize." I felt vaguely disappointed.

"It's okay," he said. "There's a lot of jokes about this place. As you can imagine."

Forget, I discovered, draws its name from Amédée Emmanuel Forget, a French-Canadian lawyer who acted as the first lieutenant-governor of Saskatchewan. The area contains a few other communities whose names are French; but in each case, local tongues smudge the meaning. Dumas has become *Doom us,* Roche Percée is known as

11

Rush Percy, and the coal-mining village of Bienfait suffers as *Bean fate.* Forget alone maintains a semblance of the first pronunciation.

"So how many people live here, anyway?"

"Oh, about a hundred, I suppose. Maybe less."

The province's official guidebook gives the total as eighty-eight. Three years ago the population was ninety-one.

"But it's growing," the bartender added defensively. "Like, a few of the old farmers have moved into town. And there's a guy who's talking about opening up a store."

I was still the only customer. "Most of the time," he confided, "I drive a milk truck for Palm Dairies."

Sentiment defeated reason: I ordered another Boh.

"What are you doing here?" the bartender inquired. "If you don't mind my asking." He had wanted to fire the question ever since he saw me, but politeness forbade it during the first beer.

"Travelling around," I said. "I'd like to visit different parts of the west. Different kinds of towns and landscapes. I want to find out what the prairies really look like."

"Well, there's not a hell of a lot to see in Forget."

Another boy, also with a slight moustache and a cheery manner, had come in while we talked. "You ought to meet my Aunt Florentine," he said. "Well, she's not exactly my aunt. She can tell you everything about this town. I mean, she's been here forever."

"Does she live nearby?"

It was a very stupid question. Everything in Forget is nearby. I followed the boy across the street and up to a little house with cracked white paint. He flung the side door open—"Auntie, it's me, Daniel!"—and without pausing led the way into a long kitchen where an old man and an older woman were sitting at the table.

"This is Mark," he announced. "I met him just now in, well, you know where I met him, Auntie." The pair rose slowly. Daniel turned to me. "This is my Aunt Florentine and Hubert, her son. She doesn't speak very good English, I'm afraid."

The beers had loosened my tongue; they might even have improved my accent.

"Mais j'habite à Montréal, je peux parler français si c'est mieux . . ."

Florentine thanked me. Daniel looked bewildered.

12

"Hey, what's going on? I can't speak any of that. Look, if you're going to jabber away in French, I'll get back to the bar."

He carried out his threat, calling out *"Au revoir!"* as the door banged. A faint voice continued from outside: "That's the only word I can remember . . ."

"None of the young ones speak French," Florentine said gently. "They don't see any reason." She took hold of a metal walking-frame and hobbled to an old gas stove where potatoes were browning over a low flame. White bread, thinly sliced and buttered, waited on the table, along with a couple of fried eggs. Arthritis had hunched the woman so deeply that when she walked, her face was parallel to the floor.

"You come from Montreal, eh?" Hubert, unshaven in a white undershirt, had been inspecting me in silence. The years had dislodged none of his wiry grey hair, but most of his teeth.

"I live there now," I said. "Is that where you're from, too?"

"*Oh* no," Hubert said. A glance passed between them as Florentine shuffled back to the table, frying pan in hand. "My mother grew up in Lorraine. You know where that is? I went there once . . ." When his chapped voice had trailed away, I could hear a radio playing old dance music in another room. ". . . But then I came back. I've got a farm about a mile out of town."

"And you want to know something about Forget?" Florentine was not unfriendly, merely puzzled.

"Sure," I answered, trying not to look at their meagre dinner cooling before my eyes.

"I arrived here as a girl," she said in a high, translucent voice, "and the whole village spoke French. When the church was burnt by lightning after the war—"

"The first war," Hubert added.

"After the first war, the men rebuilt it brick by brick. To the very same design! You know the spire is more than twenty-five metres high?"

"No," I said.

"But you must have seen the shrine behind the church—Our Lady of LaSalette. Every year the sisters used to teach a hundred children. Some years, more."

13

"And the children now?"

"Oh, they go in buses to other towns."

She spoke without rancour or resentment, her blue eyes still bright in her bowed white head as though she continued to believe, against the evidence, that God had a purpose for Forget. To me the incorrect, English meaning appeared more and more precise.

Had I stayed longer, the eggs would have become inedible. Hubert saw me out with relief.

"Come back," he said, "anytime . . ."

In the evening twilight, two cars were parked on the main street. It looked broad enough to be an eight-lane highway. A false wooden front tried and failed to give the hotel an illusion of height. I drove back to the highway on an unlit gravel road, stopping only to decipher the sign propped up against a wire fence far beyond the last house:

THE VILLAGE OF

FORGET

VACATION TRAIL 1

·V·

In the night I woke to a steady rain and random thunder. Sheets of lightning stretched away to the wooded plateau known, with poetic licence, as Moose Mountain. Yet by breakfast-time it was hard to tell that any rain had fallen. The fierce wind that ushered in the sun forced me to concentrate at the wheel, even as I headed south from Stoughton along a road that fed its two horizons without a single bend. A horde of tumbleweeds cartwheeled over the highway like scampering porcupines; a wire fence held dozens in its grip.

Here the sky seems even broader than it does near Saskatoon. The land's dryness encourages farmers to raise cattle as well as grain. On this seemingly endless sentence of earth, the cows' bodies act as punctuation: brown for the Herefords, black for the Aberdeen Angus, and white for the growing number of massive Charolais. To run a flock of sheep would be to risk both insolvency and contempt.

I could have crossed the American border in less than an hour; the car radio was pulling in Montana loud and clear. But the strongest signal came from CKSL, Saskatchewan's "Country Giant." Every few minutes its disc jockey rehearsed the details of a new competition. To be eligible, a listener had to obtain a CKSL sticker, shaped like a heart, and glue it to his car. The prizes? A car stereo, a side of beef and a weekend for two in North Dakota.

Almost against my will, I was acquiring a relish for country and western. In these huge spaces, where the nervous pulsations of rock sound as ridiculous as a Rossini opera, country music fits. Most of its songs accommodate a flush vein of narrative; they tell familiar tales; they keep an oral tradition alive. The music has little to do with the grand passions, the tropical excitements of life. It attends instead to adult themes of loss, disappointment and sheer daily fatigue. While the writers of country lyrics are guilty of constant sentimentality, they rarely whip up a frenzy of sterile excitement. If rock music is a rampant illusion, country is a distorted truth. Its awareness of hard work enables it to soften a lot of pain.

Or so I was thinking to myself north of the low suburbs of Estevan, a dreary town that calls itself a city, as the deep blue of the sky mingled gradually with brown. I had been wearing sunglasses against the glare but now, as the visibility shortened from miles to yards, I resorted to the Dodge's headlights. A cloud of topsoil swirled around me for a few seconds and drifted eastward, gathering land as it went. The world brightened; my attention expanded again from the highway, and I caught a jingle for pizza on the radio. Then the dark fog arrived with a vengeance.

At one moment, a calm landscape of pastures, sprawling fields

15

and faraway houses unfolded before me. The next, it vanished in a brownout. Dust storms, like rivers of lava, disturb the mind; they subvert what we assume to be the natural order of the elements. A few feet ahead of me, the car's lights died in a turmoil that extinguished the sun. I grounded the brakes and waited for the road to return.

Dust storms like this were common in the 1930s. A drought, an economic depression, a plague of wheat rust, an infestation of grasshoppers that surged to mythic proportions (the insects would even munch the sweaty handles of pitchforks—or so the story goes): farmers endured them all. Conditions in the grain belt of Saskatchewan grew so extreme that after the harvest failed in 1937, two in three farmers were destitute. The experience remains central to the psychology of the prairie west; more than the intermittent affluence of postwar decades, it tints a westerner's outlook on life. He continues to live in Next Year Country, where he smokes a pack of hope a day.

In southern Saskatchewan, the 1980s too have proved hard. Rainfall, snowfall and grain prices shrink; erosion steals the topsoil; grasshoppers and cutworms swarm. Surrounded by a brown cloud, I had the grim suspicion that I was inching through the future. Even in a closed car, protected from the rasp of dirt against my skin, the bruising whistle of the wind and the choking taste of solid air, I felt helpless in the storm's blind eye.

The weather cleared enough for me to slink through Estevan and turn eastward, keeping a few miles above the 49th Parallel. Around Bienfait and Roche Percée, gusts of coal dust joined the soil in the sky. Jutting out of the raw canyons of the Souris River, the village of Roche Percée wears a sour, mean face. I passed a short alley that led up from the road to a house, without a tree in sight. The signpost read: Elm Drive.

"Did you know this is where the Bronfmans got started?"

"Really?" I said.

"They may be millionaires now," Jenny said, shaking her grey head, "but when they first came over from Europe they were Saskatchewan farmers."

The point was not lost on me but, in case I had overlooked it, Frank took up the same idea: "There's more money to be made from rum-running across the border than there ever was from growing wheat round here." His smile gave him a quizzical expression: while the left eyebrow and the left side of his mouth squeezed up, the right portion of his face stayed motionless.

I was staying on their farm, a mixture of wheat, barley and cattle, modest by the standards of Saskatchewan: only seven quarters of land in active use, little more than eleven hundred acres. The dining room faced the falling sun. When Jenny had carried in a heavy bowl of corn, Frank bowed his face to his plate in order to say grace. The table was already loaded with food before the corn arrived.

"Of course," I suggested, "you couldn't get any crop insurance back around the turn of the century."

It was not the right remark. Frank looked embarrassed. Jenny fixed me with a kindly glare.

"Last year," she began, "he didn't take out any insurance. Even on a small farm like this, it would have cost $900. And then the rains didn't come. His entire field of barley was on the point of withering up. Finally he got a neighbour to come and take it off, so he could buy it cheap as a hay crop. And then"—Frank was nodding rueful agreement—"wouldn't you know it, about a week later the rain just poured down. Well, if he'd gone and bought some crop insurance, he'd have probably kept that barley and made some profit in the end."

"I guess you'll be taking out a policy this year," I said.

Frank beamed at us both. "Haven't made my mind up yet!"

"It's hard to gamble on the weather," I said neutrally.

Frank said, "That's the definition of farming." Jenny had lost her tongue.

He passed me a jug of ice water: "Don't worry, it's not from the tap." The tap water arrives from a well that receives, every spring, poisonous chemicals in the runoff. Weeks after the thaw, the water smells of Javex bleach.

"Were the Bronfmans from down at Hirsch, by any chance?"

"No," Jenny said, "they lived up Wapella-way. So did you come through Hirsch this afternoon?"

"What's left of it," I said.

It lies a few yards off the highway where the highway, unexpectedly, curves: two streets, five or six stricken houses, a boarded-up school and a locked general store with *Read Star Weekly* on the door. But also: a parked school bus, a truck pulling away and a few homes that might still be inhabited. I rang a couple of doorbells, to no response. Even if Hirsch is not quite a ghost town, it makes Forget seem a metropolis by comparison.

For half a century this frazzled village was a farming colony. It was founded in 1892 so that refugees from the Russian pogroms could remake themselves into food growers of the British Empire. Their bones are encamped a mile down the highway, in the Hirsch Community Jewish Cemetery. The newest resident, Ida Muscovitch, joined her son and husband there in 1961. A plaque forbids any burials in the future. The fifty-odd graves cluster into a corner of the fenced prairie, leaving acres open to the grass, the wind and a handful of hardy trees. Most of the inscriptions are in Hebrew, though a name and a consoling phrase often appear in English too.

The condition of the tombs defies consolation. Ground subsidence, bitter weather and a lack of maintenance have cracked some graves wide open. I saw one that lay buckled under its weight of sky as though the clouds were made of steel. Between assorted members of the Hoffer family, a red-capped lark sparrow flitted with timid curiosity. Even stone will crumble, in the end, to dust.

Hirsch was by no means the only attempt to build Jewish communities in the rural west. The village is named for a Bavarian aristocrat, Baron Maurice de Hirsch, the patron of a handsome charity that resettled thousands of eastern Europe's Jews. About fifteen settlements sprang up across the prairies despite the hostility of many Canadians, including the country's first prime minister; Sir John A. Macdonald predicted that Jewish immigration would establish "a missing link . . . between Canada and Sidonia." He was alluding, no doubt, to Ezekiel 28: "Son of man, set thy face against Zidon, and prophesy against it. . . . For I will send into her pestilence, and blood into her streets."

Many of the Jewish farms thrived, for a while. But the urban tradition, its memory, its opportunities proved too strong. The villages dwindled, leaving Hirsch as a graveyard for the baron's ideal, a dream that had also haunted Kafka in the thin streets of Prague: that a life of healthy labour on the land would regenerate his people. Some Jewish writers of distinction grew up in southern Saskatchewan. None of them lives there now.

Both Jenny and Frank were born within a mile of their red and white house. I tramped through the fields at dusk to digest the beef, the many vegetables, the bread, the salad, the pickles, the ice cream and the tea. Their farm is a haphazard museum of machinery rusting gently back to the soil; every path bypasses a cultivator, a binder or a ruined car. By the banks of a quivering creek, I almost stepped on the fly-eaten body of a calf. The head was still intact. The stomach and the back were not.

Night fell and the stars streamed out. Despite the chill in the air, a company of frogs was burping behind the poplars. As I picked my way back to the farmhouse, a shimmer of Northern Lights shone palely overhead: ribbons dangling across the sky from a wide white collar in the north.

Jenny was watching "Dallas" in the living room. Whenever the Ewing family appears on TV, Zimbabwe is said to grind to a halt: Belgrade follows suit for "Dynasty." I decided to join the rest of mankind. In Saskatchewan the advertisements that fracture and sustain these fantasies of Texan royalty depict herbicides and farm equipment. A love affair broke up, another one began, a lovely woman stooped to drunken folly: Jenny observed it all impassively. I glanced into her kitchen and noticed, on top of the refrigerator, a block of wood inscribed with a quotation from Ring Lardner: "The years skip along easily, it's the days that are tough."

·VII·

It was raining when an earlier traveller camped north of the land that Frank and Jenny farm today. James Carnegie, the ninth Earl of Southesk, came to the west in 1859 for his own pleasure, and his pleasure was the slaughter of buffalo, antelope, bighorn sheep, mountain goats, grouse, geese, passenger pigeons, skunks and a variety of other "game." He took the heads of the finest specimens back to his Scottish castle, where he wrote *The Origins of Pictish Symbolism*. When Southesk wasn't poisoning the west with lead, he spent much of his time making detailed notes on Shakespeare. "Why is it," he inquired in a wilderness which would become Saskatchewan, "that one is inclined to have more sympathy for Imogen than for Desdemona?" He answered his own question: "Say what you will, a union between a white woman and a black man is revolting."

Southesk's twin impulses to contemplate and eradicate the wonders of nature collide in his stylish book *Saskatchewan and the Rocky Mountains*. A migration of ducks down the Saskatchewan River inspired him by its "poetic charm." On the other hand, "travellers view things practically"; so he and his men hauled out the guns, "and immense blazing at the ducks went on." The west that Southesk saw, apart from some riverside farms in what is now southeastern Manitoba, was an extravagant domain of forests, grasslands and mountains, interrupted by a handful of fur-trading

20

forts. The earl was prepared to suffer for his sport, and by his own account he endured hardship with a stoic grace. On a wet afternoon near the Assiniboine River, he perused *Two Gentlemen of Verona* and observed: "Long wearisome riding, indifferent monotonous eating, no sport to speak of, hard bed upon the ground, hot sun, wet, no companion of my own class; nevertheless I am happier than I have been for years."

Instead of a rifle I had only a pair of eyes, but I too was travelling for my solitary pleasure. I too was hunting for impressions. On a mild Sunday morning Saskatchewan slipped into Manitoba past a quintet of wild turkeys—a species that seems to have escaped Southesk's aristocratic massacres. Their big ungainly bodies were standing just inside a fence; their blue heads were peering at the highway. A combination of chocolate, azure and the scarlet of their wattled throats made the birds look too exotic, too gaudy for the prairies. They suffer a reputation for foolishness, fly with difficulty and fare poorly in harsh winters; yet the wildlife managers have introduced flocks into southeastern Saskatchewan. I noticed, as I restarted the car, that the fence wire bore a label: NO HUNTING. Perhaps the birds are brighter than we think.

The traffic was sparse on roads flat and straight enough for a child to drive along them; many do. I found myself half-listening to a Ukrainian program from Swan River, a couple of hundred miles to the north. The show interspersed hymns with fervent preaching. Once, amid a rolling flood of Slavic consonants, I caught the words "rock and roll." The tones of invoking, imploring and imprecating are the same in every Western language. I ate an apple in a sun-dappled picnic site where a host of righteous blackbirds condemned me from a gnarled maple grove.

At noon I reached the little town of Souris. It amazed me: I didn't know that the late twentieth century allowed such places to exist. Nuclear families were taking strolls together. A father washed his Pontiac in a driveway while his boy rode a bicycle up and down the street under a spaniel's loving gaze. The town became a blur of robins, shade trees and tall frame houses with covered porches. I passed an intersection where three corners were occupied by churches. On the main street the foremost sign—an old maroon affair, nothing garish or neon—advertised The Chocolate Shop Cafe. Every Sunday, needless to say, it was closed. The only graffiti in the place was a word that some daring soul had scribbled beside the suspension bridge:

HI.

A certain Squire Sowden had the bridge made in 1904 for his own convenience, to connect the town's business quarter with his property across the Souris River, 582 feet away. Soon it became the local symbol, proof of a unique identity. I stepped gingerly across: the planks are only a yard wide, and they sag towards the rushing water. At a quick march, the sway produces a mild nausea akin to seasickness. My feet bounced on dry land.

A girl waved at me for no reason as I left Souris. It had, I felt, been a charming visit to the 1950s. I was wondering if the town had been stuffed.

Only later did I discover that Souris was the main setting for a novel that became a cause célèbre in 1960: *A Candle to Light the Sun*. Patricia Blondal called the place Mouse Bluffs, and her portrait aroused discomfort: "cleanliness was not next to godliness in Mouse Bluffs; cleanliness was equated with godliness. The town accepted almost any strange behaviour of a clean woman, a fastidious house-keeper." The novel's strange behaviour includes illegitimacy, epilepsy, suicide, promiscuity, anti-Semitism and other distasteful goings-on from which the nation preferred to avert its eyes. *Maclean's* inquired of Souris: "Is it Canada's *Peyton Place?*" The author had tarnished the sentimental ideal of small-town virtue. Her hero, David Newman, confesses that "we have all the sins and depravities in Mouse Bluffs, only I think we're more honest about them." Blondal had nothing to lose by her honesty; the novel was accepted a month before she died of cancer. She was thirty-three years old.

I drove on from Souris through the miles of farmland with a growling stomach. When I reached the town of Glenboro I stopped to order a cheap "downhome special"—corned-beef hash with vegetables, poached eggs, coffee and toast—in the Camel Inn.

There are no camels in Glenboro; there have never been camels in Glenboro. But nine miles to the north lie the shifting, shrinking sand dunes of the Bald Head Hills. The hills are the relic of a fan-shaped delta that once joined the Assiniboine River to a prehistoric lake. They attract an amphibian and two kinds of reptile that live nowhere else in Manitoba. They also attract visitors. The town of Carberry, across the dunes, has a good claim to serve the tourists; Carberry contains the headquarters of the Spruce Woods Provincial Park, and it boasts the homestead of Ernest Thompson Seton, whose animal tales first drew attention to the sand hills. But Glenboro, not Carberry, has grasped the bountiful potential of what its promotional brochure calls (wrongly) a "real desert." And in a bid to seal its priority, Glenboro erected a statue of a camel where a pair of highways skirt the town.

The camel, whose name is Sara, is a fibreglass beast. She stands more than twenty feet high on a platform in an empty field. Sara sports a coat of tawny paint and lavish black eye shadow. Grey lipstick adorns her thick protruding mouth. A fluffy mane points down towards her knobbly knees. She gazes heavenward, as well she might.

Glenboro could have commissioned a statue of an elk. A local woodcarver suggested the idea; elk are common in the park. Not every town can have its own suspension bridge, and an elk would have made a fine, distinctive symbol. But the Chamber of Commerce had other plans.

"Who ever heard of an elk running around in the desert?"

So the businessmen paid an outsider to fabricate a camel. The man's credentials were immaculate; he had already built a giant turtle, which wobbles on its hind legs at Turtle Mountain. His camel proved to be so unforgettably ugly that the Chamber of Commerce was delighted.

I was still eating my toast when the waitress in the Camel Inn began to prowl around the table. Soon she was brandishing the bill. She said hopefully, "That'll be all?"

Indifferent monotonous eating, long wearisome driving, no sport to speak of, no companion; nevertheless I was happy.

·VIII·

The Bald Head Hills have changed their name. The provincial authorities felt that the old phrase was too undignified, and nowadays the sands bear the title "Spirit Hills." Gentility is alive and well in southern Manitoba. I wanted to explore more of the fragile dunes than casual visitors are allowed to see. On the first hot morning of the year I arranged to meet a warden at a shop outside the park.

The Spruceland Groceteria was empty. But a middle-aged man was working with a shovel fifty yards behind the store. From a distance he looked fluorescent: a pink shirt below a yellow baseball cap; red rubber boots under black swimming trunks. Though it seemed unlikely he was a warden, I approached.

"Wilf Brock? Nope, the only Wilfred I know comes from down in Belmont. He works at the body shop in Glenboro. Is that the guy you're looking for?"

It was not.

"Nobody's ever called me by the name of Wilf."

He beamed at the idea.

"Far as I know!"

His large abdomen was quivering over the trunks like a jellyfish eluding a predator.

"I've had this place near on fifteen years. And I've never heard of Wilf Brock!"

I retreated in disarray and drove back to the park's entrance. A sign informed the empty parking lot: CAUTION. FORMER MILITARY AREA. ACCESS COURTESY DEPARTMENT OF NATIONAL DEFENCE. . . . THIS AREA MAY CONTAIN UNEXPLODED PROJECTILES. DO NOT HANDLE ANY STRANGE OBJECTS. STAY ON MARKED TRAILS ONLY.

The trails proved to be sandy ruts that slithered through gently rising meadows and bare deciduous woods. The meadows were spattered with prairie crocuses, the first wildflowers of the year: purple when the young flowers push up from the earth, whitish-mauve

24

once the petals are blown. Last year's shrivelled berries clung to the juniper shrubs. The sand began to insinuate itself into my shoes.

This landscape is acting out a drama that suggests, in allegorical miniature, a history of white settlement across the west. The play features sand dunes in the leading role of wilderness; straggling plants like stemgrass and ground cedar co-star as pioneers; forests make a late appearance, a cameo of towns and cities. For I was climbing through a region where the dunes had reigned unchallenged. Gradually the pioneers took hold, refusing to accept defeat. Their struggles made possible the invasion of more and more followers, from crocuses up to the silver birches and skyscraping conifers. The dunes retreated to high fastnesses which no plant, as yet, has colonized. But a glance downward shows their eerie, hidden power. Even these proud spruce trees, sticky with the damp gum of spring, are growing out of sand.

I clambered up a final ridge, kicked off my shoes and socks, and ran across the dunes. A winter-long cramp seemed to have fled my muscles. The sand was packed enough, and the wind low enough, to prevent any grains from whirling into my face. I left the marked trails far behind.

The dunes are a quirk of geography: ten square miles that persist in spite of rainfall and snowfall too heavy for a true desert. Wildlife abounds. Lying on my back in a warm hollow, lapping up the sun, I opened my eyes to find a Swainson's hawk flapping slowly over the rim of sand. I saw his russet breast and cloud-white belly before, catching sight of me, he changed course abruptly. Maybe I did the hawk a favour, for he turned towards the dune where a flock of juncos, ten minutes earlier, had been skittering and preening.

I clambered, slid and trudged across the sand, searching for nothing in particular. What I found was a strange, silent oasis of conifers nestling at the base of a dune. A big red butterfly had folded its wings on a trunk. The wind died among the needles; the world held its breath. Under the filtered light, the sand cooled my toes. It was a spring day of any year in the last eight thousand, and I was an intruding animal: a fly in the sun's green web.

Climbing back, I thought I was following my original route. But the breeze had smothered my prints. The new path brought me to a

25

stubby hill where a cob of grey metal glinted in a bed of sand. "Litterbugs," I thought, and then remembered.

The hills stop short at the Assiniboine River, curling down from eastern Saskatchewan to its merger, or extinction, in Winnipeg. A long cold drink had refreshed me; on impulse I decided to cross and recross the Assiniboine on the last two ferries that still ply the waters of southern Manitoba. Boats appeal to me, especially on the prairies. All I had to do was leave the highway below the village of Stockton, traverse the river, and take an unmarked road along the far bank to reach the Treesbank ferry. I forgot a prairie adage: never trust an unmarked road.

The Stockton boat lay beyond a brown expanse of grain fields and pastureland. Every mile or two I passed a farmer who, convinced that winter had beaten a final retreat, was ploughing the cold soil. A few minutes after I left the highway, handmade signs marked FERRY began to punctuate the fences. They led me over dusty gravel and into a wooded valley that cut a rough incision across the skin of the land.

A house lay tucked at the bottom of the valley near a noticeboard and an electric bell. The notice said: "Closed for lunch 12-12:30." But I didn't need to ring: a tanned man with cropped grey hair was already emerging from the door. I nosed the car onto a thin, blue and white platform that slid along a cable at the instigation of the boatman. He peered at me from a nest of crow's-foot wrinkles, asked me no questions and told me only what I asked.

"How much does the trip cost?"

"It's free."

"Do you operate most of the year?"

"April through to early November."

"How many hours a day?"

"Twenty-three and a half."

Ah, the laconic eloquence of the west! By then the ride was over, the Assiniboine being little more than thirty yards wide. I wanted to ask the man what he did for the rest of the year and for whose benefit he worked the ferry so far from any towns; but he promptly lowered the bow, and I drove off into oblivion.

A gentle oblivion, at first. I climbed to the crest of a small hill

26

and stopped to overlook a slender oxbow lake. Beyond a farmhouse in the shimmering distance a tractor was striping a field. Through binoculars I could make out the green sweater at the wheel.

There was, indeed, a road ahead. I was confident it would bring me to Treesbank through a large domain that both the Manitoba highway map and Glenboro's tourist brochure identify as Spruce Woods Provincial Forest. But the maps are wrong. The maps lie. As a bilingual sign suddenly announced, I had entered a Military Training Area of the Department of National Defence. NO TRESPASSING required two languages. DANGER needed but one.

The woods died away and the land became an open, unploughed prairie. I drove across it slowly, looking for a way out. Half a mile ahead, a large dog loped over the road. He swung his pointed head back at me from a grassy knoll, and I realized he too was a trespasser: a coyote, "God's dog," a small prairie wolf. When the car approached, he cantered off, a grey blur below the sky. I saw a lone sign to the right, facing the opposite direction, and as I passed I turned to read: DANGER—TANK CROSSING—3 MILES.

Images of flat tires and broken fan-belts began to haunt me. The prospect of a breakdown in this armoured wilderness brought back all my insecurities about driving. In theory I knew roughly how to change a tire; in practice I could no sooner have used a jack than a trapeze. The surface was a rough gravel, speckled with rocks and hollows. My imagination magnified the rocks into knife-edged boulders and the road into an obstacle course, the only prize for a safe passage being permanent escape. A row of luminous targets bordered the road, orange circles against yellow, no doubt for artillery firing. I cursed the maps and I cursed the ferryman. I cursed the government. I cursed myself.

I was contemplating what action to take if my car met a convoy of tanks when the prairie began to sprout dogwood bushes, aspens and spindly birches. A mile farther, and the bushes became a forest amid a faint odour of skunk, like musk mixed with old blue cheese. Now a wire fence severed the road from the meadows and the forest; every fourth fencepost wore a nest box. When an eastern bluebird dived for home, I stopped the car and waited for the bird to emerge. Blue plumage above, red-brown below: it echoed and intensified the colours of the prairie. It also slowed my pounding heart. The DANGER signs had vanished. I was safe, I thought, in an honest-to-goodness Provincial Forest.

Yet the road carried on: no signpost to Treesbank, no glimpse of the Assiniboine, no hints of distance or direction. The fences dwindled out of my rearview mirror. Again the forest broke up into undulating grassland. Again bilingual notices warned me not to trespass. Soon a green sign pointed across the plain—to Köln. A few minutes later, and I could have turned right to Aachen; another few minutes, and Berlin lay on the left. I kept glancing in the mirror in case a squadron of land rovers or missile launchers should appear.

But aside from the inexplicable green signs, nothing appeared until I met an encampment of corrugated huts beside the road. The huts were surrounded by high barbed wire and overlooked by a tower. In the late afternoon sun, the high-powered lamps were off. The incongruity of a prisoner-of-war camp in the empty prairie of southwestern Manitoba made me snort with a somewhat desperate laughter. Had I blundered onto the set for *The Great Escape?*

The position of the sun told me that I must be heading north. Another tank crossing came and went without a trace of tanks. As the road surface began to improve, I gained an escort: six snow buntings, dapper in black and white for the arctic summer, dipped and climbed in the breeze a few yards ahead of the car. They led me into a gradual valley and up a small hill. From its cusp, I could distinguish white buildings against the sky's rim; then the birds zipped away on business of their own. I had never been so pleased to see military barracks.

They belong to the Canadian Forces Base of Shilo, which has the stolid, functional look of any army town. The street names—Aldershot, Portsmouth, Dorking—suggest an outpost of the English south. But the only men in view wore the black, red and yellow flag of Germany on the shoulders of their green uniforms. A sign told me that all visitors must report to a guard station; it failed to say where I could find such a thing. I drove up the same road twice. Finally I noticed a Canadian officer in his shirt-sleeves. Without apparent surprise or curiosity, he told me a way out.

Not until I reached the Trans-Canada Highway and picked up speed amid an anonymous forest of commercial trucks and pensioners' trailers did I start to calm down. It was a fifty-mile detour from Shilo back to Glenboro. That journey has become a blank. All I remember is an old reaping machine that stood in the village of Douglas: the final image of a long, perplexing day. It rested in front of a pale bungalow like a poor man's equivalent of a Henry Moore nude. The machine had been painted black. White letters on its side announced: THE GRIM REAPER.

·IX·

Not far from the Treesbank ferry lived one of the oddest men who ever came to western Canada. Percy Criddle was a middle-aged merchant enjoying the suburban comfort of Addlestone, Surrey, when suddenly, in 1882, he emigrated to a half-section of land near the Assiniboine River. A financial crisis may have provoked the move; no one has ever been sure. His wife Alice and her four children accompanied him in a private cabin of the S.S. *Wisconsin*. His mistress Elise brought her five children over in steerage.

In Manitoba the two households merged, sharing a tent, then a log house. But soon Percy's offbeat propriety exerted itself, and Elise's family was exiled a few fields away from the homemade mansion that he called St. Albans. Percy implanted a succession of flagpoles, each one taller than its predecessor, but he refused to fly the Union Jack. The poles sported a banner of his own design: a gold cross against a black background, with a gold crown in the upper right-hand corner. No one knows what the design signifies.

Percy became a skilful farmer, raising grain, dairy cows, pigs, chickens, vegetables and other fare. He was helped by the unpaid labour of his sons, whom he treated nearly as tyrannically as his animals. (When he died in 1918 he still thought of his children as "the Infants" of "the Governor.") But it was the astonishing diversity of his interests, not his modest success at farming, that set the man apart.

In the best Victorian tradition, Percy was a naturalist, a meteorologist, an astronomer. He also acted as the local justice of the peace. As a student he had learned some medicine in Heidelberg, and the immigrants around Treesbank were quick to take advantage of his talents as a doctor. He was a prolific diarist and an aspiring novelist (unfortunately, "the chapters hang like damp clothes on a line"). Most of all, he was a musician.

St. Albans included a room devoted to music, where Percy installed a harmonium. There he composed a potpourri of waltzes, songs, trios and organ chorales. He also wrote a handful of arias for an opera about Undine, the water sprite, and sketched out its libretto. A former recitalist in Surrey and a former tenor in the Royal Albert Hall Choral Society, Percy found the musical isolation of rural Manitoba hard to bear. Briefly, he served as the organist-choirmaster of a nearby church, but he soon relinquished the position—perhaps because of his terrible temper, and perhaps because of his atheism.

Percy had little respect for Christianity. He saw it as "a parcel of falsehoods and forgeries." The Anglican sacrament of confirmation reminded him of a cattle branding. He liked to bait believers, and was delighted to elicit a confession from a worthy neighbour: "Oh, no, I never said I was a Christian. I belong to the Church of England and will have nothing to do with any other religion."

Although he flouted the morality of the age in an impressive variety of ways, Percy remained an imperialist and a snob: "Don't mind the *men* calling on *me* but I certainly dislike the *women* — or at any rate most of them, coming near my Wife—*She* is still an English lady." As a mark of this exalted status he obliged Alice to wear shoes a size too small, for he regarded little feet as a sign of ladylike grace. He kept his sons and daughters ignorant of the blood tie between the two families, until one of Alice's children fell in love with one of Elise's; to prevent an incestuous marriage, the truth had to come out. How the disclosure affected his children, no one can tell.

When I first heard about the Criddles, the extraordinary character of Percy struck me with the greatest force. He seemed like a rough sketch for a tragic hero—to whom nothing tragic happened. A despot riddled with interesting flaws, he never received his come-uppance. Percy's life was often confused, his opinions contradictory, his values chaotic; but thanks to his luck and his lack of self-doubt, he accomplished a vast amount. His confidence in his own powers verged on the sublime. He would have made a first-rate fascist.

A photograph taken in 1909 suggests something of his pride and elderly swagger: a bushy, salt-and-pepper beard; large, active hands; an uncomplicated smile. The unpredictable element in the picture is the expression of Alice, who stands an arm's length from her man. She seems ready to back out of view, leaving the merest suggestion of a long white dress behind. Though she was six years younger than Percy, her eyes are set more deeply into her pallid face. Alice had studied at a women's college in Cambridge; before becoming Mrs. Criddle, she had learned Sanskrit, German, Italian and French. That lengthening of her mouth could mean a lot of things: exasperation, regret, resignation. Or simply a hard-won smile.

The only sharp photograph of Elise dates from 1863. She was a dark-haired beauty, originally from Mannheim, who left her homeland because of Percy to settle in the wilds of London. Then she emigrated again, a single mother with a brood of illegitimate children. Her reward was to gain a rare mention in Percy's diaries as "the Dutchman," "the Arch Empress of Muddlers," and an "eyesore." No one knows what he really thought of her.

The easy line would be: Percy became so remarkable a tyrant because of these two women. But I wonder now: what might the two women have become except for Percy Criddle?

Manitoba closed his lady and his eyesore into their own families. At the same time, it opened up for him a range of endeavour that lay beyond the frontiers of possibility in a City office and a Surrey villa. In England Percy would never have built his own house (twice) nor would he have made much use of his medical skills. Probably he would have recorded little original news about skies, animals and weather. He might never have learned the rudiments of farming. While Canada narrowed his women, it broadened him.

The price was a loss of culture, a failure of sensitivity. His mental agility lessened. His opinions grew more extreme. And his musical gifts began to wither.

Percy had exiled himself from a society where the arts were as natural as bread and beer. In the isolation of St. Albans his in-dividuality—his eccentricity—burgeoned. The triumph of western Canada is that it continues to allow that florescence of solitary talent. Marshall McLuhan, Joni Mitchell, Jon Vickers, Gabrielle Roy, and a host of other gifted men and women have grown up here. Grown up, and gone. The failure of western Canada is that it has never grown into a community worthy of its individual talents. A scientist or an artist in most of the prairies still has the mixed blessing of working as a pioneer. Whether the rewards outweigh the drawbacks, I don't know.

There is a final reason to remember Percy Criddle. One of his "Infants" was a tall, shy, celibate man with a passion for natural his-tory. After Percy died, the man became an entomologist for the fed-eral government. Grasshoppers, at the time, were becoming a plague that reminded more than a few Bible-reading westerners of Egypt's wanton locusts. The entomologist remembered his father's command to clean out the manure from the barns every morning. He remembered the armies of grasshoppers that glistened on the moist excrement. And he had an idea: to develop a poisonous bait that could be spread like murderous honey across the dung of the prairies.

The idea worked.

Norman Criddle was among the saviours of western farming.

·X·

"The everlasting plain is enough to send one mad," Percy Criddle observed a few days after reaching Manitoba. "Water there is doubtless plenty of . . . but wood: none; beauty: none; variety: none." As first impressions go, Percy's bemusement is standard. It takes a visitor from England or New England, Brunswick or New Brunswick, courage and time to make the mental leap necessary to appreciate the prairies. Early landscape painters in the west found that the country defied their conventions. Almost invariably, they chose to maintain the conventions. They inserted brooks and gentle valleys into a rural canvas; they diffused the brilliant light; they contracted the alarming distances. The cost was visual truthfulness. But the truth is hard to think and harder still to paint.

Percy's mental leap was a large one. For unlike many newcomers —including a high proportion of the Icelanders, Ukrainians and French-Canadians—he chose a tract of fertile, lightly wooded soil in preference to poor land with forests, hills and scenic variety. A loving admirer of English downs and copses, he staked his fortune on the flatlands. St. Albans grew on the bed of what was once Lake Agassiz. Percy retained a constant nostalgia for landscapes on a human scale. But eventually, his perceptions of the west altered: "The Prairie and woods now team with lovely flowers and the weather is charming—very heavy morning dews being the rule—hot days and cool nights. Slight Aurora this evening and lots of fireflies." The prairies had invaded and settled in his mind.

I drove east from Glenboro fuming, hardly noticing the hot day. Over breakfast I had been listening idly to a radio station that calls itself "the voice of southwestern Manitoba." But its daily commentary about public affairs does not originate in Winnipeg or Brandon or Ottawa. It comes from Chicago. The speaker that morning had proclaimed the need for "our" Congress to pay and succour a terrorist army to sabotage the people of Nicaragua. His lies offended me, as did the knowledge that his polemic goes out every

33

day, without change or apology, on Canadian radio. To live in English Canada is, like it or not, to absorb the profound insecurity and the profounder mimicry of a colonized nation. I often have to battle a British colonialism within myself, a quality from which most of Canada has escaped; but escape has led it only to a grovelling dependence on the U.S.A. "When you get right down to it," according to the afternoon's Winnipeg *Free Press,* "the most important Canadian TV people could be the handful of executives who visit California in May to decide what imports you'll see on the screens in the coming months and years."

Political frustration leads nowhere; driving a car gives the sweet sensation of control. That morning I punished an innocent highway. According to the usual cliché, the family car has become an extension of the home. I think it offers something more: masterhood. Sexually, spiritually, financially, your life may be "going nowhere." But by climbing onto the driver's seat and taking the car for a spin, you elude the numbness of a dead end. The dominance over a sophisticated machine makes up for impotence in its copious forms. Not only has the car superseded the horse; it has also replaced the maid, the butler and the slave.

Driving restored me to the shining world. I turned south from Holland towards Bruxelles, and immediately the road began to clamber through the pastures of the Pembina Hills. The glaciers moulded this land into abrupt, unpredictable drumlins, slow to rise in one direction, quick to drop in another. Stands of birch and aspen lurked in the valleys and around the reedy sloughs. Near a passing monastery a gravel road led off towards the town of Notre Dame de Lourdes, and I followed it. The odd car or half-ton truck was visible miles away as a cloud of dust and smoke, each vehicle hurrying inside a cloak of brown, airy grit. I killed my cloud and climbed a field to examine the day.

The everlasting plain had relaxed into a peaceable kingdom of fields, ponds and woods. Last year's strands of yellow grass outnumbered the new green stalks in the pasture, and a smatter of rose-hips still pushed out from scraggly, isolated bushes. I counted seven farms, each one sheltered by a belt of budding trees against the

34

prevailing wind. Three long lines of hay bales lay piled on the ground. Somewhere the crickets were in full voice. The hills made the curved horizons seem finite and benign; I could have been sitting in Europe, my flask of tea a bottle of *vin de pays,* my jar of raisins a hunk of cheese. . . . It was, for once, a landscape without menace or awe. No wonder the French settled here.

Though the land is fertile, the towns are failing. Notre Dame de Lourdes showed a few signs of life but the next village, Cardinal, saddened me. The railway has forsaken it; the grain elevators, the café, the hotel are gone. Fewer than a dozen of Cardinal's white homes looked occupied. Many others were tumbling slowly back to the land: a sagging roof, a vanished door, an empty window frame. A garage still carried on its business, selling fuel to the district's farms, and the slim spire of a graceful church still pointed at the sky; but the paint on the church's walls was peeling away, exposing bare wood. I should, perhaps, have strolled round the village and struck up a conversation with the garage mechanic, yet that morning I had no appetite for another history of decay. I wanted to let the town die with dignity and silence.

In 1928 a teenaged girl arrived in Cardinal for her first year of work. In those days, before the Depression, the dust bowl and the second war, the community absorbed a dependable trickle of immigrants from France. The new teacher had grown up on the edge of Winnipeg seventy miles away, and she was surprised to find that half her pupils came from Brittany or the Auvergne. Much later she would write, "it was as if I had spent that year in the *Massif central* or some retreat in the Morbihan. I had every opportunity to learn certain richly regional expressions. How marvellous, when one went to teach in a village, to receive more than one gave!" The year remained vivid till her death. In her last work of fiction, *Children of My Heart,* Gabrielle Roy turned her memories of Cardinal and the Pembina Hills into bittersweet, nostalgic art.

I eased out of the village past the low valley of a seasonal creek. Over it a railway bridge had once connected Cardinal with the outside world. The bridge had fallen; the tracks had been removed. A handful of ravaged girders remained to prop up the air. One day they too will collapse. But for the moment they seemed a kind of monument: the art of industry and weather; the wooden ghosts of a dream.

There are still a few places in Manitoba where the dream survives. If the French language on the prairies can last for another generation, it will do so where it began: in the valleys of the Red and Rat, south and east of Winnipeg. I drove back onto the plain and rolled eastward on a highway as flat and straight as a floorboard. A branch line of the railway continues to serve the tidy Anglo-Saxon towns. Outside Miami—a place named after the band of Indians, rather than the hot city of vice and winter holidays—I passed a sign:

SOUTH & EAST HEREFORD

FEMALE
PERFORMANCE PROJECT
Visitors Welcome!

Thanks, but no thanks.

I had a cup of coffee in Morris, a town so littered with fast-food takeaways and drive-in businesses that it struck me as the ugliest in the west. It has an excuse, I guess: the devastation it endured in the spring of 1950, when the Red River overflowed its scanty banks and fanned out to a width of fifteen miles. Only two upper floors in the town remained dry. I did not linger on Morris's splay streets, but drove relentlessly onward till I found what I was searching for: a café named Le Routier, a square called Place des Colons, a credit union known as a *caisse populaire*.

I checked in at a little hotel with aspirations to elegance. But then, it wasn't exactly a hotel; it was the Auberge St.-Pierre.

·XI·

The mistake is to walk into St.-Pierre Jolys expecting to discover a fragment of old Quebec that survives amid the dark soil of the prairies. The men drinking coffee in the *auberge* wore the flexible uniform of farmers throughout the west: casual shirts and slacks, windbreakers and peaked caps with a blunt message across the hairline, HAROLD WOLFE CRUSHING or EXPLORE JOHN DEERE PERFORMANCE or simply POOL. Here, as in every prairie town, the caps act as both a badge of individuality and a sign of belonging. The new houses on the margin of St.-Pierre, like those in Morris, Glenboro and Souris, are long, ground-hugging bungalows: the kind of languid architecture that real-estate salesmen dignify with the label "ranch style." I found the drinkers in the bar watching the Oilers outskate the Jets on English-language television. During the intermissions they discussed beers, bears and breakdowns—standard prairie fare.

Most of the residents of St.-Pierre are French-Canadian. All of them are westerners. As a result, outsiders tend to find the place impenetrable and, in some way, disappointing.

Until recently, St.-Pierre and its adjacent villages—La Rochelle, St. Malo, Aubigny and a modicum of others—seemed a closed society. Whatever else the residents may have forgotten, they remembered that Manitoba entered Canada as a predominantly French-speaking province. Its prime mover was Louis Riel, the doomed leader of the Métis (or "halfbreeds"), a man who couched his poems, prayers and petitions in French. After 1870 his language lost ground. Legislation depleted its power. But until recently, the people of St.-Pierre had no intention of compromising their last linguistic rights.

By contrast, the Germans and Ukrainians who settled nearby still use old tongues in some of their churches and homes, but they accept English as the natural language of the west. And they resent any suggestion that their neighbours should be free to deal with courts and governments in French. "Why can't they just be *Canadian?*" a well-meaning merchant asked me in Steinbach. His

37

imagination split the prairies into a vast, serene majority ("Canadian") and a tiny, trouble-making minority ("French"). The division—the difference—offended him.

St.-Pierre's few visitors from France and Quebec take an opposite view. They are offended by the ease and appetite with which the townspeople have adopted prairie customs, costumes and values. Curling, peaked caps and country music alienate them. And no doubt they have reason to see the effortless bilingualism of the town's young people as a threat. Among themselves the young often use English; they resort to their native language in the presence of a grandparent, a mother. Even the signs on the streets—*Frenchie's Tire Shop* or *Welcome to St.-Pierre. Chez Tony*—betray a self-consciousness about the town's identity. Its summer festival goes by the abashed, defiant name Frog Follies.

One day I drove south from St.-Pierre towards the sun. The grain fields were interspersed with bushland—thin, low, densely packed poplars that the earth wore like a coat of bristles. Three times the highway crossed the petite valley of the Rat, sparkling from the blue flame of a kingfisher and the gold in a flicker's wing. Catkins were slowly bursting out of willows as the water hurried its cargo of dead leaves over the luminous stones. The highway enticed me onward, the river coaxed me to stay, but hunger diverted me off the beaten track to the only restaurant in the village of St. Malo: Chez Normand.

I entered to find the owner, waiter, cook and bottle-washer smoking a cigarette in an empty room. An old black-and-white TV was his companion. He slid the Winnipeg *Free Press* to his knees and watched me sit before a wary, gruff "Hello" emerged from the jowls under his reading glasses. The menu, wrapped in plastic, was written in English. But when he finally heaved across the restaurant, I asked Normand for a meal in French.

The effect was drastic. Along with the hot sandwich came a free plate of apple crumble, a refill of coffee and a stream of information. Only a few *anglais* inhabit St. Malo, Normand told me. The population is steady: nearly seven hundred. Unemployment has caused some grief, but nobody wants to leave. And everyone speaks French at home.

38

I took his remarks, though not his excellent crumble, with a grain of salt. For I knew that the 1981 census had revealed a profound crisis among Franco-Manitobans. It showed that some 52,000 people in the province have French as their mother tongue; yet only 27,000 use it as their primary, everyday language. The pressure of English is unrelenting: a perpetual incoming tide against an islet of soft sandstone. Year by year, more of the land crumbles away.

Not only is English the language of commerce in southeastern Manitoba, it is also the medium of entertainment. Shoppers in St.-Pierre's drugstore and St. Malo's grocery hear background radio in English. Even Normand, so insistent that his village was a bastion, had been scanning an English-language paper and watching an American soap.

There is, to be sure, a public radio network that functions in French across the country. But most of its programs come from Montreal and have a marginal interest, at best, for westerners. In Quebec, where the vast majority of its listeners reside, Radio-Canada acts as a necessary alternative to the rock music, "easy listening," sports and breathless advertising that comprise commercial radio in French. Out west, those kinds of popular stations exist only in the other language. Radio-Canada's analyses of Berber life in Morocco, and the voice of Kathleen Ferrier, and the writings of Jacques Ferron pleased me as I drove across Manitoba; yet I sometimes wondered if I was the only listener. The day I arrived in St.-Pierre, the lunchtime newscast began with the words, *"Le Ministre du Finance, M. Yves Duhaime . . ."* It was budget day in Quebec City. But what do Franco-Manitobans care about somebody else's finance minister?

Normand hauled his blue-shirted paunch to the till. He scribbled a bill for $2.95. I paid, then asked if I could keep the receipt. He smiled at me slyly and wrote out another—this time for $4.25. The last thing anybody expects in St. Malo is a stranger who can speak French.

I walked down the street to the twin-spired church, the town's landmark for any voyager lost in the doubtful immensity of prairie. Columns of bare, pollarded trees lead up to the rose window. Inside the building, dismal paintings of Old Testament dramas glut the side walls. Dozens of pews, stretching in waves to the altar, look as though they could accommodate every man, woman and child in St. Malo. At Easter and Christmas, perhaps they do.

The Roman Catholic church used to be the light and fire of French-speaking communities across the west. In the face of prejudice and oppression—for many years the Manitoba Schools Act outlawed public instruction in French—the church nurtured a flame of resistance. It inspired the ideal of a sacred mission on the prairies. "Strange as it may seem today," Gabrielle Roy wrote in 1970, "I owe to Manitoba the good fortune of having been born and raised in a francophone area of exceptional fervour."

"I suppose," she added, "this enthusiasm, like a wick turned too high, could not burn forever." Nowadays, despite Normand's reassurance, it's sputtering out. St. Malo and St.-Pierre are in a condition of linguistic unrest; for the first time, the schools have been teaching more French than parents want. A week after I left St.-Pierre, 330 residents signed a petition demanding that the high school function in English. "Let's be practical," a spokesman told the press. "We simply don't accept and won't accept any longer to be railroaded into becoming francophones."

Tolerance, in short, has accomplished what repression failed to achieve: the re-evaluation of a people's identity; their absorption into the dominant culture. I felt a sadness akin to the grief one feels at the disappearance of the Inaccessible Island bunting or Cuvier's gazelle: something precious, irreplaceable and (in rational terms) useless was vanishing from the earth. The current state of easy bilingualism in St.-Pierre will not last long. In a generation or two, only the old women will speak more than a pittance of French.

I was learning to cherish the diversity of the west, its hidden swaths of tradition and perception, at a moment when they stand exposed to the advance of the continent's routines. All across the prairies the monoculture of a single language, like the botanical monoculture of wheat, continues to uproot thickets, reeds and forests that have formed part of the social landscape since white settlement began. It is, unfortunately, only a fragment of a worldwide

40

trend. In the first St. Malo, the intricate, stone-hard language of the Bretons has been chopped away by French.

At St. Malo, Manitoba, even the church is bilingual. A table at the back proffered old booklets in French about vocations to the contemplative life; it also held a glossy collection of anti-abortion tracts in English. Next to the brochures I noticed a cap. The insignia showed a monstrous fish about to overturn a canoe and a couple of shuddering fishermen. The cap had no words of explanation in any language. Was it meant to be symbolic?

·XII·

"We went to Yellowstone Park last summer," Hilda said, looking at me evenly. "One day we just climbed up those mountains. And then we had fish for supper. I couldn't eat fish since. That was too much mountains for me."

I ate another mouthful of lamb chop and nodded. It seemed odd that a wistful painting of the Rockies should be hanging on the wall. The mountains as myth and decoration are one thing, however; as a pile-up of rocks, cliffs and glaciers, they are something else again. Hilda rose and walked to the stove to fetch me a second helping of corn and potatoes. We were still sizing each other up, and to refuse her home-grown food would have been unwise.

"So how did you hear about Mom and Dad?" Lena asked. I felt less than comfortable devouring a hefty meal under the gaze of the two women. They had eaten at five o'clock sharp, an hour before I arrived.

41

"Through the Farm Vacation Association," I answered. What I did not say, when I phoned to book my room, was that I had chosen the Penners only because I wanted to stay in a Mennonite home. What Hilda did not say was that she lived on a hobby farm of only a few acres and that her husband Isaac would be away all evening. He had driven to Winnipeg, accompanied by a son and a seven-year-old grandson, to watch the professional wrestling. "Rassling," Hilda pronounced it, with a sigh of distaste. Lena had driven over to keep her mother company. In the rural west, a car is as needful as a winter coat.

Hilda folded her big hands into some cavity of her plain grey dress and began to talk about her family. I had already inspected their framed photographs throughout the living room, where they battled for prominence with a tank of tropical fish, a massive television and a birdcage with a open door. The budgie stayed close to home, but the cockatoo zoomed about the room at odd angles and was liable to perch on any convenient shoulder.

"I have eight children and eleven grandchildren," she said, "so far. My oldest son, he drives a garbage truck." Hilda saw nothing odd in announcing the fact to a stranger; to her the job was worthy of respect. It was Lena who felt a rush of embarrassment and added, "Mom, he does more than that!"

Hilda looked blank for a moment and then said, peacefully, "Oh ja."

I took a walk after supper on their property. The path to the aspen wood led down a muddy pasture charged with tame, doomed animals: three calves, a few goats, five or six lambs pursuing each other's tails. Before their slaughter, the animals were destined to amuse busloads of schoolchildren, who would return to Winnipeg in the fond belief that they had explored a typical farm. I strolled to the wire fence at the wood's end and watched the sun going down. Overhead, the high clouds were a mild silvery blue. A hawk soared in the gathering twilight and whinnied like an airborne colt.

I was about to retrace my steps when the farthest sky turned scarlet. A meadowlark chose that moment to rise from a tuft of grass and flutter westward across the empty field. He sang as he flew, a lucid raga that lasted fifteen or twenty seconds, far longer than his usual melody, before he landed in silence. No doubt the behaviour-ists can explain away his song as territorial instinct, a response to an aggressive impulse; I prefer to think of it as pure exhilaration at his consciousness of life, light, spring. Or else it was a weather warn-ing: a squall of cold rain rolled up from nowhere as I padded back through the dark trees to the house.

Four generations of Mennonites awaited me in the living room. In spite of my Anglican past, I felt like a lion thrown to the Chris-tians. I was introduced first to Hilda's mother-in-law, a presence in black who spoke only the Mennonite *Plautdietsch* (a strain of Low German). Then Hilda's brother-in-law Henry, a pig farmer, and Henry's wife Agatha, both of them fluent in German and English alike. Then one of Hilda's sons, a burly businessman called Ed, and two of her daughters-in-law; for this generation *Plautdietsch* is a for-eign language used out of respect to the elders. And four children, ranging from two to nine, well dressed, well mannered and sharp-eyed. Evidently the cohesiveness of the Penner clan stretched beyond its heritage of language.

The family seemed so rooted in the prairie west that I had to force myself to remember: for any Mennonite believer, heaven is the only homeland. Almost as much as the Jews—another people of rare in-telligence, musicianship and commercial acumen, though with a more obvious sense of humour—the Mennonites have found the en-tire world to be a foreign country. From Switzerland the first of them moved in the sixteenth century to Holland, from there to East Prussia and on, eventually, to Ukraine. Along the way they became an ethnic group as much as a religious sect. They liked to be the silent ones, *die Stillen im Lande,* isolating themselves from their neighbours and labouring to create a private Kingdom of God. They became, in a sense, a caste of prosperous untouchables.

Sooner or later their hosts always restricted their land, culture or political autonomy, and the Mennonites fled. In the 1870s, threat-ened by conscription and Russian education, many of them looked for a refuge. And as luck, or God, would have it, the government of Canada was searching for settlers in the new west. Their success at converting wilderness to fertile farms in Prussia and Ukraine made the Mennonites ideal candidates, and eight thousand arrived in southern Manitoba to break the free land. Eventually, fortified by some twenty thousand refugees from Soviet violence, they spread across the prairies. But in the process, they adapted their customs to the Anglo-Saxon continent more closely than to any foreign culture in their history.

Mennonite beliefs are similar in essence to those of the Amish and the Hutterites. They share a common origin: the Anabaptist movement of the Reformation. The members of all three groups believe in adult baptism, a resistance to military service and a life of simplicity—although their interpretations of that phrase diverge. The Amish, who live mainly in Pennsylvania and Ohio, reject modern machinery; Hutterites and Mennonites accept it. Yet the Christian communism of the Hutterite brotherhood is a far cry from the capitalist system that a majority of Mennonites now endorse. "I tell you," Henry Penner said with scorn, "those Hutterites have no sense of the value of time. I tell 'em to bring over a load of weanlings to my farm at one o'clock, and they'll show up at two-thirty. Then they want to stay around all afternoon and watch TV!"

At first I suspected that Henry's dislike of Hutterites was a question of economics—a different notion, perhaps, of "the value of time"—but I soon realized it went deeper. "You know," he added, leaning forward, "they twist the German language something terrible. Sometimes it's hard to even understand what they're saying. They don't have a dictionary in the whole colony, so they can pronounce a word any darn way they want." Ed took up the attack: "And they're drinkers. Oh yes! There's more than one of the colonies that's been ruined by liquor. The Hutterites aren't so holy as people think."

The men nodded at each other, and I wondered what underlay their contempt. Perhaps it was a distaste for "backwardness": the uneasy derision that people who have broken from centuries of seclusion feel towards insular communes. In the eyes of most Canadians, the Mennonites have done well in the west. But is that enough for them? Maybe the Mennonites' aversion to their fellow Anabaptists is born from a secret, unspoken fear that the Hutterites might be doing better in the eye of God.

Hilda brought in plates of cake and sweet bread, bowls of chocolate ice cream and mugs of coffee. It was a signal for the children to emerge from a side room, trying not to show their fatigue, and to subside in a neat sprawl. The adults' conversation went on without a break; they could take the children's courtesy for granted. I saw two of the little girls glance sideways at me and giggle. Any new man was a novelty, but a visitor with a black beard belonged to the realm of dream.

I sipped the coffee and listened again to the musical, rolling *Plautdietsch*. Henry noticed. "You know," he said, "when I was a boy, if the teacher caught us speaking German when any other kid was around, she would make us stay after school and write a composition. In English. But when I got home, if I ever used a word of English when my grandmother was around, boy, would I get punished!"

A few of the women and children departed in somebody's car, but most of the Penner family stayed in place. Near midnight I retreated downstairs. The talk carried on above my head. No doubt it would continue till Isaac had returned from the wrestling, for Hilda could not be left alone with a strange man. The basement contained a pool table, a rumpus room, guest bedrooms and a bathroom; what it lacked was a mirror. I slumped into bed and pulled up a quilt of astonishing beauty and complexity. "In the morning," I told myself, "I'll look at it closely . . ."

On the shelf above my head, a plaster statue of a buffalo pointed his horns at a plastic bouquet. The only other furnishing was a black copy of *The New Chain Reference Bible*, fourth improved edition. Sleep welcomed me into its heavy arms.

·XIII·

I was dreaming of ice-capped mountains when somebody banged three times on the basement door. The room shone with a thin, pallid light under which the round face of my watch told me it was seven o'clock. I got up unwillingly, feeling as though I had been ripped from the womb of a revelation, and drew aside the curtain of the high window onto a world of snow. A ruff of flakes was fluttering to the white soil. I took a shower to bring myself round from the snug peaks of sleep, hoping that the snow was a remnant of the dream, and as the hot water slapped my head three more bangs resounded on the door.

Though I rose to the kitchen before seven-thirty, Hilda and Isaac had finished their breakfast. Again my table manners had to endure the scrutiny of four thoughtful eyes. Isaac was an iron-haired man with fingers thicker than my thumb; his toughness was undamaged by age. When he retired from farming he undertook to drive a school bus around the backroads five days a week, ten months a year.

"That's a beautiful quilt on the bed," I ventured through an egg.

"It has a story," Hilda answered, and glanced to her husband for approval before saying more. "Years ago, Isaac's father was preaching on a Sunday morning. And he had a heart attack. He just fell over dead in the pulpit. Well then, his wife—you met her last evening, ja—she started to make quilts. She made one for all of her children. It took years. But when she was done with her quilts, she was done with her mourning also."

I remembered a story that I had heard from a friend in Saskatoon, the granddaughter of a Mennonite farmer who moved to Canada as a boy in 1905. The farmer reached a great age before his health broke. He died in a cold, early winter when the earth below the snowdrifts was frozen. Only then did the farmer's relatives discover that he had dug his own grave, secretly in the previous summer, and had filled it with hay.

"You want to see the hatchery?" Isaac asked without warning.

46

Travellers are game for anything. I arranged to meet him in the local café at nine o'clock, by which time he would have delivered a pack of kids to school.

The car slithered through the wet snow like a cat unwilling to sully its paws. I tried to disbelieve the weather. Overnight the land had grown austere, morose, its fields as white as the low sky, its brush forest a dull grey. "The whole country," the Earl of Southesk observed, "may be described as trying to break out into a wood, and half succeeding." I reached the town of Grunthal five minutes early, turned off the lights, the wipers and the engine, and marched into the café.

The conversations died at once. Although I had put on my best camouflage—corduroy trousers, a grey windbreaker, a baseball cap—I stood out, the unknown quantity in a room of friends and co-believers. On a normal working morning late in April, the farmers would be on the land. Snow had given a few dozen the idea of driving into town in search of gossip and companionship. Their excuse was a cup of coffee and, perhaps, a slice of toast. I had barged into a morning ritual. Outsiders, I suspected, were unwelcome. Luckily there was still an empty table.

But when Isaac walked in, he greeted me warmly and bought me a refill of coffee. I started to relax. He introduced me to a brother, a brace of cousins and a nephew—a burly young man who wore a small moustache above his lean lips. Alone of all the coffee drinkers, John Thiessen was bare-headed. Perhaps it was a proof of grace? For John was a minister.

"How many people would you expect to see in your congregation?" I asked. "On a typical Sunday."

Grunthal has a population of 572.

"About two hundred, I would say."

"You must be the biggest church for miles."

"No. The church just up the road here has bigger numbers than we do. And then there are the two other churches in Grunthal. One of them has its worship in German. They're also doing well, I think."

"That's amazing," I said.

The minister looked puzzled.

47

"Last year in our church," Isaac said, "thirteen children were dedicated to God. And you know, twelve of them were the great-grandchildren of my mother!"

"That's not the same as baptism, eh?"

"No, no," Isaac said. "Only adults can be baptized."

"Are *you* baptized?" John asked.

"Well, I was baptized as an infant, and then I was confirmed at about twelve, I guess."

A shaking of heads. I began to wish the conversation had taken another turn.

"As a rule," John said, "we don't baptize anybody younger than seventeen. A person has to be old enough to make his own personal commitment to the Lord."

"Is that right?"

"We believe that infant baptism is un-Scriptural."

The talk at a couple of adjacent tables seemed to have died down.

"Well," I said, "maybe I'd better be on my way."

Isaac rose as well. "We gotta see that hatchery," he told the minister.

With a cheese factory and a posse of small businesses, Grunthal has an unusually sprightly economy for the rural west. But the poultry plant is Isaac's pride. I drove him down a few slippery streets to a windowless building on the edge of town. In the company of four middle-aged farmers, we waited in the entrance hall for the manager. Two of the men were called Jacob Klassen. Both Jacob Klassens wore a green windbreaker and blue jeans, but their caps were different.

"Morning, Jake. Dirty wind today."

"So how was the wrestling, Isaac?"

Isaac smiled broadly.

"Pretty mean," he said.

The manager led us to his office. A calendar of the Rocky Mountains surmounted a cluttered desk; an arm's length away, a plate-glass window faced an enormous room. In its fluorescent light, two young men were hauling boxloads of baby chickens down from high stacks and emptying them onto metal trays. Each tray contained a hundred or more birds, shoving each other for position, peering in bewilderment and calling shrilly. The birds looked terrified. The room looked immaculate. The tray disappeared on a conveyor belt.

"That's the hatchery," Isaac said happily.

"You interested in chicken farming?" the manager asked.

I dropped Isaac back at the café and slid out of Grunthal with relief. East of town the farms became fewer, the ground rockier, the land more heavily forested. I resisted the temptation to forsake the district and drive straight into Winnipeg, for I still wanted to explore Steinbach, the largest Mennonite community in the west. It was with some astonishment that I noticed a pair of silver cupolas looming up above the icy road.

I should have realized: agriculture was so onerous here that the Ukrainians were sure to be around. Wherever the land is stony in southeastern Manitoba, and wherever the labour of farming is enough to break the back or the heart, you find struggling Ukrainian villages: Zhoda and Vita, Prawda and Tolstoi. Cook's Creek, a moribund settlement near Winnipeg, holds a lemon-yellow church with nine black-and-blue domes and a grotto—a grand, pathetic attempt to create a Slavic Lourdes of the west, built, like Tom Sukanen's ship, using picks and horses in the Dirty Thirties. The Ukrainian impulse to elaborate a kind of three-dimensional mandala by the play of sensuous, extravagant detail bears far more kinship to Mogul or Ottoman architecture than to any church the Mennonites have erected.

I slowed down to drive through the village of Sarto. It boasted a domed Catholic church on one side of the highway and a domed Orthodox church on the other. A dozen houses skulked in their curvaceous shadow. Then it was back to rock-ribbed farms. Towards Steinbach, the land improved. Even the snow diminished.

Steinbach deceived me, baffled me, disconcerted me. I couldn't find its centre; and a city of nearly eight thousand must, I thought, *have* a centre. I drove through downtown waiting for it to begin. My mistake was to look for the features that define most prairie towns: the railway, the river, the park; the main church, the main hotel, the bars.

Steinbach has no bars. Its council has never permitted a licensed restaurant or a liquor store, let alone a beverage room. This may be one reason why the place attracts so few visitors — judging, at least, by the absence of any hotel downtown. After wandering among the headscarved women and buying a pair of cheap shoes, I retrieved the car and drove to the dry Sunset Motel on the outskirts. The only alternative was a licensed "motor inn" somewhere beyond the city limits. Mennonite backsliders often prefer to cruise to La Broquerie, a French-Canadian village that does a thriving trade in alcohol.

I remembered the pious scorn of Lena Penner: "Sure, Steinbach is dry. But there's a lot of crooked Mennonites in town. They'll drink like a fish as soon as they get on that plane to Hawaii, but they won't touch a drop at home." I remembered, too, the English town of five thousand where I lived in 1981 (a Canadian settlement of that size would stretch itself into a "city," but this town liked to be defined as a "village"). Like Steinbach, Eynsham was enveloped by farms. It had ten pubs, six shops that sold wine, and no hint of public drunkenness.

Steinbach lacks more than a central hotel. It also lacks a river, a lake, a hill or any other point of physical interest. It squats on the land with the impermanence of a resting gopher who might decide at any instant to scurry somewhere else. A railway would add solidity but Steinbach, unique among prairie cities, has no tracks. What it does have, as if to compensate, is a plethora of car dealers. Its nine firms flourish on the wealth of a wide region, attracting customers even from Winnipeg, thirty miles to the northwest. Other people drive long distances to the credit union, which offers loans at the exact rate it pays on deposits. (A particular strain of Mennonite belief, like Islam, prohibits usury.)

Once the men have arrived to do business, the women go shopping in a mall. If possible they avoid crossing Main Street. The trek required, I found, twenty-seven strides.

A stroll round Steinbach can unnerve anyone whose idea of a city embraces the concepts of pleasure, beauty or relaxation. The place does not encourage loiterers; it would no sooner boast a sidewalk café than a singles bar. Its civic sense is functional. Its aims are businesslike. Therefore the streets, the sidewalks and the malls are all in excellent condition.

Besides commerce, Steinbach exists for another purpose: prayer. It contains eighteen churches, most of them Mennonite. In them the city attends to the pleasures of devotion, the beauty of the Word.

The simplicity of Mennonite worship—congregations have severed over the introduction of a choir—extends to the architecture of the churches. They fit into Steinbach like a hand into a pocket. While the churches look trim and capacious, none seduces the eye or charms the imagination. Steinbach keeps the aesthetic sense subordinate to the moral, like a talented but fickle servant of a strict householder.

That evening I passed a dreary couple of hours in the laundromat of the Sunset Motel. Waiting to add detergent to a load of tumbling shirts, I came across a pile of pamphlets from the Gospel Tract and Bible Society, Church of God in Christ, Mennonite. *Your Destination—Where?* the first one asked me. Its opening words were sufficient: "That there is a place of torment where sinners and all they that know not God will receive their portion, we cannot doubt . . ."

Inside the German sentence structure, the old familiar damnation. But true theological die-hards look on Steinbach, and everywhere else in Manitoba, as a place of torment. By remaining in the province, even the author of *Your Destination—Where?* accepted a compromise of Mennonite ideals.

The emigrants settled, a century ago, on a pair of reserves. After early hardships their villages thrived. The Mennonites introduced

51

sunflowers, watermelons and plums to the west; they were among the first to show that farming was possible on the open prairie, away from the protection of rivers. In return for their labour, they won control over their children's education and an exemption from military service.

But as the decades passed, the pressures grew. The world war subjected German-speaking pacifists to fear and loathing, and in 1916 the government of Manitoba abolished the Mennonites' schools. Henceforth, all children had to study in English under the Union Jack. Thousands of Mennonites chose a new exile in Latin America. The remainder decided that the privileges and opportunities of Canada outweighed the betrayal of Canada's promise and the distortion of their own tradition. They compromised. They flourished.

And their ideals expanded. The Mennonites' quiet, effective work for international development strikes me as admirable; so does their passion for peace; so does the sanctuary that several congregations have given to refugees from Guatemala and El Salvador. In Saskatoon some of my best friends had come from Mennonite families: strong, stubborn people, grounded in the church but blossoming in the secular world. They had found the courage to leave the past; they had also enjoyed a coherent past to leave.

I wanted to like Steinbach more. But as a writer, I need to believe in something other than its earnest righteousness. Small, church-based communities in the past—Assisi and Chartres, Lhasa and Qom—leavened their stern morality with an outpouring of beauty, so that the cities became a visible thanksgiving for the glory of the world. Joy infiltrated fear. The spiritual and aesthetic aspirations of the builders complemented each other in a manner that strict Mennonites can only see as dangerous. The austerity of Steinbach seemed to me a ponderous denial: the wilful refusal of a gift.

I was feeling tense and obscurely annoyed when I left Steinbach behind. It had not destroyed my respect for Mennonites, but neither had it provoked affection. Or a desire to return.

·XV·

Maybe it's the space of the west, the ease with which the earth and the vaulted sky conspire to make a man feel insignificant. Out of that terror, a liberation can arise. The past can fall away like a torn shirt. Or maybe (more likely) it's the newness of western society: the openness, the flexibility, the absence of a fixed class structure. The world converged on a region it saw as primitive and empty, forcing settlers from Ulster and Ukraine, Ontario and Lithuania into an abrupt proximity. The frontier looked like the future; no one wanted to excavate the past. The questions were too many, the answers too complicated. Usually it was better not to ask.

The settlement of the west under the Union Jack entailed, among other things, a massive alteration of names. A majority of newcomers finally converted their lives to English, or their children did the converting for them. Across the prairies, *Johanssen* and *Boisvert* and *Schmidt* turned into *Johnson, Greenwood* and *Smith*. A name was no longer the baggage of history; it was a label you were known by, a word you gave like a right hand. Identity became a flexible commodity, something a man could break or reclaim.

For a century the prairies have welcomed a stream of spiritual fugitives, refugees of the mind. The goal of all the settlers was independence—a fresh start, a freedom from the constraints and humiliations of whatever had gone before. As a rule the newcomers found it enough, of course, to forget. Only the most tormented, imaginative immigrants were driven beyond forgetfulness to the creation of a non-existent past.

Something about the west made the region a haven for such men. "Charlatans," "impostors," "pathological liars": all these terms have been applied to a strange quartet of writers who found in Manitoba, Alberta and Saskatchewan a refuge from their previous selves. The west allowed each of them the liberty to wear a new skin until it had become his own. Their lives became a kind of art. Their final text was themselves.

53

The first of these men, in time and talent alike, was a German poet and novelist called Felix Paul Greve. He grew up in Hamburg, the son of a tram conductor, and dabbled in everything from Sanskrit to oceanography at university in Bonn. The young man moved to Munich and spent wildly; in 1903 he went to prison for fraud. His first novel, *Fanny Essler,* appeared two years later. It was the tale of a fallen woman who suffers a legion of humiliations, takes a sea voyage at the age of thirty and dies. Out of prison, Greve worked at a furious rate, translating Balzac, Cervantes, H. G. Wells and many other writers into German (in the 1970s his version of the *Arabian Nights* would be republished in both East and West Germany). Yet his debts were still mountainous. In 1909, at the age of thirty, he took a sea voyage to Sweden, leaving a note to tell his wife he would never reach shore. Life, it seemed, had imitated art.

Felix Paul Greve was dead. But in December 1912, Frederick Philip Grove secured an interview with the Deputy Minister of Education in the province of Manitoba. He did not inform Mr. Fletcher that he was an author, or even a German; already he was fabricating a past. He became the school principal in the Mennonite town of Winkler, and in 1914 he married a Mennonite girl. For the next ten years the couple taught in a variety of communities across southern Manitoba. The experience gave him an intimate knowledge of the contours of the land and the psychology of its settlers. *Over Prairie Trails,* a selection of his essays, appeared in 1922; Grove pretended it was his first book. A "first" novel, *Settlers of the Marsh,* followed in 1925 and offended many. Nobody questioned the author's command of English or his understanding of the harsh west. It was his frankness about sexual unhappiness that created dismay. Yet despite the hostility of the prudent, he continued to write realistic fiction with a prairie setting. The region suited his gifts. Grove's forthright analyses of the culture of pioneering made him, for Canada, a literary pioneer.

His "autobiography" *In Search of Myself* won the Governor General's Award of 1946 for (ironically) nonfiction. There he elaborated the tale of his past that he had been assembling for decades. Grove claimed an Anglo-Swedish father; he claimed a Russian birthplace;

and he claimed to have explored Madagascar, Siberia, Australia and other exotic lands late in the nineteenth century, long before he found a home in Manitoba. He disguised his age, his nationality, his mother tongue. And Canadians believed. A quarter of a century elapsed after his death in 1948 before the truth unravelled.

Grove had been meticulous in covering most of his tracks: "I have travelled," he observed in *Over Prairie Trails,* "rather far for a single lifetime." In 1938 he saw the contempt that was heaped on another stubborn loner, the dead Archie Belaney. He knew how much the public needs and enjoys its myths, and how much it hates to be fooled.

Archie was brought up in the English town of Hastings by a severe pair of spinster aunts. In 1906, at seventeen, he sailed to Nova Scotia and began the slow process of obliterating his middle-class childhood. He worked as a canoeist and mailman in northern Ontario, learning woodcraft from a band of Ojibwa who still followed a traditional way of life. Then he took up trapping. He also fathered children by at least two Indian women, one of whom he married.

The war pulled him back to England as a soldier in the Black Watch. He was wounded in battle and he married again; but when Belaney returned to Canada, he left his English wife behind. He immersed himself afresh in the forests and Indian ways. In 1926 an old chief conducted him through yet another marriage ceremony, tying him to a spirited Iroquois girl called Gertrude Bernard (or Anahareo). She believed his deception: that Archie Belaney was a Métis of the woods, the child of a Scotsman and an Apache woman. Spurred by Anahareo, he switched careers: from trapper to naturalist. Soon he started to write eloquent prose about the wild.

He also switched identities. As late as 1929 *Country Life* was publishing his articles under the name of A. S. Belaney. Yet for nearly twenty years the man had tried to live native, and he finally altered his name to match his buckskinned, plaited, moccasinned appearance. Out of the remnants of a Sussex rebel, a wanderer called Grey Owl was born. And now his pleas for conservation reached a public avid to hear.

In 1931 Grey Owl, Anahareo and their small colony of beavers moved westward, first to Manitoba, then to Prince Albert National Park in central Saskatchewan. He had the title of "honorary park warden" and the freedom to live as he pleased. He made a log cabin his home. There he wrote the handful of books that stirred the imagination of America and, especially, Britain. Just as Frederick Philip Grove had used his German artistic education to mould fiction about the prairies, so did Grey Owl invoke the cadences and metaphors of literary English in order to make tangible an Indian view of life. Both men—outsiders, intruders—interpreted a culture about which the "authentic" voices seemed inarticulate.

Grey Owl grew rich. As a lecturer in Britain he was a runaway success; he even met the king and charmed the king's young daughters. But inconvenient facts were emerging; the strains became too obvious; and it was perhaps a mercy that Belaney's heart failed in 1938, back at Grey Owl's spiritual home in Saskatchewan, just before the truth came clear.

In his book *Men of the Last Frontier,* Grey Owl praised an autobiography with the title of *Long Lance* and described its Blackfoot author as a "splendid savage." Buffalo Child Long Lance was, next to Grey Owl, the most celebrated Canadian Indian between the wars. Unfortunately, he proved to be neither a Canadian nor an Indian. Like Greve and Belaney, Sylvester Long had reconstructed his identity in a foreign country.

Even more than the debt-ridden novelist or the constrained teenager, Sylvester had reason to flee. He was born in 1890 in Winston, North Carolina, and although his ancestry was a mixture of white and Cherokee—possibly infused with black—the apartheid of the time and place stamped him as "coloured." To say the least, his prospects were limited. The boy quit school at thirteen and laboured as a janitor. But he also ran off with a circus and gained a taste for a free life on the move.

By some sharp half-truths and self-promotion, the young man gained entrance to a school for full-blooded Indians and a small military academy. As his own country was still at peace, he took a train up to Montreal where, using the name Sylvester Long Lance, he enlisted in the Canadian Expeditionary Force and sailed for war-eaten Europe. He fought at Vimy Ridge, was wounded in battle and

56

served as a sergeant in army intelligence. A few years later he was claiming the rank of a captain and the award of a Croix de Guerre.

Discharged in 1919, Long Lance arrived in the young city of Calgary, where he pretended to be a Cherokee war hero from West Point. He joined the staff of the *Herald* and honed his craft as a journalist by covering boxing, civic politics and other recreations. He also wrote a thoughtful series of articles about Alberta's Indian reserves. North of Cardston the Bloods—part of the Blackfoot Confederacy—adopted him as an honorary member and gave him the Blackfoot name Buffalo Child. Long Lance had escaped his past by lying. As his lies grew more and more compulsive, his success would grow more and more astounding. Even his dismissal from the *Herald* proved a liberation. An extrovert, a showman, a feeder off attention, he realized fast that a "Blackfoot" could outdraw a "Cherokee." Maybe he ceased to remember who he was.

By trading on his Blackfoot name, Long Lance turned into a professional Indian: a full-time noble savage. He became a publicity agent for the Calgary Stampede, a writer for *Cosmopolitan* and an effortless social climber. Costumed as a Blackfoot chief with a picturesque, mixed-up regalia, he lectured with aplomb across the admiring continent. His copper-coloured skin, black hair and conspicuous cheekbones made the deception plausible; like Grey Owl, he looked his part. By 1926 American journalists were reporting that "Chief Buffalo Child Long Lance" was the "big boss" of all the Indian tribes on the Canadian prairies. Long Lance had left Alberta behind, though he returned to one of its Blackfoot reserves to research his "autobiography."

It sold superbly. He went on to play the muscular hero in *The Silent Enemy,* a feature film about Ojibwa life in the forests of northern Canada. (Grey Owl's reaction to the movie is unknown.) But when the news trickled out that its pet Blackfoot chief was truly a colored Southerner, the adoration of New York's *beau monde* turned to contempt. Sylvester had left too many loose ends. Unlike Grove and Grey Owl, he had never lived by the identity he wore. He had made himself into nobody. He shot himself in the head.

His story contains more pathos than tragedy. Yet Long Lance, like Grey Owl, achieved some good through his lectures and writings. At a time when treaty Indians in the Canadian west suffered even worse discrimination under law than blacks in the American south, Long Lance evoked a fraction of their culture with pride and flair. They began, through him, to command respect. In Alberta, a bewildered man found a people among whom he deserved to feel at home.

There is an odd, ironic coda to the lives of Greve, Belaney and Long, whose deceptions paid off thanks to the freedom from conformity and expectation that distinguished the west. In the small towns, that freedom has dwindled; many of them have become intolerant of eccentrics. But in the large cities, the collision of cultures remains intense and unpredictable. Downtown Edmonton contains something called the Weinberg and Gee Wok and Bagel Haven. Rules are still evolving; dreams hang in the air. Even in a time of credit cards and computers, a man can still invent a history in order to escape the past.

After the Second World War, an Englishman called Cyril Hoskins became obsessed by the lovely, betrayed culture of Tibet. He was the son of a Devon plumber. But when his "autobiography," *The Third Eye,* appeared in 1956, the author's name was T. Lobsang Rampa. The graphic descriptions of his boyhood in the Potala monastery overlooking Lhasa seduced many readers into accepting T. Lobsang's fables as authentic. He even claimed to have advised the Dalai Lama. The man went on to write twenty or so books on esoteric subjects, many of them quintessentially English: *Living With the Lama* purported to be the work of a Mrs. Fifi Greywhiskers, translated by T. Lobsang from the language of Siamese cats.

He was nothing if not audacious. Confronted with the evidence of an unspectacular past, he retorted that the spirit of a Tibetan mystic had taken over the body of Cyril Hoskins—a statement that defies both belief and refutation. He and his wife Sarah emigrated to Canada, living in five provinces and many towns. But only in his last years did he discover a measure of tranquillity. The dedication to *As It Was!,* published in 1976, reads: "To the City of Calgary, where I have had peace and quiet and freedom from interference in my personal affairs. Thank you, City of Calgary."

Five years later the "lama" was dead. His final refuge lay within sight of Canada's snow peaks. Escaping all his pasts he had become, in the end, a westerner.

·XVI·

"Great jazz on Saturday afternoons," Thomas said, "in the strangest place." So we rolled down the Pembina Highway past the junk-food dealers and the gas stations till we found the Ramada Inn. Its shaggy lobby, ferned with Muzak, made me nervous. An unobtrusive door took us to the cocktail lounge. The light died and I stopped, waiting for my eyes to cope.

My ears knew at once. Either we were in the wrong bar, or we were in the right bar at the wrong time, or Thomas had a unique conception of jazz. His vision was better than mine in the darkness, and he discovered a little table confronting the bar. The bartender was a girl in a white cowboy hat. A dark cascade of hair flowed from the hat over a denim vest and a remarkable figure. Unfortunately, it was a young man in a black shirt who took our order.

"Hi there," he said. "Welcome to the Ramada Country Jamboree."

By craning my head sideways, I could see a little platform at the room's end. Three men of an indeterminate age stood crammed below a glimmer in the ceiling. They wore a kind of uniform: white shirts, string ties, jeans with a gargantuan belt buckle, boots. One was fingering an electric guitar, the second an electric bass, and the

59

third a microphone. *"Lord,"* he crooned, *"I know this day is good
. . ."*

I grieved for them on Monday mornings.

". . . But Lord, I feel misunderstood."

"Used to be great jazz on a Saturday afternoon," Thomas said in a
respite of silence, "and nobody ever came to listen. I haven't been
down this way for months."

My eyes had adjusted. The room was threaded with listeners from
adolescence to old age. One small table had three generations
stitched around it.

"Think I could put in a request?" Thomas said.

"What is it you want to hear?"

"Drop kick me, Jesus, through the goal posts of life."

In the middle of the room was a little space. I had assumed it
served the convenience of the waiters. But when a few rough twangs
signalled another song, a man and a woman rose from a corner.
They walked stiffly to the open space. She joined her hands around
his collared neck, and they began to shuffle in a private circle. A
spotlight, singling the couple out, provoked a good-humoured
blare of applause. The dancers kept on revolving.

The crowd was in a jovial, weekend mood. They knew this song;
they knew every song. The singer beamed from the depths of his
moustache:

"Let's chase each other round the room tonight."

* * *

I liked the oddness of Winnipeg, its paradoxes, its nonchalant complexity. I admired the extravagance of its history and the abundance
of its rivers: the Red, the Assiniboine, the Seine, the La Salle and a
dribble of creeks, one of which rises on the international airport. I
appreciated the city's refusal to disclose its character and secrets at
first sight. Though I wasn't sure about its motto—"Commerce,
Prudence, Industry"—I was happy to find that a city with such a
slogan could produce a ghoulish rock group called the Chocolate
Bunnies From Hell.

Winnipeg is the only inescapable place on the prairies. Farther west, Calgary and Edmonton have boomed to a slightly larger population (above 600,000) and sprawl across an even greater space; yet somehow those cities are optional, not essential. You can avoid one of them and still gain a sense of the character of Alberta or the psychology of the west. But Winnipeg stands where the white west began, and for a long time it was the only metropolis between the Pacific and Lake Ontario. It dominates its province, its political hinterland, more than any city on the continent. Three-fifths of Manitoba's people live here; no other city is even seven per cent as large. The province, as a result, has an ungainly, unbalanced feel, as though its makers had joined the head of a moose to the body of a raccoon.

Winnipeg is still the prairies' gatehouse. Roads lead out of it to little towns in all directions; anyone with an urge to drive northeast has a choice of three divided highways. The system of movement inside the city is more problematic. Its most important vessel, Portage Avenue, which begins life as the Trans-Canada Highway and flows in triumph to the city's heart past a succession of golf courses, parks, malls, government buildings, a university and many gleaming shops, terminates at Main Street in a wall. The point of land that overlooks the natural pivot of the city—the Assiniboine's fusion with the Red—is an inaccessible forest of railyards. Winnipeg continues to pay for the deal that ensured its growth: its poaching of the transcontinental railway from the village of Selkirk twenty miles north, the surveyors' original choice for the crossing of the Red.

Architecturally, politically, emotionally, the city is a jumble. But the jumble has life and style. Its real-estate prices are low. Its murder rate is not.

* * *

I sauntered into the Fiesta Beverage Room of the McLaren Hotel just off Main Street. A working morning in a working day, yet eighty or ninety men and women were loudly at their play. The majority were Indian and Métis. A parade of customers glided between the cramped lobby and the bar.

61

A small bald waiter slapped a hand on my shoulder. He kept it there while he asked me my pleasure, while I told him, while he repeated the brand and while he assured me it was coming right up. I watched him: regardless of age and appearance, every man got the treatment. Serving a woman, the waiter kept his fingers on his tray.

The noise and vibrancy of the atmosphere, the crowd's hum of glad anticipation, mocked the drabness of the room. What unwritten law makes prairie bars so meagre for the eye? The Fiesta's carpets, tables, chairs, ceilings and walls were all maroon or black. In the corner a game of pool seemed to progress at random: any passerby could take a pot shot.

Nobody was watching the children's show on the little TV. Big Bird explained the letter B on a shelf above a cluster of excited Indian girls, a couple of sullen men, a boisterous boy in a red jacket, and a white woman at least sixty pounds overweight.

Nobody paid attention when a grey-haired woman in a yellow dress began to weave between the tables, glancing at one drinker after another and calling in a furry mezzo-soprano: "I want to cool off or I want to die! I want to cool off or I want to die!"

She sat down and was served. She cooled off and shut up.

*   *   *

In prairie terms, Winnipeg is an ancient city. It arose near the site of Fort Rouge, a fur-trading post that la Vérendrye established in 1737 on his futile quest for the western sea. Another aristocrat—Thomas Douglas, the fifth Earl of Selkirk, a friend of Sir Walter Scott—founded the Red River Colony here in 1812. He saw emigration as a mode of relieving the hardships of his subsistence farmers. Those early settlers met even greater hardship on the plains (twenty-one of them died in a battle with the Métis), but the Scottish outpost endured. The Earl of Southesk found "houses enough to form a sort of scattered town" under the protection of Fort Garry, "a great parallelogram of lofty stone walls with circular bastion towers."

It was, however, not an aristocrat but an Irish-Canadian businessman who had the bright idea of opening a store where the fur trail down the Assiniboine (in other words, Portage Avenue) met the fur trail up the Red (Main Street, in short). Henry McKenny's shop became the nucleus of a community that by 1872 included more than a thousand men and 448 intrepid women. The town ate up Fort Garry to the south, it swallowed Point Douglas to the north, and it became the political, commercial, financial mouth of the plains.

Winnipeg's days of growth and glory lasted, but for the odd crash, until the First World War. Money flowed like rye. Main Street soon encompassed sixty hotels, in whose "free admission parlours" a man could choose between target practice, slot machines, a silent movie or a whore. The city developed its own banks, trust companies, insurance firms, even a stock exchange. The porticoed banks and ornate office buildings recall Renaissance Rome and the City of London in some of their architectural details. Their exalted proportions and cocksure grandeur even suggest a mercantile thirst to rival St. Peter's or St. Paul's. Winnipeg became Canada's third-largest city and sponsored its first civic gallery.

Along with the riches came the slums. John Marlyn, in his novel *Under the Ribs of Death,* saw in Winnipeg "an endless grey expanse of mouldering ruin, a heap seething with unwashed children, sick men in grey underwear, vast sweating women in vaster petticoats." Few of these fat women and ill men were native to Britain, Canada or the U.S.A., and the city fathers did little to heal the squalor. Its outdoor toilets and open sewers gave Winnipeg a higher rate of death from typhoid fever than any major city in Europe or North America. Nowhere in Canada west of Montreal was the contrast between rich and poor so hard to ignore, or to forgive.

In 1914 the Panama Canal opened for business, and Vancouver began to challenge Winnipeg as a grain-trading centre. Other prairie cities unfurled their own industries, reducing Winnipeg's dominance over the region. Meanwhile, the bitter poverty that festered amid such immoderate wealth made this the ideal location for Canada's most radical experiment in union power: a general strike, which shut down the city for six weeks in 1919. It finished with a confrontation in which the mounted police shot a couple of strikers to death and injured many others. Winnipeg's businessmen had won; they had forestalled industry-wide bargaining, the threat of

"One Big Union." But the legacy of bitterness and bad will, combined with an absence of economic leadership, led the city to a long stagnation.

Probably the pain and stagnation go a fair way towards explaining why Winnipeg appealed to me: it has a maturity that Alberta's gangling, gum-chewing cities lack. The only sources of good literature are places where people have suffered hard. Winnipeg, like rural Saskatchewan, has produced a disproportionately large number of writers. The sleek suburbs of Calgary have produced next to none.

*   *   *

"The McLaren, that's nothing," said Will. "Come on, you can find the McLaren anywhere in the west. You gotta see the Roblin, that's the real survivor. The last of its kind."

The Roblin Hotel takes its name from Manitoba's most distinguished political family. Once, no doubt, its guests had wealth and power. But its tone fell. By now it no longer warrants a mention in the supposedly inclusive lists of *Travel Manitoba,* where the Ramada Inn sports five stars and even the McLaren picks up three. The Roblin faces Kerr's Fun ral Chapel. Although it advertises a banquet hall, perhaps for revellers after the fun ral, it hasn't served a banquet for years. We arrived to find the front door locked. Not to be deterred, Will opened a side door into Winnipeg's final all-male bar.

The refuge. The end of the line. Around the borders of a bare room, a couple of dozen derelict men slumped over their draught beers, one or two to a table, mumbling.

"One time," said Will, "a friend of mine from Toronto came into town. Don't think he saw the Roblin, though. He didn't need to. Inside of three days he'd decided that Winnipeggers do more talking to themselves than any other people in the world."

A lank, mournful waiter called Tex brought us our beers without a word. A monstrous change purse hung from his belt like a holster. Put him onstage, and he would be ideal in the role of Lucky. I could imagine him exploding into an incomprehensible tirade and then remaining silent for a month.

I couldn't tell at first why this bar felt so different from all the others. It wasn't just the lack of carpets and women—

"Owner and his son run this place almost like a charity," said Will. "They actually take care of these guys. Put them to bed if necessary. To force this place to change, the Human Rights Commission would have to receive a complaint. And who in God's name would complain about discrimination at the Roblin? I mean, can you imagine any woman *wanting* to come in here?"

—The lack of music! The lack of muzak. The lack of electronic games. The total absence of sound except for the clinking of somebody's glass against a table or a denture, and the low perpetual murmuring from the walls.

"Got to go to the can," said Will. "You want to leave already? Sure, okay," disappointed, "just be sure to look at the lobby before you go outside."

When I entered the green, peeling lobby, the bar's faint stink of urine rose to a dank clamour. A grey man was doddering below the stuffed head of a moose. He looked as though some nightmare of the trenches had driven him to incontinence. A deer's head protruding from a second wall was the happiest item in view. Halfway up the stairs a man in a felt hat was speaking softly to himself—". . . no use telling them they could find it down the hall because they wouldn't want to see it even if I . . ."—not moving.

*　　*　　*

I liked the lingering bravado of Winnipeg. One bright morning I strolled around the North End, a district of modest, tightly packed homes and churches and small, struggling businesses. Their signs announced Perogy Corner or Russell's Corner Store ("Come In and Freshify"). The North End was the traditional home of Poles, Ukrainians and socialists; so many Jews lived in the neighbourhood that it went by the scornful nickname "New Jerusalem." *Under the Ribs of Death* was set here in the 1920s. The North End became a womb of writers: a matrix of brainpower, rage and passion among the disinherited; a prairie St. Urbain.

I didn't see any horsemen. But I did come across four Indians lounging beside an old apartment block in whose broken windows a few green shutters nudged shards of glass. Above its dusty lintel the building wore a nameplate: North Panama.

·XVII·

The air cooled. The city dissipated. I took a day's diversion westward to find a pile of stones and an owl. Nowadays the old road to Portage la Prairie is little travelled, for it massages the shoulders of the Assiniboine instead of spearing the belly of the plain. The names on its mailboxes tell a familiar tale of settlement: Poirier, Desjardins, Allard. I had a snack of juice and raisins beside the wavering river, thinking at first I was alone among the wild mint and the boulders except for a black determined spider with a body like a miniature tank.

Wait in silence, and the birds will come. I watched a crow harass a soaring red-tailed hawk and a sandpiper twitch along the shore. Across the water a white-throated sparrow, pausing from his voyage to the boreal forest, sang what I heard as a plaintive adieu to April from a greening ash. In the corner of my eye, below a dove in flight, something surfaced. I looked down. It was gone.

The river flowed smooth and steady, confident of its direction. I carried on upstream and rented a dingy hotel room in the floundering town of Portage. Near the turn of the century it had verve and hope; expecting a current of profit, the Bank of Montreal built a stately, elaborate office with a coat of arms in stone. Today the building acts as a "Kosy Korner" for the old. Most of Portage's surviving businesses are cheapskate firms — Army and Navy, Metropolitan, Lo-Cost Drugs — that serve an impoverished clientele. I bought some high-priced lotion for my contact lenses and drove north to the Delta marshes: a tract of grassy swamp where Lake Manitoba and the prairies fight to a precarious truce.

The marshes occupy more than seventy square miles. They rank among the most valuable breeding grounds for geese and ducks on the plains. I explored them in the velvet light of early evening from the passenger seat of a half-ton. Its driver was Al Hochbaum, a naturalist, artist and author who directed the Delta Waterfowl Research Station for thirty-two years. I was grateful for the ride and delighted with the company. Al knew the wet, sandy labyrinth of trails like the back of his big, hard hands. They looked more apt for poultry farming than for painting in egg tempera.

The track twined towards a wooded ridge above the far, frozen lake. Al was searching for white-tailed deer, the subject of an unfinished canvas. Whenever I saw a smear of red-brown movement, he slammed the brakes and lifted his binoculars. The deer's caution stopped short of fear. Long before we discovered them, their dark eyes were peering for us across the reedy swamp and their delicate ears stood alert.

In my charmed eyes, the stretches of open water were afire with birds. But I had no way to measure the company of wild adventurers, no memories on which to base a judgement. Al shook his head and gestured at the air. "When I came up here in '38," he said, suddenly old, "the spring sky would be covered with birds. Clouds of ducks. Not any more."

"Why?"

"Overhunting," he said. "And the draining of wetlands."

A private road brought us home. From its picture window, Al and Joan Hochbaum oversee the marshes. Their sloping lawn supports a heap of rocks arranged to form an *inukshuk:* a stylized man with a head, two legs, and a large hole in the heart. An Inuit man from Hudson Bay once converted some Delta stones and boulders into a sculpture. It may look unbalanced, as though a slight breeze from the marshes would overthrow it, yet the structure has withstood the punishments of prairie weather intact. In the desolate immensity of the barren lands, inukshuks served as landmarks for hunters. They were proof of human passage, a sign of consciousness.

"Got anything that might need some luck?" Al asked unexpectedly.

To pass an object through the cavity in an inukshuk is to bless it, to bring it luck. Celtic dolmens worked on the same principle. I took a gold Papermate and slipped it through.

"Use it," Al said, "when you're suffering from writer's block."

"Listen," said Joan.

In the blue-black freshness a tumult of crickets, frogs and the first mosquitoes of the year vibrated against the distant, juicy clamour of birds. Why do we give their cries a label—"honk," "quack," "hoot," "chirp"—that mocks them? It was the sixth night of creation. The moon glittered off the marshes. My car thudded away like artillery.

Back in Portage I found myself up against the amplified clamour of a dance in the hotel. It smelt of beer and sweat and cologne. A tattooed bouncer stalked the entranceway. I dozed off long after midnight above the pump and thrust of rock.

"Pretty rowdy," said the desk clerk at 5:05 A.M. I was feeling dismal. But I had made a private vow to watch the sun's rebirth on May Day, and the sky was already growing pale. "A vanload of Indians came in last evening from the country." He put down his paperback of *Absalom, Absalom!* and unlocked the door into the late, cold night.

I took the curling road to Lynch's Point, following a slender river with the unglamorous name of Squirrel Creek. Sure enough, a couple of red squirrels at the creek's mouth chattered like rowdy choirboys. F. P. Grove had taught in a nearby town long before the roads were paved. I left the car and shivered up and down an empty campground. The barbecue pits and rain shelters, unused since September, had the aloofness of museum implements. Gulls and a squadron of teal floated on a strip of open water that lay pressed between the beach and seventy-five miles of ice. I tramped towards the Delta marshes through a forest of *Phragmites*—quill grass, "queen of the prairie," its reedy stems stretching seven feet up to feathery tufts in mid-air.

By the flamboyant standards of the evening, dawn was ladylike, polite, genteel. Streaks of orange and pink slowly, deferentially, took on the shape of clouds. A watercolour grace until the sun emerged: a rough, red-gold stain. It stood on the horizon like a wounded iceberg far beyond the quill grass. Then it climbed again and lost its colour and devoured its limits.

The light grew hard. A hornet buzzed my head in some obscure fury. High in a clump of budding maples, a great horned owl saw me out with a massive silence. Everything but him was on the move.

Driving back, drowsy and elated, yearning for a coffee, I passed a roadside graveyard. Its only occupants were two young children who died a century ago. A plaque honoured a priest from Quebec who came west in 1831, ministered to the prairie Métis, and accompanied many of them to the Dakota Territory when Canada spurned their claims. Before he left, Father Belcourt wrote a dictionary of the "Saulteaux" language.

·XVIII·

On a blue summer's day when I was seven, I was driven through the ptarmigan heights of the Logan Pass. I perched between my parents in a wide back seat. The driver was a friend of theirs, Albert Hart, a big man with a strong bass voice. Albert's wife Verna sat beside him. I recall her as small with sharp glasses.

We were greenhorns, newcomers, outsiders. I had never visited Glacier Park; the small city of Lethbridge was world enough for me, never mind the surrounding prairies of Alberta. My eyes were big about everything. I had all the time on earth.

I remember the mountains growing in the windshield as the long golden fields and the highway began to look unkempt. Some wooden shacks teetered near the road. A smashed car protruded from the ditch. Verna went on the warpath:

"Indians. Dirty people. Look at the mess they've made of this reserve. Got more good land than they know what to do with. And they drink like fish—"

Now I'm inventing. I don't remember her exact scorn. But I still feel my childish outrage when, glancing back at us over her left shoulder:

"They almost wiped out the buffalo, you know. That's right! Most of the time they never used the dead animals, they just left 'em to rot in the wilderness. If it hadn't been for the white man coming in and saving a few, the Indians would have killed every last one."

Was that my first lesson in adult prejudice? Kindly grown-ups "weren't supposed" to tell malicious lies. But at seven, with shorts and a half-English accent and my polite mother an inch away, I couldn't lean forward and say:

"Mrs. Hart, you're an ignorant bigot!"

I twisted and fumed. I may have cried.

She spoiled the mountains.

In the twenty-three years since that drive, I had never —never!—visited an Indian reserve.

* * *

You are now entering the First Nation of Fort Alexander
Land of the Anishinapek— —of the Algonquin Nation
Pop. 2,800   Acreage 22,000

"That includes the land the government stole from us," Dave said.

The smokestack of Abitibi-Price's paper mill receded in the rear-view mirror. The Winnipeg River, from whose banks the mill rises beside a pyramid of broken wood, disappeared behind a railway track. A few bright houses, yellow or turquoise or sky blue, lay at crazy angles off the highway.

"The Pine Falls sewage used to be dumped straight into the river," Dave said. "That means it came to us. And there was one old woman who would hunt through the garbage when it drifted onto the shore. Beachcombing, I guess you'd call it. Well, one time she found a whole heap of condoms. And she figured they were bal-loons! So when she'd cleaned 'em and blown 'em up, she hung 'em in her home above a statue of the Virgin Mary."

But he wasn't laughing. A thin, tight smile occupied the edges of his mouth. His dark eyes watched me steadily.

"Why don't you stop for this guy?"

It was a command as much as a question. The boy pulled in his thumb and jogged to the car. He was the first hitch-hiker I had seen in the west. When the boy had slumped into the back seat, Dave swivelled his shoulder painfully and said, "How come you're not in school?"

"Where I'm goin'."

"You miss the bus this morning?"

"Yeah."

Dave didn't probe any further. "The school's a few miles up the road," he said to me. "In the townsite of Fort Alec."

"So do the kids in school still learn the Saulteaux language?"

"Absolutely," he said. "But we don't call it that. It's the Ojibwa language. That's what we are, Ojibwa, part of the Algonquin na-tion. 'Saulteaux' was the French word, it doesn't mean anything to us."

"But you still talk about Fort Alexander. That's another colonial name."

Dave nodded. "The real name of this place is Sagkeeng—'the mouth of the river.' It's why we've got businesses here called Sag-keeng Furniture and Sagkeeng Crafts."

We passed a stretch of peat swamp before the houses became commoner. Almost none had paths or gardens. Most of them fol-

71

lowed a curt design from the federal Department of Indian Affairs: low wooden bungalows resting on unpainted foundations of cement. Their outhouses lay a few yards to the rear. Across Canada, less than half of Indian homes enjoy indoor plumbing and sewage. The river reappeared on the right, broader as it swept towards Lake Winnipeg.

"Yeah, I used to work for Abitibi," Dave said sourly. "When there were fires out of control in the summer, they'd hire Indians for a flat rate. Three dollars a day. Take it or leave it. So we'd take it, and we'd be fighting shoulder to shoulder beside white men on union contracts. Same amount of labour. Eight times more pay."

We approached the townsite, which the highway tears. On the right lie the Catholic church, its rectory, a graveyard and a school ("You gonna miss the bus tomorrow morning?" "No"—and he was gone, a scamper of blue jeans and scarlet sneakers). I pulled off to the left, where houses spatter the land like costume jewellery, and parked beside the band's offices.

"Had an arena here a while ago," Dave said. "But it burned down."

Inside the building a few men in caps, windbreakers and check shirts were gossiping or waiting for appointments. They could have been farmers. But the chief—Dave's young cousin, a burly man called Ken—wore a fawn sports jacket and a black turtleneck labelled *Serge Saint Yves* at the collar. His black hair was fixed in a ponytail. We chatted inconsequentially about weather and hockey till I asked about unemployment at Fort Alexander.

"It's high," he said simply. "Very high. At certain times of the year it's up above eighty per cent. That's why our people are so dependent on the government. You think we like it that way?"

None of my questions touched on the news Ken wanted to tell me. When he judged the moment right, he looked at me hard for the first time. "In our culture," he said softly, "we have some people that we call dreamers. I guess other groups might use the term clairvoyants. And these people are telling us that pretty soon, man is going to find himself on an island. *With nothing to drink.*"

I left the office with Dave and drove slowly around the townsite. "Over there," he said heavily, "is where they're going to build the

72

Rehabilitation Centre. For native people from all over Manitoba who've got severe problems with alcohol or drugs. The idea is to get them into a healthy environment where we can deal with them ourselves. In our own way. There might be fifty jobs in it."

"It's going to be pretty close to the town," I said.

Dave nodded. "Lots of people are nervous. I've always said it's a mistake to build an economy on the misery and dependence of our people."

"But you've got to find the jobs somewhere."

His nostrils flared, and his voice grew tense.

"I've been to Kuwait," he said unexpectedly. "I've seen what the Arabs have done. Now I've got some very important friends there. If they invest in Sagkeeng Enterprises, there's all kinds of things we can accomplish. We've got a sawmill already—why couldn't we make wooden fences for Chicago? They need 'em bad down there. Lobster traps for the east-coast fishery. I'd like to see a marina built. No reason why we couldn't start up a lodge for tourists. The fishing's good enough . . ."

But along the beach lay a black, sticky scum, a gift from Abitibi-Price.

"Want to show you the house I'm building," he said.

It stood outside the townsite: the wooden skeleton of a two-storey home overlooking the river. Many of Dave's relatives live a short walk from the building, in obedience to the Ojibwa networks of family and clan. The Department of Indian Affairs prefers a checkerboard pattern of housing that violates native custom. On many reserves its external tidiness has provoked and hidden chaos.

We clambered up the staircase and Dave chatted in his own language with a couple of workmen. The climb had tired him. Against the backdrop of the grey river and the remote pines, he seemed just an old, weary man, no longer the former Grand Chief of the Manitoba Indian Brotherhood, a leader known for his militancy. His painful back and semiparalyzed leg made me doubt the wisdom of a home with stairs. It might soon be inappropriate, even impossible for his body.

But his spirit needed that house. As a symbol of his rise above the low expectations of his underemployed, humiliated people. As a

73

defence against the corrosive bitterness of a lifetime of grievance. As proof that at least one of his dreams could come true.

Dave insisted on limping down the stairs to see me off. "Remember," leaning through the driver's window, still fastening his tough gaze on me, "*native control* doesn't mean a thing by itself. Oh, it's a nice phrase, sure. But the government can still screw us around. What we've got to acquire is *native self-sufficiency.*"

So I left the reserve. In the company town of Pine Falls the streets had grace and permanence. Bearing names like Walnut, Elm and Empress, they rose from the river to a park that called itself a "village green." The tall houses around the green were built of stucco and old brick. I sat on a bench, thinking hard, enveloped by a flock of robins listening for food in the cold soil. A flurry of voluble grosbeaks occupied a nearby conifer like black-and-yellow puppets on some invisible string.

It wasn't enough. I needed to see more. Especially, I wanted to learn how Ojibwa traditions were faring. In the coffee shop of the Papertown Motel, the place mat was a map of the region ("Home of the Paper, Power, Pea & Pickerel Festival") on which the white businesses in nine small towns were named and plotted: Muskey Propane, Susie's Penthouse Hair Boutique, Aquarius Chip Stand . . . But the three Indian reserves were nebulous dark blotches. No doubt South African place mats treat black townships in a similar fashion. Dave had mentioned the existence of a Fort Alexander Cultural Centre. I drove back past the smokestack and the wooden pyramid to search it out.

This time I was struck less by what I saw—the gaudy, peeling, higgledy-piggledy houses—than by what I did not see: vandalism. Broken bottles. Herds of extinct cars. Drunks roaming the townsite. Schoolchildren playing hooky.

The cultural centre, a nondescript box of a building, lurked behind the Catholic church. I climbed the concrete steps and introduced myself.

"Oh," the man said slowly. "Art Beaubard isn't here."

"Well, is there anybody else I could talk to?"

He thought and thought.

"Yep, I guess so."

74

I waited. The man's crow-coloured hair protruded from a pony-tail below his baseball cap. He had a creased face and an odd, slurred speech.

"Come on in!"

The room reminded me of a church basement. It contained the same tables and metal chairs, the bright forlorn pictures that did not quite fill the walls, the low ceiling, an uncarpeted floor. The man's shoulders were stiff as a fence.

"I'll . . . look out some things for you."

And he set off to forage among some files. I remembered the Earl of Southesk's reaction to an Ojibwa man he met in 1859: "no favourable specimen,—a miserable object, half naked and quite drunk, a bloated, disgusting savage." The white tendency to look on these people as disgusting savages may be disappearing, finally. But the impulse to see them as specimens, as objects, as primitives, remains as strong as ever.

"Hello!"

A younger man, wearing a blue shirt and a loose leather tie, had padded in without a sound. His hair slid over his forehead and stretched below his collar.

"My father told me about you," the man said. "I'm Dave Cour-chene Jr. I'm the superintendent of schools here."

But how did he know to find me at the cultural centre?

Dave's responsibilities include two elementary schools and a high school, which instruct an impressive, alarming total of seven hundred pupils. "Impressive" because, unlike the great majority of reserves in Manitoba, Fort Alexander keeps most of its young people in school. "Alarming" because more than half the population is under twenty—and houses are in as short supply as jobs.

"The prairies are Canada's Third World," I had been told in Winnipeg. A glib remark, for even if power and style begin elsewhere in the country, most westerners enjoy a standard of living that in Senegal or Peru—never mind Ethiopia or Bangladesh—belongs to the realm of fantasy. But the fantasy breaks on the reserves. Hundreds of thousands of native people endure poverty and frustration of the sort other Canadians associate with tropical squalor. Across the country one in three young Indians tries to commit

75

suicide, and on a per capita basis more than six times as many Indians as whites succeed. A third of all Indians in Canada will meet a violent death. For decades the policies of the government and the attitudes of white citizens have combined to deprive native people of their languages, their faith, their self-respect and their hope. Yet no matter what the pitch of misery, native people in western Canada have not rebelled since the uprisings of Riel and Wandering Spirit collapsed in 1885.

"Why do you stay?" I asked. Dave was gifted. He could doubtless have "done well" outside a reserve.

"Because I feel a responsibility," he said. "To my grandfathers and my great-grandfathers. They were given life for a purpose. And it's my purpose to pass on their knowledge to the children." He paused; maybe I was looking startled. "The children are not ours. They're only lent to us."

A pleasantry or two, and he padded off. I had nearly forgotten the stiff-shouldered man in the corner. But all the time, the man had been gathering material for me: reminiscences of elders; a paper on the spiritual meaning of the tipi; another on Indian pipes.

"So it's not just the Protestants against the Catholics?" I asked.

"Oh no," the man said. "Our own practices are . . ."—he always looked beside my face, rather than at it—"very much alive."

I glanced at the memories of Beatrice Guimond: "Medicine is found all over. We step on it and we don't know it. When I want medicine, I look for it, find it, and talk to it like I would to anybody. I would tell it what I want to use it for."

"Are your own healers in touch with the ones on other reserves?"

"They communicate." A smile narrowed the man's eyes to a couple of slits. Then they widened again. "They don't need to visit each other."

But he added nothing. We walked slowly out to the fresh evening. I was about to bid the man farewell when he pulled a small, inconspicuous leaf from a pocket of his denim jacket.

"You see this? It's a kind of . . . wild mint. You can smell the menthol, eh? The plant won't grow round here. It comes from a special area of wetland. A swamp, I guess you'd say. We mix it with tobacco in some of our ceremonies."

76

Why had he shown it to me now, six feet from my car?

"Goodbye," I said. "And thanks."

"Yeah," he said. And walked away.

I was back on the highway before it dawned on me: he was a medicine man.

·XIX·

Gimli seduced me. All I meant to do was pause for a very late lunch, or a very early supper, and then roll on. The highway flits between the western shore of Lake Winnipeg and a branch line of the CPR: three northbound stripes that divide the white world of the frozen water from the brown-green of the land. An image from Mondrian, if you rise high enough overhead.

I turned off the highway and parked in the town. Nestling along the vast lake, it appealed to me at first sight. And first touch, for Gimli's air had a moist freshness to it, a kind of seaside glisten minus the salt. I could sense the pores in my face, closed against the prairie's dust, opening with a wary gratitude. The resemblances to an Atlantic fishing town were uncanny: the rumour of gulls in a grey sky; the pier stretching out to a watery horizon; the little shops promising fresh fish or ice cream; the working boats (now being refurbished in dry dock) and the sandy beach. The afternoon was cool enough for me to imagine a likeness to Iceland. Even the floes seemed to fit.

The café near the harbour looked unprepossessing from the outside, and its seats contained the usual quota of high-school girls sipping Coke and middle-aged men in caps, on the other side of the room, pondering coffee. I ordered the daily special—soup, fish and chips, coffee—and inspected the scene. A sculpture of a fish hung on top of a door; a second door was overlaid by a colour photograph of a tall ship. The waitress shoved the masts to enter the kitchen. By twisting my neck I could see the mural above me: Lake Winnipeg attacked by a wind.

The soup was wonderful.

"Can you tell me what this is?"

"It's cream of beer," the waitress said.

"I beg your pardon."

"Cream of beer!"

Chunks of bacon and vegetables were floating in a rich, malty stock—the first original dish I had encountered in a prairie restaurant. And the fish was breaded pickerel. And the price was low.

I tramped the town, more and more delighted. The little cinema on a side street promised some distinguished films—*The Killing Fields* and *The River,* not just the standard *Rambo* and *Commando*—five nights a week. Every second home seemed to have a birdhouse in its backyard. By the harbour stood a tower for purple martins, an Emmenthal of an edifice with holes to welcome two hundred pairs. Gimli calls itself "the purple martin capital of Manitoba." I just hope the birds use their free hotel. It was a little early for them to be back from their insect-ridden winter quarters in South America, and a crowd of rowdy sparrows was already in residence.

I liked the vivid kiosks for posters and advertisements, which gave one of Gimli's streets the feeling of a miniature Amsterdam. I liked the variety of residents out for a jog beside the lake. I liked the odour of malt that drifted in from the Seagram distillery beyond town when the wind changed. To my surprise, I even liked the statue of the bearded Viking.

He was sculpted in stone (no fibreglass replicas for Gimli!) by Gissur Eliasson and unveiled by the president of Iceland in 1967. The statue recalls the Vikings' discovery of Markland—Newfoundland, or Canada, or America, depending on your point of view—half a millennium before Columbus. A solemn figure, burdened that afternoon by a gull on his helmeted head, he stares away from

78

Lake Winnipeg towards an old people's residence, as though bemused by fate and time. A few yards from the Viking lies the low-slung shore. In the distance: a faint tinkling, as though hundreds of wine glasses were toasting the breeze. The months of ice were finishing at last.

After a few drastic winters, Markland was abandoned. The same fate nearly befell the Republic of New Iceland, a self-governing reserve which Canada set aside here in 1875 for immigrants from the oldest democracy on earth. Disaster after disaster—a plague that killed hundreds of thousands of sheep, a succession of wintry summers, a volcanic eruption that dressed the country's farmland in a shroud of ash—led to a mass departure Iceland could ill afford. Thousands came to Lake Winnipeg. They met smallpox, a severe flood, summer frosts (again), and a religious war in their own ranks that struck some of the cruellest blows of all.

Ploughing, tree-felling and road-building were foreign skills to the New Icelanders. They had to be tough, resourceful and intelligent just to survive. Eventually most of them moved on to drier, less stony pastures elsewhere in Canada. But with the bulwark of further immigration, from the dispossessed Ukrainians in particular, their first village grew into one of the most attractive, graceful communities in the west.

I had found, at last, a little town where I could imagine feeling at home. The only thing I didn't like about the place was that everything from a drugstore to a fishing boat, a travel agency to a hotel, bore the name of Viking.

I walked back to the martins' tower past a bookstore that had, unfortunately, shut its doors at five o'clock. Most prairie towns of two thousand people have nowhere to buy books except, perhaps, a rack of thrillers and Harlequin romances that keeps deodorants away from shampoos in the local pharmacy; but Gimli, bless its collective soul, contained a pair of bookstores. Or rather, the general store that sold an eclectic range of shoes, scarves, souvenirs and sweaters also dealt in books. Reluctantly I stayed clear of its thirteen heroic sagas: Hrafnkel, King Harald, Gudrun and the rest would have to wait for me another year. I bought, instead, the translated poetry of Stephan G. Stephansson, known in the vicinity of Reykjavik as a major poet and known in the vicinity of Markerville, Alberta, as a thrifty pioneer.

A cheerful, good-looking girl rang up the sale on a heavy metal cash register that had, she said, been in service since 1910. In most prairie towns, such a contraption would have been thrown away as an old-fashioned nuisance or donated to a pioneer museum. At H. P. Tergesen & Sons, it was used and treasured. The girl's black-and-white cat, brushing my jeans with its fluffy tail, accepted a morsel of apple with apparent delight.

"So what does 'Gimli' mean, anyway?"

I knew the term only from *The Lord of the Rings,* where Tolkien gave it to the most admirable of dwarfs.

"It's Icelandic," she said. "It means 'paradise.' "

·XX·

"So," she added, "you'll be heading up the Interlake tomorrow?"

"I hope so."

"Why not stop in at Narcisse?"

"What is there at Narcisse?"

"It's where the snakes come out."

How could I refuse? On a crisp, windswept morning I left the Viking Motor Hotel and penetrated an unkempt, pockmarked land. A collision of roads sporadically provoked a church or a forsaken schoolhouse. Low and dense, the aspen woods jostled pastures that were spattered with mounds of rocks like the foundations of extinct villages. The mounds attest to a recent archaeology of courage and perseverance: they are the hard proof, the heaped-up evidence of the settlers' clearance of the soil. A lot of prairie towns contain an official cairn of homage. These giant informal cairns—six, ten, even twelve to a field—pay tribute to a struggle that men and women undertook out of a sheer hunger to survive.

To a farmer, Lake Winnipeg and Lake Manitoba sandwich a bad land: meagre, stony, damp. Although it tolerates cattle, it discourages grain. Narcisse is a moribund village. Its name, I guessed, must refer to the plethora of sloughs and small lakes. I guessed wrong: it honours Narcisse Leven, a promoter of Jewish settlement in rural Manitoba. A few miles north of its tumble-down buildings, I turned onto a brief, bumpy trail that led to the local "community pasture." An old blue bus and a couple of cars at the trail's end suggested the snakes were not alone.

I hiked across the prairie to a remote commotion in the bushes. The crocuses made a sudden constellation, the buttercups a galaxy in the silver-green grass below my feet. I approached a cackle of laughter in down-filled jackets: the Selkirk and District Senior Citizens' Club. The shallow basin of rocks and earth in front of them clasped about four hundred twisting, wriggling snakes.

"Watch out at your feet there, Doris!"

Doris jumped. She looked pleased, then annoyed to find that one of her cohorts was playing a practical joke. She turned her attention to the bus driver, a genial man in a windbreaker with a snake around his left arm. A scarlet tongue, darting over his wrist, gave the illusion of danger. The snake was a foot long: a handsome animal with a black body and a pinkish-red shading on the margin of two yellow stripes. His colouring nearly belied the term "red-sided garter snake."

The creature had passed a dry winter beneath us, in a collapsed limestone cave where the warmth of underground tunnels protected his cold blood. Late in April he glided from the months of darkness into this tussle of boulders. There he and hundreds of other males waited for the females to emerge. In spring the glands of female snakes emit a scent that drives male snakes wild. Each female must slide a gauntlet of males who coil around her, fasten onto her and swarm all over her in a frenzy to mate. But the males are thin and

81

small, and within a few hours most females escape from the pit and emigrate to a marsh. Lascivious, the males remain.

The driver let his captive go at last. Within a few seconds the snake was oblivious to manhandling; his world had contracted to the shape of an ancient imperative.

A flock of children, ten- and eleven-year-olds from a school in the Interlake, romped up. Rapt and excited, they called advice to each other—"See this little guy jumpin' down?"—and to their favourite snakes—"Come on, she's gonna escape, catch hold of her!" Yet the pensioners with their Pentaxes seemed as agile as the children with their pencils, and were somewhat less inhibited about clambering into the pit. One old-timer crouched beside his anxious grandson over a nest of snakes. A young biologist kept an eye on the crowd and assuaged its doubts:

"No, ma'am, they aren't slippery. They feel like leather. No, sir, they're beneficial to farmers. Yes, ma'am, the females are the big ones."

The festive atmosphere intrigued me, the sense that I had stumbled on a rite of spring. Somehow the spectacle drew the crowd together, transforming its individuals into a stirred community. Their knowledge had dispelled paranoia. For when it comes to snakes, ignorance breeds fear. Knowledge gave the crowd the confidence to watch the sinuous dance; and the dancers, it was clear, took no interest in human beings apart from eluding their feet and hands.

"Look at that female tryin' to get away!"

The snakes were here for sex. And the senior ladies of Selkirk took a sly glee in the mating—or else in the patient work of the young biologist. Behind his back, the driven animals continued to wrap each other up. Benign, unfamiliar, non-erotic, the sexuality of the event encouraged a sweet banter.

"So the males don't think about nothing else for weeks! Typical, eh, Arthur?"

I hiked to another snake pit along a path that coursed through bearberry meadows for a flat, speckled mile. The year's first avens shone purplish-red in the grass. From its black roots, Indians brewed up a tea against coughs, colds and cankers.

The aspens were already in leaf: spring was quick, precocious. I sat on a sandy hill to watch more animals writhe amid the crannies of lime. The sight, I realized, confounded the familiar image, whereby a snake lurks alone in the grass with a venomous desire. Such is the power of mythology that I promptly felt uneasy and glanced behind me twice. As soon as I quit the safety of a crowd, the old archetypes began to slither back. I was relieved when a teen-aged boy chugged up on a trail bike to join me above the boulders and the leathery coils.

"That ball of them over there hasn't moved in the last five minutes," I said. Not from a need to pass on information, but from the urge to establish a kind of relation.

"Is that right?"

Thereafter we looked on in amiable silence. His shadow leaned across a cool knot of snakes.

A mourning cloak butterfly fluttered into the pit, attracted by the warmth of the sun against stones. Its dark wings, like a garter snake's back, were emblazoned with yellow. The butterfly settled on a rock to bask. "Dangerous," I thought. But the snakes, six inches away, were too preoccupied to care.

·XXI·

Canada too has its narrow roads to a deep north: the ropes of asphalt that untwine, with a heroism that totters, sometimes, on the brink of madness and futility, up to Fort McMurray or Fort St. John or Manicouagan. Roads that leave the domain of loneliness—a light flickering in the woods—and broach the realm of solitude. Roads that tunnel through the ore of wilderness as though it were a green mine. "In the midst of the roaring wind and driving clouds," Basho noted after a pilgrimage to the deep north of Japan, "I felt myself to be in a world totally different from the one I was accustomed to." The radical simplicity of water and pines makes every breath a traveller of eternity.

First hour. Near the village of Poplarfield I looked away from the road at a stone angel in the graveyard. That instant, a thin kestrel flew over the angel's head. It was searching, no doubt, for voles and crickets in the grass. But the synchronicity—hawk and statue, feathers and rock, a winged killer and a promise of mercy—filled me with a glance.

Second hour. I stopped at Grahamdale. Within living memory the Interlake's northwest was unsettled; the first white families, many of them German, survived on jack rabbits and snowshoe hares. After leaving his homestead in the summer to work on a harvest crew, a man would spend the fall and winter in Manitoba's sawmills or Ontario's lumber camps. His springs were for the family. This was, perhaps, the pattern of life for a local pioneer called Armand Lemiez; but Monsieur Lemiez was also an artist. I tried the Grahamdale Hotel for news.

I waited a couple of minutes, tapping on the beer-sales counter. Nothing happened. Finally, a sallow woman in her forties emerged grinning from the bar. A button on her white T-shirt announced *It's About Fucking Time*—an ambiguous phrase, I thought.

"Does Armand Lemiez still live in the area?"

"No, he passed away a while ago."

"But can I look at his paintings?"

"They're in security down in Winnipeg."

"You mean there isn't anything left at Grahamdale?"

"Sure, there's the sculptures all around his house."

This sounded hopeful.

"How do I get there?"

Her two suggestions left me a choice between a probably impassable road and a hike through a succession of wet, barbed fields.

"Just watch out for the cops," she added. "They keep a real close eye on the place."

84

"Okay, thanks a lot."

"And don't tell anybody I told you the way!"

But my discretion overpowered my valour. In this grudging countryside, the nearest town of a thousand people was already more than eighty miles away. I wanted neither an arrest in a pasture nor a breakdown on a liquid road. The sculptures of Armand Lemiez joined the church at Forget and the Treesbank ferry as icons on my mental screen of Next Year Country.

Third hour. What keeps a driver alert in the flat, wooded emptiness are the small red flags by the side of the road. Sometimes they signal a pothole, sometimes a patch of gravel, sometimes a swooping bump and sometimes nothing at all. Sometimes they flutter on the west bank, sometimes on the east and sometimes both. Sometimes, too, a pothole detonates the highway without a flag in sight.

I listened to a country lament from a crackling station in Dauphin: "She's got a-hold of me where it hurts / And she won't let go."

On my left: Devils Lake. Blind Lake. Soul Lake. On my right: Wicked Point.

Two ravens peered up from the ditch, eating.

Fourth hour. The land is an exception, a bone in a pool of blood. The rule is water. Below me, the constrained waters of the Saskatchewan River were rushing to embrace Lake Winnipeg. The fur traders knew the value of an outpost in this green, spectacular valley. Before the cities of Saskatoon and Regina existed, before the province of Manitoba was more than a postage stamp on the map, Grand Rapids had a wharf, warehouses and a tramway. Men manufactured lime here and fished for profit, and later built a generating station for hydroelectric power. The components were in place for a great city.

Two centuries after its foundation, Grand Rapids houses fewer than six hundred people. Another three hundred live on the adjacent lands of the Cree. Unemployment is epidemic. To drive about the ramshackle town on a gusty afternoon is to hear the whispers of the dead mingling with the petitions of the unborn, the never-to-be-born: "Build here!" "Have faith!" "Give this place a chance!" "Give it your life!"

I ate a sandwich in the Esso café and fed the car a drink of gas. A handwritten notice by the cash-desk instructed me: HAVE A GOOD NICE DAY.

Fifth hour. North of Grand Rapids the aspens and poplars lost their buds and reverted to a wintry nakedness. Thirty miles disappeared before I saw another car. The highway pierced a wilderness unbroken by mines or villages, camps or parks.

"Wilderness" was once a misnomer, a cultural anxiety. The vast scale of the landscape provoked white fright. But to the Indians who used these forests and waters as a thoroughfare, who knew them with the intimacy of lifelong wayfarers, "wilderness" was a foreign concept.

Their descendants belong on reserves or the skid rows of cities. For better or worse, they have accepted the notion of permanent settlement. Even men who still fish, hunt and trap use their reserves as a base. And in the hundreds of square miles I was driving through, no reserves exist. Nowadays the land may be "wilder," may be emptier of human consciousness than at any time since the glaciers left.

Yet the experience of speed negates the shock of the land. It kills the massive stillness, the evergreen poise. It destroys the silence and the solo improvisations of water. And it distorts the natural values of northern space, the arterial quality of lakes and rivers. Charging ahead like a manic bull, a car makes the world around it irrelevant.

For dozens of miles the road accompanied the wires and giant silver pylons that carry the breath of power to the south. The shape of these pylons interested me: two diagonal poles that rise like spread legs into a torso of metal, from which a vertical pole emerges at the neck. Such metallic landmarks, fixed at regular intervals against the forest, establish the presence of technological man in an alien, alienating land. They are symbols of domination in a stylized human form.

They are, in brief, our inukshuks.

Sixth hour. Still driving. In the shadow of the pylons the radio faded, leaving me with nothing except my voice and the engine's voracious purr. We talked to each other. We answered back.

Seventh hour. The highway split against a wall of forest near the

86

tiny settlement of Ponton. I took the right-hand fork. A few miles later, a dark shape loomed at the roadside. I skidded to a stop five yards away from a black bear on its hind legs. To my surprise it remained, looking. Its big, inquisitive face showed no sign of fear. After a minute, probably bored, it dropped to all fours, trotted through the wet ditch and scrambled up a bank into the forest. There it paused and gazed at the car, as though hoping for an answer to some important puzzle of its own.

A campground, a picnic site, the odd village thinned the emptiness. The turning to Wabowden came and went. It sounded, I thought, like an Indian name—the word, perhaps, for "curious bear." The next day I learned the truth: an engineer on the rail-building crew was called W. A. Bowden.

Eighth hour. Still driving. I caught up with winter's retreat in the shape of a weary ridge of snow prodding the highway. A flock of goldeneye flew fast and low above the final ice-floe of the Grass River, then settled warily onto the surging water near the bridge.

I took the gravel track down to Pisew Falls. Its name comes from the Cree term for a lynx's hiss. But the water hisses only from a distant safety; close up, the noise suggests an amplified roar. Every second, twenty-five thousand gallons of water suffer a forty-foot drop. The water never freezes, even in the abyss of January. Its spray has created a microclimate ideal for mosses, ferns and lichens. White spruces tower above the tumbling river from a height they are never supposed to achieve north of the 55th Parallel.

Legs creaking, I left the car for the first time since Grand Rapids. The damp air smelt sweet. Snow on the forest floor had melted to a boggy duff. But where the spray had frozen beyond the waterfall, ice rose up like a berg. Tattered and bruised, a few small conifers protruded from the white wall. Over it a spruce's wavering shadow played in the evening light.

The barred tail of a ruffed grouse brought the woods to life. Its chirr of alarm was scarcely audible against the water's perpetual cry. I stretched and breathed, hard.

Ninth hour. Road-worn, seat-sore, I arrived at the mining town of Thompson.

·XXII·

The place is, literally, built on nickel. Tunnels from two of the International Nickel Company's shafts connect below the waste of asphalt, interrupted by shopping malls, that constitutes "downtown." Thompson's streets have mineral names: Quartz and Copper, Nickel and Silver. To resist the wind—harsh from the west, cruel from the north, vicious when it claws from Hudson Bay to the east—buildings are low. Snow is not uncommon in May and September, not unknown in June and August. Close to the surface of the land lies the permafrost. In their annual battle to grow an onion or a tulip, the residents of Thompson buy sacks of topsoil to spread like jam across the earth.

They've fought hard to make the town pleasant, to make a life here something more than a lucrative endurance test. Nowadays they can use, amid the tang of pines, a multicultural centre, a dapper library, even a French immersion program. But it's hard to forget, even for a moment, that Thompson is a company town. Much of the forest is barred to everyone except "authorized Inco personnel." To create a nearby open-pit mine, the company dredged a lake. Thompson's buildings are bland and functional; nothing in them can approach the rough grandeur of the mines, the refinery, the processing complex.

Nothing except the spindly trees, the river and the ancient rocks is more than thirty years old. In the first years of development Inco ruled this place as though it were United Fruit Company, and Canada a northerly Honduras. Thompson eventually swelled into a city of 25,000. But its fortunes cleaved to a single industry. And when, in the depression of 1982, Inco shut down for months, the population fell by half. Apartments emptied, small businesses died, mobile homes trundled away. Thousands of southerners took their scars and unemployment cheques elsewhere. The experience left the city with a permanent nervous tic, a twitching awareness of its collective mortality. When the nickel is exhausted, only the ravens and the Cree may remain.

Even if you try to overlook Thompson's origins, its purpose for existence, you won't be permitted to succeed.

A THANK YOU AND AN APOLOGY
The Thompson Festival of the Arts wishes to publicly thank Inco
Limited for its donation of $2,000 for Festival bursaries. At the
same time, the Festival Awards Committee apologizes for not
inviting Inco representative Dan McSweeney to present the awards.

I had been travelling hard. Thompson gave me a respite—a chance to recuperate from the stress of constant movement. I relaxed there. As a result, perhaps, my memories of the city are sporadic and incongruous. I recall a waitress in the Chicken Chef who seemed flabbergasted that I should ask for a "fish dinner," who brought me the dismal stuff without a knife, fork, place mat or serviette, and who had never heard of tartar sauce; but I forget two complete mornings. I recall the crescent-shaped flock of geese pushing northwest into a violent, orange-purple sunset outside my motel room; but I slept three nights in that room (or was it four?) and I can't remember it at all.

Luckily I found a couple of diversions. The first was a family from India (via East Africa and Saskatoon) who showed me kindness and a video of a wedding. Outside, the afternoon was iron-grey and the wind from some oblivion was bitter. Inside, I perched on an exquisite chair of inlaid wood—part of Anil's lavish dowry—and watched his family pose before a public building in Ahmedabad. The building bore the inscription GOVERNMENT WORK IS GOD'S WORK. Anil, a technician for Inco, pressed the fast-forward button; while his tape sprinted ahead, the TV screen reverted to a baseball game somewhere in a shirt-sleeved sun. I stayed for dinner: roast beef, to my bemusement, with broccoli and mashed potatoes, a meal that Anil and his sisters shared. But his wife and his beaming grandfather, sitting at the same table, ate shaak and chapatis and rice.

My second diversion was the newspaper. To know a place it always helps to ponder what the local journalists uncover, and what they neglect to cover. I found the RCMP report in the *Thompson Citizen*

89

enlightening. It described forty-eight hours in the middle of a working week. One attempted suicide, two assaults, three break-ins, four traffic accidents, five thefts: the litany of chaos read like a child's primer of arithmetic. Occasionally the awkward prose achieved a lumbering, taciturn eloquence:

Six persons were reported missing. Two were six-year-old children from Brandon Crescent, who were later located, and one was a lost two-year-old girl who was also located. One was a report by the Awasis Agency of a missing juvenile. There was also another report of a missing juvenile who was later located. There was also a report of a three-year-old child found in the Queens Bay area.

I read about a drunken commotion in a bar and a fight outside the Presbyterian church. The RCMP had heard about a sea gull with a broken wing, and the Department of Natural Resources had sent a man to retrieve it. Then came the oddest, saddest sentence of all:

A complaint was received of a person throwing rocks on Parkway which proved to be a female breaking windows of her own house.

·XXIII·

The old man sat down at the next table. I sipped my beer and watched him stretch a hand to the slumped woman in a black blouse and tight black trousers. Indignantly she pushed him away. He shifted his chair sideways so that

90

above the high-voltage rock, she could hear his voice. I looked elsewhere, at the white bartenders and waiters and the (mostly) Indian
drinkers observing each other in the vast room. It was, in fact, not
so much a room as a warehouse with a low ceiling, a badly stained
red carpet and dark wooden walls. "Roughest bar north of fifty-
five," a friend had said in Saskatoon. "Stay away."

The man was pointing and waving in my direction. I turned to
see who or what he wanted behind my back. He wanted me.

So I took my beer and joined him. The man pumped my right
hand with his large gnarled fingers. I understood the gesture but, in
the Saturday night hubbub of heavy music and two hundred customers, I was bemused by the workings of his mouth. Inside his
windbreaker the man wore a tie over his patterned shirt. A Via Rail
cap hid his scalp.

Finally I understood his challenge: "How come you're sitting on
your own?"

"I'm a visitor."

"What are you doing in Thompson?"

The truth was too complex to shout.

"I'm on my way up to Churchill!"

The woman spoke for the first time. Her puffed complexion,
plump body and dark, tiny eyes gave little hint of her age. She
could have been anything from twenty-five to fifty.

"I was in Churchill for two years. Churchill's where I had my first
child."

"I was in Churchill in 1933," the man said. He tried to elaborate, but the music and his drunkenness defeated him.

"My name's Mark!" I said. They nodded and smiled. We all
looked at each other.

"This here's my girlfriend," the man said at last, grinning as he
slid his left arm round her shoulder and onto a breast. His cigarette
dropped ash on her blouse.

"Don't paw me!" she shouted. "Get your fuckin' hands away!"
And to me, bending across the round black table: "He's my uncle."

"Do you work for Via Rail?" I asked him.

"I worked for CN for thirty years," he said. His glasses shook on his
nose when he nodded. "Retired in 1974."

91

"What was that?"

"I retired in '74!"

"Really," I said. Their bottles were empty and a waiter was hovering: a decision had to be made.

"I'll buy drinks all round," I said. "Another Blue for me." They welcomed my offer in desperate style: a double rye for him, a double vodka for her, and chasers of draught beer for them both. The man spoke a couple of foreign sentences which, I assumed, were Cree. But instead of answering, she leaned at me:

"You're French, aren't you?"

"No, I come from Saskatoon."

"But you're French!"

Why—my dark hair and beard? My watchfulness? My tight, crisp speech? When the woman frowned, her eyes all but vanished inside her face. The drinks arrived, the man laughed and finally, briefly, she joined in. But then:

"What you doin' tonight?"

The man locked his muscular right arm around my head and tugged it over the table, inches from his rye. He bent and began a complicated narrative. My face swam in his power. But I couldn't see his lips and I couldn't understand the furred rambling. After thirty or forty seconds, he let me go.

Baffled, I looked away. At the long bar, black-and-white photographs of eminent Indians vied for pride of place with a couple of baseball trophies. A mirror bore the label OLD VIENNA.

The rock music cascaded to a halt. In what passed for silence the woman said, "I want to read your eyes." Though she discovered nothing of interest, she had succeeded in trapping my gaze.

A quartet of men in ruffled shirts and leather boots mounted a platform at the other end of the room. Glancing around, I saw a hockey game in shades of green on a high, ignored TV. The men grated a fistful of chords and cantered off into a macho ballad. At the table the old man looked stupefied. The woman smirked and winked.

"You know how to dance?"

"Not really," I said.

"What?"

"No!"

92

But she stood, grabbed my hand and led me through a forest of bottle-barked tables to the dance floor. Three or four couples were shuffling to and fro. I felt a little nervous about the jealousy of her boyfriends, past, present or future. Yet nobody betrayed a trace of surprise. Our bodies were too distant for the woman's taste, and she pulled me against her. The tactic enabled her to lower her voice.

"We're all halfbreeds," she confided. "I hope you didn't want no full-blooded Indians."

After a couple of sluggish songs, we retrieved our drinks. An odour of alcohol was starting to overwhelm her lingering cheap perfume. The railwayman had moved to another table, from which he gave us a tough look. "He's mad at me," she said. "I don't want to sleep with him no more."

Now that she had made a kind of conquest, the woman relaxed a little. She dropped her repertoire of tics and flutters. "I love you," she said with a glimmer of drunken bravado. "Baby!"

The endearments were appeals. They arrived from some far-off memory of tenderness, as though they belonged to an alien tongue. Our hands were immobile between our touching thighs: the grip was like a proof that the woman was still good for something. But she made no move to kiss.

In the interval between a couple of cowboy songs I asked her where she lived. The mention of home—a reserve not far from Thompson—somehow recalled her brother Norman:

"I warned him not to fight with me. I told him! But he forced me. He backed me into a corner! And he's the one that ended up in hospital."

A pause.

"What happened?"

"I stabbed him."

The man heaved back to our table, showing no sign of bad will. "Hi there," he called. Perhaps he had read my reluctance.

"I fight dirty," she added, smiling. Her lips budged less than her eyes. The gesture opened up her sockets.

The man's granddaughter came over and chaffed him for a minute. She was a friendly teenager, nearly good-looking, but without a front tooth in the upper half of her mouth.

Drunkenness was overcoming the woman. In the smoky haze her relaxation crumpled her will. "You got a room?" she asked with a slur I could barely understand.

"No," I lied. Common sense and prudence and the wedding ring on my finger were buttressed by a cool absence of desire.

She nodded.

"You want to go someplace?" the man inquired.

I didn't answer. The two of them held a confused discussion about the possibility of borrowing a room at the hotel from somebody who might or might not be sleeping in it. No one said a word about money.

The country singers finished their set and the amplified rock pounded back. But the bar's turbulent pulses of human energy seemed controlled, even orderly, as though its rough public exchanges were but a preamble to the private acts of sex and violence that would ensue after midnight in black streets and alleys and the town's meaner rooms.

"Where's my handbag?" the woman asked suddenly. "Where's my jacket?"

They were lying somewhere in Thompson, and neither she nor the man could imagine where. "Goddamn lost!" she cried. For a minute her self-control guttered.

She roused herself for a final effort: "Love me, baby," with a low laugh. It was not a plea I matched. The alcohol, the music and the general confusion made replies optional. Yet she would, no doubt, even through the tumult, have taken note of the answer she craved.

I gave no comfort. Instead, I recovered my hand, rose and said, "I got to go to the toilet." There I waited an unnecessary length of time.

When I emerged, the woman and the man were gone. They had read my absence with lucidity; they had even left me some beer.

·XXIV·

I used to think that Canada's Indians had traded their broken freedom for reserves under Queen Victoria, and that they had festered or (occasionally) flourished on the same land ever since. In Manitoba I found a grimmer truth.

An Ojibwa band near Fort Garry, I learned, had helped the Earl of Selkirk's immigrants to survive. "Having rendered most essential services to the settlers in distress," Selkirk wrote in 1817, "[Chief Peguis] deserves to be treated with favour and distinction." Half a century later, when Louis Riel first rebelled against the Crown, the Ojibwa offered Colonel Dennis a hundred men to suppress the revolt. A treaty that they signed in 1871 gave them exclusive rights to 48,000 acres north of Winnipeg. "Her Majesty shall have you as her own children," the treaty said. "You have done a wonderful thing to surrender your country to Her Government and this shall stand for all time."

But in 1907, under pressure from white men who coveted the Indians' farms, the government decided to hand the region over to settlers. Its officials promised the Ojibwa more land elsewhere. They arranged an informal poll, giving two days' notice, and announced that the men of the band had approved the scheme. The Ojibwa were then shunted to the northern Interlake. Their new reserve was certainly larger than the old. But it consisted of marginal land, damp and rocky and uncleared. It had no schools, no farms and no roads. The nearest store was eight miles distant.

There the people remain.

The illusion is that such an act of treachery belongs to the remote past. Even in the deep north of Manitoba, an Indian band suffered irreparable harm at the hands of a recent government.

When the Hudson's Bay Company post at Little Duck Lake closed down in the mid-1950s, the federal Department of Indian Affairs decided that a band of Chipewyan should no longer hunt, trap and fish in the scrub forest around the lake. Caribou populations were uncertain and, in the absence of the Bay store, hardship

95

might ensue. So the Chipewyan were airlifted from their homes. Their dogs, boats, traps and sleds remained behind. The planes deposited the people in the modern town of Churchill, more than a hundred miles away on the shore of Hudson Bay.

The government had not discussed the plan with the Chipewyan, few of whom were fluent in English. Many of them had never seen Churchill, which contained a large population of Cree Indians, a traditional enemy. The Chipewyan way of life disintegrated at the stroke of a pen. They were left with no land, no bread except the government's charity, and no peace except the peace of death.

In Churchill they inhabited shacks and tents until the government transferred them to "Camp Ten." The camp was a cluster of forty-five small houses without toilets or running water, located on an exposed ridge above the local graveyard. Eventually the government moved them again, to a model ghetto called "Dene Village." Here again the Chipewyan patterns of settlement, which reflect kinship and friendship, were disregarded. The people fell into an anguish of alcoholism, violence, prostitution, poverty and sheer, mute despair. Of a community smaller than four hundred, more than seventy died in Churchill as a consequence of drinking.

Nearly twenty years after the forcible relocation, the Chipewyan started to regain some control over their lives. Most of them went back to the land, moving into log cabins by a roadless lake. The isolation and unemployment they experience at Tadoule are still preferable to the degradation they met in Churchill.

At short notice, I couldn't fly into Tadoule. But when I visited the office of the Keewatin Tribal Council, I learned that another band of northern Indians was leaving another convenient town. The Fox Lake Cree were hoping to find self-control and harmony in a new settlement called Bird. Would I care to pay a visit?

XXV

Harold Earle, an official of the Keewatin Tribal Council, arranged the flight and drove me to Thompson's little airport. On the far shore of the Burntwood River, we passed a junk-food trailer called Popeye's. Harold stretched a hand towards the slush-consumers.

"That's where my grandmother had her cabin. I know these woods. I went trapping here when I was a boy."

"The cabin isn't there anymore?"

"Naw, they bought her out with a few trinkets."

We drank coffee in the waiting room. "I used to have hundreds of caps," Harold said, glancing at my peaked head. "Then a few years back I was drinking heavily. And I started giving away caps to everybody I met when I was drunk. By the time I quit drinking I was down to fifty caps."

Three or four mechanics were lounging across the room and chatting, of all things, about England. "They just don't have the empty spaces we do. I mean," the speaker added, looking in my silent direction, "you fly out of here and there's *nothing*."

"Of course," another said, "they don't have no natives either."

Harold did not respond.

The plane was ready: a four-seat Navajo. "So long," Harold said, and walked back to his car.

The pilot tried to enlighten me about the mysteries of the control panel. But as we clattered down the runway and climbed the sky, a cacophony of engine noise preempted casual talk. I gazed downward at the free drift of a few white clouds, passing like thoughts across a mind of air. Grounded, the forest broke against a whiteness of frozen water. Occasional lakes had thawed to a numb, anaemic turquoise. It seemed a comfort that this blessed plot of earth, this womb of wolves two miles below our feet, had been marred so little by man.

We landed on a spiny airstrip near Gillam, a raw, prefabricated town of fourteen hundred. Whites are dominant here, but not by

97

much. The streets feel like pudgy lines that a methodical child once ruled across some makeshift clearing in the forest. A government building, bland as ever, holds the offices of the Fox Lake Cree. For the moment, its members were living mostly in town.

While I waited for the chief I read a notice in the corridor. It promised a weekend of spring ceremonies elsewhere in Manitoba's north. Pipe-carriers and elders would come from three provinces to engage in a series of rituals: healing, feasting, naming; smoking, sweating, sunrise-greeting. "Camp out—bring the whole family." And an afterthought: "No booze, no drugs, no etc."

The chief put down the phone, shaking his ponytailed head.

"Let's go have some lunch," he suggested.

We fed on soup and sandwiches in the Strawberry Patch Café. In a painting by the kitchen door, the world was the colour of jam.

"Ever hear tell of what happened one time down at Island Lake?" the chief said. He was young and broad and pensive. "The only whites on the reserve were a Hudson's Bay man who was a bad drinker and a missionary priest who kept dogs. Well, the weather got pretty tough for a while, and the Bay man drank all his whisky. Finished it the very morning that a plane was flying in with supplies. So when the plane had landed, the Bay man rolled up and started tearing open the crates. And there was nothing inside of them except cans and cans of Dr. Ballard's dog food!"

On our walk back to the offices we paused at a Cree bakery. Row after row of metal trays accommodated sliced white bread. I declined a loaf and accepted a roll. Pale and airy, it had no flavour.

"Good, eh?" the baker said. "We sell a lot of those."

"We also run a store," the chief said as we emerged into the streets' scent of pines and gasoline. "But probably you don't want to see it."

I was feeling downright puzzled. The motive for my journey had been to explore the new settlement of Bird. But everything I had seen so far suggested a rootedness in Gillam.

"Do you like this town?" I asked.

"Not much," the chief said. "In Gillam we're not in control of our lives. It gets hard to maintain—" He broke off and started anew. "Some of our people feel different, though." He shrugged.

98

"They'll stay."

A young woman called Betsy awaited us by the office window. Her skin, unusually pale, formed a powerful contrast against her black hair. The band had made her a councillor, an uncommon role for a woman in Manitoba, and that day her job was to drive me out to Bird in her menopausal half-ton. I boarded with suspicion. The chief followed with another councillor in a second worn machine.

But the road was a sleek asphalt. A few miles out of Gillam it overarched the wide, fast Nelson River, then swung to parallel the north bank. The evergreens here were taller and thicker than the trees away from the river, which looked like neglected bonsai. The Nelson is a continuation of the Saskatchewan River-system under a different label. If Tom Sukanen had ever got his boat off the scarred prairie and nosed it down to Hudson Bay, he would have passed these boulder-strewn shores.

"You come from Gillam?" I asked Betsy.

"No, I'm from Winnipeg," she answered. "First I moved to Thompson, then up to Gillam. And pretty soon I'll be moving out to Bird." She grinned; the gesture uncovered an immaculate line of teeth. "It's kind of opposite to the normal pattern, eh? If things carry on like this, I guess maybe I'll end up some kind of hermit in the bush."

We turned left along a gravel road about twenty miles from town. The highway barged ahead to the massive complex that was gathering near the confluence of the Limestone and Nelson rivers. Most of the electricity these Sundance turbines generate is destined to flow south to the U.S.A. Without the guarantee of American sales, the dam would have remained a dream.

The side road brought us to the tracks of the CNR and a little cluster of wooden houses. A mild assortment of débris bedaubed the land. Smoke twisted from a chimney. Beyond it, the road died in a few crescents of bungalows painted to outshine the sky.

"This is Bird!" Betsy said, her face glowing.

I scrambled out of the truck and looked around. A mean wind was shoving across this cavity in the bush. Yet the chief, like Betsy, wore a little smile.

He unlocked a front door in the wilderness and we stepped into suburbia. I recognized at once the square windows and the low ceiling; I knew the stagnant air by heart. The kitchen resembled a set for a detergent commercial. The basement boasted a washing machine and a dryer. Four sleek bedrooms wadded the house, which had space enough in the basement to insert a couple more.

"So when will you be moving in?" I said. Whatever I had expected Bird to be—a scrum of cabins on the outskirts of nowhere? —it wasn't an estate of thirty houses that could have been airlifted from the flanks of New Westminster or Kansas City.

"Maybe next month," the chief replied. "A few families have been out here for a long time, eh? The rest of us would have moved already, but we ran into problems hooking up the water."

We inspected a second house. The design was minutely different, but the same electric accessories stood on guard.

"And what will you do when you're out here?"

Their answers were a little slow.

"There's good fishing in some of the rivers," Betsy said. "Hunting too. When you get the caribou moving through . . ."

"Trapping," the chief's driver muttered.

"Then there's the Sundance project," the chief said. "The government keeps talking about how it wants to get native people involved. We're waiting, eh? They know we're here."

A blue house overflowed with bedrooms: five of them, like squat fingers probing the contours of a plywood box. In Gillam I had seen nothing to approach this derivative glamour.

"Is there a store here?"

"Not really," the chief said cryptically.

"How about a school?"

"Now that's what we're kind of upset about," he said. "The government paid for these houses, eh? And we asked them to build a permanent school. But they said no, because Sundance is just along the highway. So our kids are gonna have to catch a bus to some trailers over there. Then five, six, seven years from now, they'll haul the trailers down to Bird."

"Don't you see?" Betsy said. "The government couldn't accept that a few white kids might have to go to school on an Indian reserve!"

100

"Guess you've seen enough, eh?" the chief inquired.

"How about one of those older-looking houses?" I asked. "Away from the road. Maybe I could speak to somebody who lives here already."

An embarrassed reluctance: a looking away: a shifting silence.

"Well, I don't know," the chief said finally. He lit a cigarette and watched his fingers through the smoke.

"Might not be that good an idea," his driver added.

Betsy was nodding.

So we eased aboard the half-tons and sped back to Gillam. Optimism began to fight a war with cynicism in my head; the desire to believe skirmished a weary disappointment. The optimism said: *What you've seen at Bird is a group of people who are proud of what they're doing and confident about the future. So what if the houses aren't to your idea of taste? Maybe this will be a place where the Cree can accomplish what native peoples everywhere need to do: integrate the present with their own traditions, in their own particular way. How dare you scoff at their dignity and their hope?*

But the cynicism: *The only way these people can possibly survive out here is by taking money from the government. And what good is that for their dignity? Their old problems will still be around: Bird is pretty close to Gillam and it's even closer to Sundance, which consists mostly of young white men loaded with dollars and lusting after booze and women. This fake suburbia is just a clever use of white money to try and appease white guilt.*

And the optimism: *Come on, there'll still be families at Bird when the Sundance workers have all gone south. And it's far enough —*

Betsy was looking my way.

"You hear those geese?" she repeated.

Above the sore-throated clatter of the engine, a remote appeal in the sky.

"Yeah, they're on their way back," she said with pleasure. "My husband shot a couple of snow geese last Saturday. He was going out again today."

XXVI

That evening I wandered Gillam's silent checkerboard streets. I was waiting to catch the Polar Bear Express, the train that plods from Winnipeg to Churchill twice a week. I wanted to travel as far north as the prairie provinces allow.

Light lingered in the sky. But the air was chilly, and my only refuge was a cavernous bar near the station. I drank a solitary Export and watched four or five men playing pool. Their jokes and insults left no doubt that the men worked for Manitoba Hydro. Handwritten signs on the walls of the cavern advertised shrimp cocktail and pickled herring.

A pool player joined me at the urinal.

"You're a technician with CN," he told me.

"No, I'm not," I said. "I'm heading up to Churchill."

"Then you're with Parks Canada," he said.

"No, I'm not," I repeated, and left him standing baffled.

The train lunged timidly into the station. A locomotive with a single passenger car, it would remain in Gillam until midnight. I jogged up and down the platform a few times, then climbed aboard. The seats were deep and pliable, and most of the twenty-five passengers had stretched into a fitful, diagonal doze. Three women and a man were playing a lazy game of whist. A stylish student from Winnipeg showed the only ebullience: she was a single night away from her boyfriend.

"Can't believe how quiet it is out there," I said.

"That's on account of the curfew," she replied. "When a kid is found on the streets at night, his parents get fined."

A damp wilderness of shortening evergreens lay beyond the town's prefabricated buildings and the line of telephone wires. I wondered how many demands, pleas or loving reassurances were flitting past the stationary train. In Manitoba's north, the wires are bolstered by a network of tripods, like skeleton tipis dividing up the land. By balancing three short poles against each other, the builders guarded against the ravages of permafrost.

The CNR constructed the railway in the 1920s to furnish the prairies with a harbour: Manitoba still has no road to Hudson Bay, and no prospect of one to come. The railway gives the western plains an ocean door, a salt-water escape. Churchill, where food cannot be grown, is a farmers' port.

The darkness was intense when we deserted Gillam, and the windows showed only a mirage of the inner train. I accomplished the delicate task of removing and storing my contact lenses at my seat. Sometime around one we passed the invisible settlement of Bird. An hour later, a jolt evicted me from a dream of gardens and blossoming fruit trees: two Indian boys across the aisle gathered armfuls of gear and stumbled out towards a shimmer. I tried to find a name on a tripod. Failing, bleary, I wondered at my need for names.

It was light when I woke again. Consciousness arrived before memory, delivering a shock: the trees had vanished and the world had changed to boulders fringed with snow. It was as if I had awakened into someone else's mind. My eyes had never before seen the tundra, the subarctic barren lands: the exposed flesh and bones above the well-dressed south of the country. Then I remembered.

I bought a plastic coffee, implanted my lenses in red, protesting eyes, and watched the skin of the world. Briefly, the patches of snow occupied the tundra and shook the metallic sky. But as the train approached the estuary of the Churchill River, a stunted forest reappeared. Waist-high, chest-high, its trees were veterans from a past generation, even a past century. To grow an inch in diameter, one of these spruces needs twenty years. Each life was bending southward, as though from a mute, instinctive hunger to capture light and heat. Grey moss, like a shawl of worn-out lace, draped the trees. It deprived their scrawny branches of the colour green.

"You want to know a Churchill joke?" the student asked. The prospect of meeting her boyfriend gave her a radiance which nobody else on the train, tired after an angular sleep, could match.

"Sure."

"How many trees does it take to grow a Christmas tree?"

"?"

"Two!"

103

Looking out at the dwarf forest, I managed a grin.

The passengers began to search for scarves and gloves. To the west I glimpsed the half-frozen Churchill River, almost, by now, a coastal bay. The clutter of cabins, garbage and old machinery proved the approach of civilization. A young mother, contemplating the snowdrifts, turned to the conductor and said: "Makes you wonder why we live here, eh?"

"Don't ask me, ma'am," he replied.

"& when wee was gott in," Captain Knight wrote in 1717, "I went a shore. But I never See such a Misserable Place in all my Life."

·XXVII·

In all my life, I eventually decided, I had never seen such an odd little place. A town of the toughest individuals—many of whom are also tough-minded individualists—the modern Churchill is a government's creation, and it exists at the government's mercy. Its inhabitants—true believers in the north, its beauty, its way of life, its potential—seem to come from everywhere except the north. Hanging by its teeth onto Next Year Country, Churchill depends for its living on a threat to its residents: polar bears. The town defies generalization. It reminds me of nowhere else. It is a true original.

I decided all this after a few days. But when I stepped off the train, the first thing I realized was that a woollen sweater, a waterproof jacket, a light scarf, a cap and gloves were barely sufficient for early May. Asleep, I seemed to have moved back a season. The temperature that day (58° in Winnipeg, 53° in Thompson) never climbed to the thawing point in Churchill, buffeted by a cold front and a bay wind. I hunched around the streets, looking for the Arctic Inn and not finding it amid the disorderly jumble of low, bright houses and sheds. Their concrete foundations were visible above the earth. Some of the front yards comprised brittle snowdrifts as high as my waist while others, facing the sun, lay awash in puddles. A tangle of snowmobiles, bicycles, egg cartons, beer cartons, tires, toys and tied-up dogs furnished the gravel yards anywhere the snow and the water left some free space.

The dogs are a sensitive issue. Numbed by half an hour of wandering, I retreated for warmth inside the black fortress of the Town Centre. A bulletin board displayed a stern letter from the Resident Administrator of the Local Government District: "The streets in Churchill are very unsightly in appearance, due to the large number of dogs turned loose to find their own bathroom facility. It is a poor reflection on our Community when the streets are lined with the evidence of defecating dogs."

I asked directions from a sightly passer-by and set off for the sky-blue walls of the Arctic Inn.

"What a miserable time of year," Larry said by way of greeting.

"I hope you've got a room free," I answered.

"Oh sure," he said. "Hey, would you like a piece of toast? Just step into the office and help yourself."

I accepted. The Arctic Inn was the first hotel I had encountered where the videos, the toast, the coffee and the limousine (a euphemism for the shuddering van) cost nothing.

"Why is it so miserable now?"

" 'Cause everywhere else is enjoying spring," Larry said. Asian by descent, he had grown up in Trinidad. "After a while you start to get restless."

But Churchill too was in the throes of spring. Because of the season, indeed, I became a prisoner of the town and its little web of nearby roads. Surrounded by melting ice on the barrens, I was too late for snowmobiles and too early for the big-wheeled "tundra buggies" that gingerly slide across the permafrost in summer without gouging holes in the land. Nor could I cross the estuary. Its fast,

105

floe-ridden waters barred me from the preposterous stone folly, Fort Prince of Wales, that commands the entrance to the harbour. The Hudson's Bay Company completed the fort in 1771: a grandeur rivalled only by Quebec and the broken Louisbourg, guarding absolutely nothing. The outer walls alone, speckled with forty cannons, rose sixteen feet above the desolate peninsula. Briefly, the structure seemed impregnable; then a raiding party of unimpressed Frenchmen appeared in 1782, and Samuel Hearne surrendered at once. The raiders spiked the cannons, blew up a chunk of wall, torched the inner fort and sailed away. When the Hudson's Bay Company reopened the trading post, its men bypassed the superb ruins and built a modest base upstream. The stones remained, a perpetual reminder of one of the earliest and largest of Churchill's multitude of squandered dreams.

The recorded history of the place goes back even further, to a Danish seafarer called Jens Munck who left Copenhagen in 1619 to search for the Northwest Passage and the spices of the tropical east. He found, instead, the Churchill River, where he and his dying men wintered over. From a crew of sixty-four, Munck and two companions survived. Abandoning the *Unicorn,* they sailed home on a sloop called the *Lamprey* to horrify Scandinavia with tales of a bone-crushing, heart-breaking coast and the "rare and extraordinary" disease that produced "great pains in the loins as if a thousand knives had been thrust there."

From a gravel road a few miles south of Churchill, I looked across the river towards Munck's wintering site. It was my only escape from the town: a birding expedition with a trapper's daughter who guides tourists for money and watches birds for joy. On the drive to Goose Creek, Betty and I conducted an abstruse conversation about thrushes while her client, a Viennese businessman, fumed at the lack of bears.

"Wrong time of year," Betty said cheerfully. "Come back in the fall. See that rough-legged over the water?"

"Excuse me, no?"

Churchill bored Hans. He had hoped to set foot in a romantic wilderness replete with wolves. The sight of half a dozen cranes, a dozen hawks, three hundred ducks and more than a thousand snow geese in the tundra marshes failed to appease him.

"Alaska, that is better," he confided when Betty was a few yards distant. "South Africa also. There is however no reason to bother with Ja-*pain*."

Yet I could understand his disappointment with the town. Apart from the absence of shade trees, it conforms to the superficial pattern of innumerable settlements across the west. Churchill even has a grain elevator—the massive white building, as powerful and immovable as a resting bear, where the railway tracks approach the river's mouth.

If, far to the southeast, the estuary of the Nelson River had been able to accommodate freighters, Churchill today might be a wilderness more akin to the reveries of Hans. The modern town was born because of a government decision: to create a port on Hudson Bay closer to western grain farms than are Halifax and Montreal. Construction of the grain terminal and the Polar Bear Railway breathed spirit and money into the district, even though it hastened the death of the old trading post upstream.

Churchill was a boom town once. War brought the U.S. Air Force; peace brought a rocket station, where the National Research Council of Canada used to maintain a staff of two hundred. But nowadays the rocket range stands in virtual abandonment. The American military withdrew; the Canadian military came and went; the CBC followed suit. A vocational school for Inuit students opened its doors, and shut them. Even the local paper, the *Taiga Times,* folded up. From a population of six thousand, Churchill drooped to its present level of twelve hundred. Some of the disused buildings have been bulldozed into oblivion.

Once the bringer of sustenance to Churchill, the government has recently behaved as though the town should die. It survives thanks to the port and the tourists—and even the future of the port is open to question. The Canadian Wheat Board encourages ships to travel the St. Lawrence Seaway, and the CNR's hopper cars are too heavy for the Polar Bear railbed. In 1985 a mere thirteen freighters would carry grain up the bay to Europe. Soon the great white elevator—visible, I was told, from forty miles—may be a great white elephant.

Churchill's health centre still serves Inuit communities far up the

107

western coast of Hudson Bay. At the Arctic Inn a man and his two small sons, their treatment complete, were awaiting a flight to Rankin Inlet. I discovered the younger child staring raptly at Larry's black-and-white kitten, which was bird-watching with a glum, predatory alertness. The boy was bundled up in a coat and hood to almost spherical proportions. If I had seen him in southern Canada, I would have taken him for a Tibetan.

Up north, the Hudson's Bay Company, in its current incarnation as a retail chain, continues to exercise power. "The Bay," a Métis woman called Rose McAuliffe told me, "has got the only store at Rankin. And you know how much they charge for a grapefruit?" I shook my head. "Ten bucks. Ten bucks! But they sell chocolate bars and Pepsi at about the same price as everywhere else. And you know another thing?" I shook my head again. "On the supply barges that go forth from Churchill every summer, the most popular items are soft drinks, potato chips and Pampers. Yeah, they've done to the Eskimos in twenty years what it took them two hundred to do to the Indians."

One day I sat on an ancient, lichen-coated boulder above the frozen shore. My feet pressed lightly against an island of spongy moss. The running water, audible from someplace among the multicoloured rocks, was nowhere in view. I found it hard to imagine the bay free of ice. And indeed, the most celebrated explorer of Hudson Bay defined the region by its garish frosts and icy mountains. Thomas James, who sailed along this coast on the same futile quest as Jens Munck, passed the winter of 1631-32 on Charlton Island far to the southeast. He survived to write a popular account of the ordeal: *The Strange and Dangerous Voyage.* The scientist Robert Boyle would allude to it often in his "Experimental History of Cold." James was not a man to understate his hardships. The mast-high bergs, oval-shaped suns, star-dogged moons, thunderous ice and other perceptions of that ancient mariner appear in a poem about an even stranger voyage written by a townsman of Thomas James: Samuel Taylor Coleridge.

I scoured the white horizon with binoculars, hoping to find a ringed seal hauled up on the solid bay. But three Churchillians were zooming over ice and land in their motorized fat tricycles ("all-terrain cycle," or ATC, is the official term), deterring life. Half a million seals swim in Hudson Bay; their juicy presence accounts for the multitude of polar bears. In September and October, while hundreds of hungry bears prowl the coast, waiting for the water to freeze, Churchill overflows with tourists. The townspeople used to fear the bears. Then they realized that the animals support much of their economy. Many residents of Churchill now find the polar bears easier to handle than the federal government.

I climbed a few hundred yards from the ice and stepped into the Anglican church to warm up. A stained-glass window in a lucid Victorian geometry proved to be Lady Franklin's memorial to her lost explorer husband. At Churchill, more than anywhere else in the Canadian west, history envelops you like air.

From a table behind the font I bought *Northern Kitchen,* a recipe book compiled by the Ladies' Aid of St. Paul's Mission. The book was unexpectedly droll. A single page juxtaposed the "Chewy Chip Bars" of Sue Stretch and the "Crumb Cake" of Betty Sollid. Father Capon's ruminations on grace ("Your company is an earthly image of the Divine Sociality of the Godhead") followed a poetic "Recipe For Living" ("Mix fresh eggs from the Dove of Peace / With the Milk of Kindness, and lightly beat"). Among the casseroles, Betty Sollid was back with "Salmon Roly Poly," and a Mrs. Gill submitted "Tuna Fish Pie." The ingredients for "The Archbishop's Flaming Plum Pudding" started with two pounds of beef-kidney suet and finished with a pint of brandy. But my favourite recipes were the northern dishes—caribou tenderloin, ragout of arctic hare, roast ptarmigan, and savoury seal hearts ("Trim off the fat, large veins and thread-like cords"). Was there a dish in Churchill known as sweet seal hearts?

It wouldn't shock me. After a couple of days I felt that nothing about Churchill would shock me. I was growing to recognize a certain style about the place: an ability to take normal discourse to its limits and leave it dangling at the border of absurdity. An outsider was left wondering how far, if at all, the speaker's tongue was up his cheek.

The tendency showed in a recipe for bannock that appeared in *Northern Kitchen:* "Make an open fire in the ground, put a chunk of

109

dough in a hole, cover it over and let cook. Throw away the outer covering when cooked." It showed in an old man's slow inquiry as he searched his pockets for small change: "Now do I want the beaver or the caribou?" It showed in a cryptic sentence from a book of local history: "A house of joy, at first in a tent, came into operation." To err on the side of charity, the tendency was also manifest in a tawdry totem pole that decorates a side street.

Aside from the ATCs tearing up the coast, that painted pole was the only thing in Churchill I resented. Totems are a function of a Pacific civilization. They gather meaning from the context of the rain forest, whereas Churchill contains nothing grander than midget spruces and knee-high willows. The Churchill pole, like the Glenboro camel, reveals a divorce of symbols from facts.

Unless its implanters kept their tongues ear-high, the pole is merely false. And everything else I saw in town, no matter how incongruous or paradoxical, had the stamp of the real. A painting in the Catholic church captures Jesus in a shaft of light about to ascend not only from His startled disciples but also from a pair of native hunters; its message that the Word goes out to all the nations appears in Latin, English and Inuktituk. Outside its walls, a chained dog howled and a frozen engine hacked. I liked such anomalies: unlike the imported totem pole, they spoke of an authentic strangeness, a balancing-act between a merciless environment and a keen, fragmented culture. The town is ripe for a subarctic Marquez.

On my final evening in Churchill, Rose McAuliffe and her husband Walt cooked me an impromptu banquet of arctic char, wild rice, bannock and tundra mushrooms. The accompaniments included French wine, Brazilian coffee and American cheese. We dined in an elegance which hovered somewhere between the suburban and the urban, gazing at twilight across the snowdrifts that still encrusted Munck Street. In the northerly Cree dialect used around Churchill, the word for window means "a thing to look out from"; but to the woodland Cree of central Saskatchewan, where Rose grew up, a window is "a thing to let in light."

Until she was eight years old, Rose spoke nothing but Cree. She was born near Cumberland House, the earliest trading post in the western interior; Samuel Hearne, journeying inland from Hudson

110

Bay, founded it in 1774. The town was all but forgotten forty years ago when Rose was a child. No roads led into the place; no marker commemorated the *Northcote,* a steamship that plied the Saskatchewan River and carried troops for General Middleton in the uprising of 1885. Aground at Cumberland House, the *Northcote* became a playground and a local resource. "The little boys," Rose said, "would piss on girls through the holes in the timbers. And whenever my mother was in need of kindling, she'd give me the hatchet and tell me to go fetch some wood from the ship!"

Today a highway connects Cumberland House with the motorized world. Nothing remains of the *Northcote* except its metal boiler, hauled onto dry land and adorned by a respectful plaque.

No roads lead into Churchill. But ten miles out of town, a wrecked freighter called the *Ithaca* is rusting away in peace. "It's a wonderful town," Rose said. "I came north on a visit thirty years ago and I couldn't drag myself away."

When I strolled back to the Arctic Inn, the wind was small and the dark air held a crisp, maritime freshness. The barking was a rumour now, the engines still. Among the shuddering stars the town seemed an eye of light. And I understood suddenly why Samuel Hearne, dry and warm in the apparent security of Fort Prince of Wales, wrote home to say, "Myself and the other People are as usual all in good health but that is no wonder since the pureness of the air and the wholesomeness of the Diet makes it the healthiest part in the known world and what is very extraordinary at this place some of us think we never grow any older."

·XXVIII·

Two days before my thirtieth birthday, I almost killed myself. I had warning: on the train ride from Churchill back to Thompson, I dozed into a dream that carried me along Clarence Avenue in the middle of Saskatoon. While my car moved from the riverbank towards 8th Street, gathering pace, I couldn't find its brake. In the dream I approached the clotted traffic of 8th Street expecting disaster, and the car threaded the free spaces like an engine-powered needle. I relaxed—but the car continued to speed down the tranquil suburban avenue. When it was out of control and racing across a sidewalk, I woke up sweating, the unpaved wilderness serenely all around.

In Thompson I had a long night's sleep and a fatty breakfast. It was the eve of Mother's Day, and I wanted to make good headway on the drive to Saskatoon. Unfortunately I had to wait for a bank to open. Churchill had emptied my wallet.

"Are you up here for business or pleasure?" the bank clerk inquired.

"It's sort of business."

She nodded sympathetically. "Nobody comes here for pleasure in May."

I drove then for three hours without stopping. The paucity of traffic and the day's cool brightness combined to make wildlife abundant: a swimming muskrat in a soaking ditch; a pair of mergansers; a spruce grouse immobile by the roadside, its black breast and barred belly vivid even at a glance. By the highway's side, the railway line to Soab Lake was unused. It stands on a high embankment from which, in three or four places, the gravel has crumbled away, leaving yards of track exposed crazily in midair. I thought of a long bone that had lost its flesh.

At Ponton I continued west, rather than following the main highway south towards Grand Rapids. More than a hundred miles of trees, boulders and water awaited me, unbroken by a town or village: an asphalt tunnel through the green world. By the time I met another vehicle—a red station wagon heading my way, twenty-five miles out of Ponton—it seemed a hallucination, a trick of the coniferous light. The forest bowed and produced, for its next act, a sandhill crane above the road, turning as though lost, flapping slowly south to the Mitishto River. I pondered its direction, and the highway turned pink. From sandstone, not embarrassment, I assume.

When the road was grey again, I switched on the radio. The only signal that could penetrate the tunnel came from the mining town of Flin Flon far to the northwest. Out of the mouths of zinc and copper came the program "Meet the Legion." I listened to a song called "Mr. Sandman, Bring Me a Dream." Then I paused for a rest.

That lakeshore picnic site in the Grass River Provincial Park has lodged in my mind with absolute clarity: the clearing in the woods, the feeble pier, the white-throated sparrows with their treble yearnings, the stained brown table where I munched my raisins and sipped my northern water. The car sat quietly on its gravel sofa, ready for a few more thousand miles in the weeks to come. I had great plans for it in the newborn summer of the prairies and the western foothills. The farther I drove that day, the more I was recapturing spring: already the domain of needles and leafless branches had given way to a forest studded with green poplars. I looked up once from the leaves and the lake to find a flock of thirteen snow geese turning lazily against a high cloud. When the sun caught them, their feathers flashed a brilliant white. They turned again, and a serration of black wings appeared to cut the sky. I got back into the car and regained the straight, empty road.

It was early afternoon. The Flin Flon station was broadcasting a country-and-western lament. The male voice whined, the forest gleamed in the sun, and I looked down at the highway map to see how much longer this road would go on before I had to turn south to The Pas. I felt glazed by all the green. Or could I take a different route? I revolved the map, glanced up, and found that the car had left the asphalt and was hurtling over the gravel shoulder at more than sixty miles an hour.

I veered left to escape the ditch, slammed my foot on the brake and lost control. The car swung onto the wrong side of the highway, lurched back towards the right shoulder and pulled left again. The singer whined as the Dodge fought the road. Everything was happening so fast that I had no time to panic; my only emotion was a numb amazement that such chaos could emerge from nowhere. My sporadic fears of big-city pile-ups, slippery blacktop, treacherous backroads, misplaced wildlife and drunken drivers had left no space in the imagination for me to abandon an excellent highway without another vehicle in sight. My body refused to believe the danger. I recovered concentration too late to scream or pray.

The only thing that flashed before my eyes was a green line of trees turning upside-down as the car deserted the road. It flipped in midair and landed on its rear. An instant later, the front of the car joined the back in a grassy ditch, and the world fell silent. Maybe, for a second or two, I lost consciousness.

I found myself sitting in an upright wreck, stunned. If the first feeling was relief—*alive, can move, not in pain, not burning*—the second was shame. *What happened, why did it, how could I?*

My mind battled for order. After I had removed the keys from the ignition, I switched off the silent radio and pushed the gear lever from "drive" to "park." Then I unstrapped the seat belt, which had possibly saved my life, and tried to open the door. It was jammed. But the glass had shattered out from the side windows, allowing me to clamber across the passenger seat and jump to earth. I could hear nothing other than a small breeze playing through the forest.

The car was ruined. Its windshield lay in fragments, its roof was bent, and its hindquarters had the crumpled appearance of a shed skin. It looked like the surprised victim of some monstrous rite of spring. Or was it a rite of passage? The impact had forced open the trunk, and my belongings—everything from a hefty blue suitcase to a couple of fifty-dollar bills—lay scattered like old fillings in the jaw of the ditch. My first impulse was to gather up the money and the small objects that had rested, along with my wallet, on the passenger seat: an address book, a journal, a little camera, the map. I was still doing this when I noticed the distant throb of an engine.

It was approaching, I thought, from the west. I stepped into the highway and started to wave when the throbs became visible. A

114

blue half-ton truck, empty except for the driver, a middle-aged man with short brown hair and a face of dismay, slowed and stopped.

"I've had an accident," I said through his window. "That was my car."

"Is there anyone inside?"

"No, I didn't have any passengers. I just drove off the road."

He looked relieved.

"How long ago did it happen?"

"Don't know. A couple of minutes?"

The man climbed out of his truck. "I'll take you into The Pas," he said. "Let's load up the back."

"But that's where you're coming from," I said.

He gazed at me and silently, gently, shook his head.

I had my directions completely askew. Only at that moment did I understand: after flipping over, the car had landed off the wrong side of the road, facing east. The half-ton had been following my path.

We lifted my possessions into the truck and sped away. I sat in the passenger seat of the cabin, my hair stuffed with shards of gravel, pressing a Kleenex against my only wound: a tiny cut on the left ear. Behind me, a sleeve of my plaid dressing gown protruded from the ripped suitcase and flapped for fifty miles until The Pas. In retrospect, I was beginning to feel afraid.

Apart from some loose change, there was only one item we had failed to discover, either in the car's shell or in the ditch: the golden pen I had been using to write my daily journal. I had passed the pen through Al Hochbaum's inukshuk to bring good luck. Perhaps it had accomplished its task.

My rescuer, chauffeur and benefactor was the Shell dealer in (of all places) Gillam, who was in the process of driving six hundred miles to his mother. Among the greatest of my blessings that afternoon was Roger. He took me to the RCMP station in The Pas, he waited while I filled a report and answered a constable's questions, he found me a hotel; and never did he reproach me for my foolishness. When Roger renewed his own journey to Saskatchewan, I felt more than alone: I felt lonely.

"You should get a checkup at the hospital," he said. The constable agreed. But time had become an enemy; the blue afternoon was drawing in, and I was carless in an outlying town. A ponytailed taximan who looked and talked like a refugee from Woodstock drove me twenty miles to a little airport where I could rent a new car. The eagerness with which the agent handed over the keys astounded me, considering the thoroughness with which, four hours earlier, I had eliminated another of her firm's machines. A stiffness was growing in my neck, and perfunctory combing had done little to rid my hair of small débris. I eased away from the parking lot with qualms.

Back in The Pas I still intended to visit the hospital. My stomach, however, complained that I had fed it nothing more than a few handfuls of raisins since breakfast. It was Saturday night in a forestry town; I strolled down the main street. Among the locked shops I passed a closed restaurant; a second; a third. Surely graveyards could be livelier? Some native boys and girls lolled in doorways and watched me without delight. The only possibilities appeared to be a dingy Chinese café and a Kentucky Fried Chicken franchise. I bought a small bucket of battered poultry and removed it to the privacy of my hotel room; there I drew the curtains and settled down to chew. The only table faced a mirror. By turning the chair sideways and leaning left to eat, I could avoid looking at myself.

I was not the first traveller to suffer an accident in the western wilderness. In 1859 the Earl of Southesk's ride through Saskatchewan came to a halt when "a loud crash burst upon my ears, and I beheld McBeath bounding from his cart, just clearing it as it upset and rolled over and over in its progress to the bottom of a hill." It was scarcely an important mishap: Southesk could depend on McBeath and his fellow porters to mend the broken axle. Their labour enabled the earl to pass the time feasting on wild strawberries above the wooded banks of a lake. There, in "the adorable melancholy of loneliness," he finished *The Winter's Tale*. "Are we to hold," he inquired in his journal, "that a mere fit of indigestion communicated prophetical lore to Antigonus?"

I ate everything, even the sodden salad, and drank water from a glass which some invisible chambermaid had wrapped in an absurd paper envelope "for my personal protection." By the time I was full, the room stank of Colonel Sanders's eleven herbs and spices. The loneliness and melancholy were swelling fast. A walk through the night to the nearby hospital seemed an impossible task. Instead I tried to phone Annie in Montreal: no reply. In succession I had a shower, a hot bath and a sauna. A fit of indigestion came and went, communicating nothing. I took to my bed. But when I closed my eyes I saw a whirling sequence of gravel, asphalt and sky. Better to open them into the semidarkness of a sterilized, foul-smelling room. After a while I found some rock videos on TV. One of them, a visual duet of Alice and the Mad Hatter in which sizes and shapes kept changing without warning, seemed appropriate. Eventually I slept.

Morning arrived with a drizzle. I loaded the wounded suitcase, the grit-filled books, the ripped map and the rest of my paraphernalia into the new vehicle and set off for Saskatoon. My mind felt lucid, refreshed, determined. I closed it off from the random impressions that enliven a normal day at the wheel, and concentrated on nothing but the long road to the south.

Hours passed. The drizzle turned to rain, and the conifers disappeared in favour of a rolling deciduous forest. I wanted neutral scenery, but gradually the woods took hold and I began to notice their grace. Not far from Mafeking I swung right towards Saskatchewan. The first village along the thin, verdant highway was called

117

Baden. I drove for ten minutes in an agony of suspense to find if the next settlement would be Powell.

It was. Just beyond it came a leafy village with an enterprising sign:

WELCOME TO BARROWS
POPULATION 999,800
SHORT OF A 1,000,000

Tempting, but I pressed on, torn between misery at the pitted, potholed road and delight at the charming landscape. I could easily have been pottering through Moravia. Grain fields and dairy pastures alternated with woodland through which even the rivers—the Armit, the Little Armit and the North Armit—flowed on an Old World scale. Yet memories of the previous day hardened me against a sideways glance.

The road improved when a town with grandiose pretensions and a misleading name grew near:

WELCOME TO HUDSON BAY
MOOSE CAPITAL OF THE WORLD

Westward still, through a smooth domain of farms and reduced woods. The shortness of the growing season has led these northern farmers to nurture faster grains than wheat, their favourite substitute being rapeseed. Late summer turns a horde of acres a fierce, flamboyant yellow. Unfortunately, the connotations of the term caused the grain industry to rename the stuff "canola"—a bland word, redolent of packaging and marketing, not of the earth from which canola grows. Only in the middle of a weather-beaten sign beside a highway in eastern Saskatchewan does the old name stand on guard:

WELCOME TO TISDALE
LAND OF RAPE AND HONEY

The farmers raise bees too.

118

Amid the wide spaces west and south of Tisdale, my mind drew back into itself, heedless of the grey weather and the infant grain. Some names alone stay with me, like a pocketful of coins from a crowd of nations that make up, in their jumbled combination, the currency of the prairies: Bruno and Valparaiso, Muenster and Carmel, Star City and Lac Vert . . . I stopped at none. Near Saskatoon the glacial drumlins were like three-dimensional memories: old afternoons ploughed into the dark, dark brown of the soil. The car swooped and loped across the hills until at suppertime, glancing towards a luminous cloud, I caught sight of the green city stretching out from its river bank below.

And so, at the end of my thirtieth year, having drunk my shame to its fill, I came back once more to the bridged water, the changed haunts, the elusive dreams.

·XXX·

The first European to penetrate the western plains was a young Englishman named Henry Kelsey. A sloop dropped him at Fort Nelson in 1684: a boy of fourteen on the brink of an unexplored subcontinent. While England was changing dynasties, Kelsey was scouting for furs on the tundra, some two hundred miles beyond Jens Munck's wintering site. The results were unpromising, but the wanderlust endured. When the youth again left Hudson Bay, he and a party of amicable Cree travelled west and south. He would not see a white face for two years.

Now Reader Read for I am well assur'd
Thou dost not know the hardships I endur'd
In this same desert where Ever that I have been
Nor wilt thou me believe without that thou had seen
The Emynent Dangers that did often me attend

The journey was heroic, even though Kelsey was alert to keep many
of his activities in the "desert" a mystery. To transcribe the hardships and dangers would have been to undercut the tone of his
report.

He voyaged up the Nelson River-system towards the complicated
network of streams and lakes into which the Saskatchewan subsides.
Waterfalls and rapids along the route demanded that Kelsey and his
companions make thirty-three portages. Somewhere near the modern town of The Pas, he set up a cross. Then it was west again, and
south again. The youth was pleased by the berries of the forest and
delighted by the wildlife of the plain, particularly its buffalo and its
silver-furred, "outgrown Bear":

> His skin to gett I have used all the ways I can
> He is mans food & he makes food of man
> His hide they would not me it preserve
> But said it was a god & they should Starve
> This plain affords nothing but Beast & grass
> And over it in three days time we past
> getting unto the woods on the other side

Kelsey had attained the parkland, a fertile belt where trees and
meadows alternate. Despite the excitement of a buffalo hunt "on the
Barren ground," he preferred the forest to the plains.

But he travelled under orders: "to discover & bring to a Commerce the Naywatame poets." And in search of them, he perhaps
roamed as far as the Touchwood Hills in what is nowadays southern
Saskatchewan.

Who the Naywatame were, whether they required Kelsey's discovery, and why they seemed poetic remain uncertain. In fact an
ambiguity underlies all of Kelsey's dealings with the native peoples

of the west. His account of his travels reveals a mixture of motives and emotions that would typify white reactions for centuries to come.

> In sixteen hundred & ninety'th year
> I set forth as plainly may appear
> Through Gods assistance for to understand
> The natives language & to see their land

In the following line he came cleaner: it was "for my masters interest" that he undertook the trip, his master being the Governor and Company of Adventurers of England Trading into Hudson's Bay. A knowledge of the natives' language was a useful instrument to gain their fur. And although Kelsey recognized the west as "their land," "their Country," he also took possession of it in the British name.

While the traders wanted pelts and robes, the Indians coveted weapons. Kelsey's role is again ambiguous. Apparently he tried to make peace between two warring bands; yet he also took pleasure that "our English guns do make them flie." It was, perhaps, his utility as an arms trader that gave him power over the Indians. In his prose journal for August 1691, he described a cluster of eighty tents on the plain: "Now we are altogether they made a feast the which they Invited me to so they desired leave of me for them to go to wars but I told them that I could not grant them their request . . . so we lay still today."

Whatever his degree of authority, Kelsey relied on the Indians. Without their guidance, he would have died in a swamp or a snowbank, or wandered forsaken through the beasts and grass, never discovering a route back to Hudson Bay. The Indians left him behind, once, and he felt "fear & terror." Yet even as he travelled in their helpful company, "I was alone & no friend could find." Friendship demands a kind of spiritual equality and, while Kelsey held the native peoples in high regard, he also thought himself superior.

Back at the maritime fort, he transformed his experiences into rhyming couplets in the vein of Denham and Dryden. Kelsey's poetry has caused needless derision ever since its eventual publication in 1929. For an explorer of twenty-three with little schooling,

121

he did an admirable job. If his rhythms were irregular and his rhymes haphazard, his images were often evocative and precise:

> This wood is poplo ridges with small ponds of water
> there is beavour in abundance but no Otter

The waters and the land, its native peoples, its animals and plants acted on a tough, practical man like a muse. Kelsey's response to his incredible journey was to make it credible through art. The west lit his imagination. On behalf of the intruders, the invaders, he began the process of making the west into a state of mind.

More than two centuries later, another brash Englishman stormed onto the prairies. He was fond of treacle and sex, fist-fights and suet pudding; his university had expelled him for bad behaviour. Sailing to Canada before his twenty-third birthday, the man had little notion what to expect. But he was forthright and adaptable, and he found enough work in the lumber camps and farms of the west to return home within a year, a wad of money in his pocket. Canada had strengthened his physique and fortified his nerve. It had also sown one of the seeds from which modern poetry would spring.

Back in London, T. E. Hulme began to associate with Gaudier-Brzeska and Ezra Pound. He lectured and translated and wrote, becoming more and more convinced that Romanticism was merely spilt religion. "I want to speak of verse in a plain way as I would of pigs," he told an astonished crowd at Kensington Town Hall in 1914.

By then Hulme's ideas were firm. They placed him in the advance guard of English modernism. He wanted a classical poetry, dry and hard, free from the moist sentiment and inert language of the Georgians and their mild precursors. Poetry should be adequate, he thought, to the flux and bluntness of experience; it should be clean of pretension. Brief poems, vibrant with images, could perhaps make their readers see afresh. Such lyrics would not purport to explain the enormous world. "The flats of Canada," he once observed, "are incomprehensible on any single theory." Their vastness had showed him human endeavour in a fresh and tiny stature.

If Hulme's awareness of the insignificance of man goes back, in part, to his months in the west, so too does his appreciation of poetry: "the first time I ever felt the necessity or inevitableness of verse, was in the desire to reproduce the peculiar quality of feeling which is induced by the flat spaces and wide horizons of the virgin prairie of Western Canada."

Hulme began to write poems. And he began to hunger for an art that would be, literally, down to earth: "To read a book which is *real clay,* moulded by fingers that had to mould something, or they would clutch the throat of their maddened author. *No* flowing on of words, but tightly clutched tense fingers leaving marks in the clay. These are the only books that matter—and where are they to be found?" His desire, unknowingly, echoes Kafka's longing that a book should serve as an axe for the frozen sea within us.

Like Henry Kelsey, Hulme had taken the west inside his consciousness. The land turned him towards a new vision of art. By the time war broke over Europe, he had come to see that poetry is the cutting edge of language, a weapon against the stagnation of the mind. Soon his cohorts, led by the irascible entrepreneur from the American west, would convert many of his ideas from heresy to a new orthodoxy. But a German shell killed T. E. Hulme in 1917. Barely a decade earlier, he had glimpsed the

> Brand of the obscene gods
> On their flying cattle,
> Roaming the sky prairie.

·XXXI·

I rested for a few days in the comfort of Saskatoon. On my birthnight the Northern Lights shimmered in a far arc above the city: a pagan halo, white on white. Hours later I woke up with a shudder, a little surprised to be alive. I handed back the Pony I had rented at an exorbitant price in The Pas and hired a Skyhawk in its place, as pale as a fingernail. A fresh decade. A clean start.

The streets were lush with spring: my eyes could roam them without fear of dust. In a riverbank park a southern breeze caressed the bareskinned joggers, picnickers and sunbathers. The water was high.

But the Ritz had closed for good. Under an earlier name, it functioned before my birth as a theatre. Then it became a hotel and tavern, cheapening over the decades as the competition grew swank. I knew the bar in its final incarnation: the Apollo Room. Oversize photographs of astronauts loomed like armoured ghosts over the little tables that attracted a motley, unpredictable crowd of blue-collar workers, students, drifters, gays, New Democrats, slumming professors, Indians, drug dealers, artists and a few incoming farmers. The draught beer was the flattest in the west. For a while, the hair was the longest.

Three or four blocks from the doomed Ritz, a recent restaurant glistened. Its name was Italian, its menu French. A string trio cavorted among the chandeliers from Toronto and the neoclassical statues from God knows where. *Mais où sont les neiges d'antan?*

When I was in some danger of drowning under a froth of nostalgia, an accountant rescued me with a hard, hooked phrase. Cary Mazankowski had left a big-city office to study biochemistry in Saskatoon. There she was living with a native man who had been born in a tent near Twin Moose Creek. The city contained some lively people, she agreed. "But after Vancouver and Toronto, being in Saskatoon is like always having a box over my head."

124

I remembered the feeling. And the sense of isolation. And the yearning.

One morning I drove fifteen miles out of the box to meet an insurance agent who had constructed his house from telephone poles. Wilf Hocking moved back to his family's land when his marriage cracked in Saskatoon. Sometime later, the telephone company introduced a system of underground wires. Wilf scoured the district in a large truck, took the downed poles back to his farm, stacked them, sawed them, and started to build. The walls of his home, mortared and insulated, are eight inches thick. A picture window that faces south and a wood-burning stove give all the heat the building needs; in January Wilf and his new wife used the stove a mere three days.

"I have trouble reading," he confessed over lunch. "I mean, I don't read much. Except for philosophy and psychology."

Across the yard an office was rising, again from telephone poles. Wilf has no training in architecture, no pretension and no fear.

"A lot of people come out from town and admire what we're doing," he said. "But they could do something similar if they really wanted to. The thing is, they're too busy making money to spend time creating anything for themselves."

I thought about the incest of money and time as I wandered Saskatoon again. The most eminent dangers are sometimes the least apparent: the hunger for wealth, for example, which makes food of man. It cost me nothing to watch a pair of falcons mating high up in a birch tree a block from my old school. The slim branch, fringed with green, looked too light for the balancing hawks; but it held. The female uttered a series of mild, chirruping cries before and after the act. Saskatoon had begun to draw me back into itself.

Once more it was time to leave. Next morning, with regret, I chose an old highway curling south past the violet-dotted woods of Beaver Creek. The rich acreages dwindled; fields broadened; homes grew rare. In a roadside graveyard, blue vetch adjoined a ring of buttercups and lemon-yellow locoweed. A pipit rehearsed his downward arpeggios high above the tombstones.

Heat and light were pouring through the car's windows as

125

though winter and darkness were a delusion, a sour rumour, a lie. Mosquitoes whined about my ears. To my relief, I felt composed at the wheel. Nearly six weeks would elapse before I could return the Skyhawk to its nest and forget the demands of the road. It carried me past miles of tawny farmland, where seeding was in slow swing, to a dam. On its far side the Saskatchewan River turns into a lake. The dam commemorates a Liberal politician, the lake celebrates a Conservative politician, and a park along the shore takes its name from a New Democratic politician. Such, I suppose, are the rewards of public service.

Beyond the bridge the highway swerved to breast the coulees and grassy hills of the Missouri Coteau. Under a variety of unflattering names—the Bad Hills, the Cactus Hills, the Bear Hills, the Dirt Hills—the Coteau slices a loamed arc through the heavy clays of western and southern Saskatchewan. Somewhere in its folds leaned the decrepit cabin of Jack Hitchcock, the region's most famous pioneer. The stories about him are legion. A few of them may even be true.

Hitchcock, according to the legends, was a cowboy of immense height and toughness. In his scorn for authority and convention, he seemed to fit the wild American west more than the ordered west above the border. Some say he was, in fact, a married engineer whose wife fled home to Massachusetts after her one and only winter on the ranch; others insist he was a bachelor. All agree that he lived in a shack with approximately twenty-eight cats and a large hole in the door.

"Don't you get cold in the winter?"

"Naw, there's always a cat goin' in or out."

During the arid summers, Hitchcock tramped the prairie wearing nothing but a loincloth and his guns. As much as possible, he lived off the land.

"How can you tell those wild mushrooms are safe to eat?"

"Well, I try 'em out on the cats first."

In his old age he bought a motorbike and rode it with panache. A highway accident in his mid-eighties nearly killed him—but the doctors patched him up, and he limped home. Rumours persist that he eventually died.

126

It is possible, of course, that behind the man's extravagance lay a certain desperation.

Hitchcock Coulee is nowadays a finger of Lake Diefenbaker, which I crossed on a long ferry. Six or seven drivers emerged from their metal boxes to drink Coke or Fanta on deck. The sunlight had the strength of steel. A wind, barely perceptible ashore, rippled the navy water sixty yards above the buried farms. As we approached the eastern bank I noticed the bumper-sticker on the half-ton in front: CHAPLIN SASK. SODIUM SULPHATE CAPITAL. If that was the only reason Chaplin could claim any limelight, the town would have to do without me.

Instead I pushed east past the Vermilion Hills, listening to CBC radio. It gave me a pleasure so intense that I parked on the shoulder to concentrate: Two-Ton Baker's country classic "I've Got Tears in My Ears from Lying on My Back in My Bed while I Cry Over You." I hummed it through a town called Eyebrow. I was still humming when an oncoming driver made a pass at an absurd moment: he swung into my lane a couple of hundred yards away and headed straight at me. If I—and the driver he was overtaking—had failed to hit the brakes at once, Two-Ton's tears would have finished in a bed of warped metal on Highway 42.

The more I thought about it, the more shaken I felt. I was halfway into Moose Jaw before I realized the city had begun. Numbed, I drove downtown and checked into the Royal Hotel. According to another prairie legend—what is it about the west that breeds yarns?—tunnels run from Moose Jaw's capacious railway station to several of River Street's hotels. They date, it is said, from the epoch when Moose Jaw was a refuge for Al Capone, a Mecca for gamblers and opium-smokers, a Jerusalem for pimps. (The Board of Trade, however, preferred to call the city "The Buckle of the Greatest Wheat Belt in the World.")

"You ever hear tell of these tunnels under here?" I asked the mousy woman at the till.

"Oh sure," she answered. "But they're all converted to rooms now."

"To *rooms*?"

"Yep, rooms in the basement."

How far was her tongue up her cheek?

127

"A few years back they struck one on Main Street, why, twenty feet down it was." A younger man had emerged from the office without the trace of a twinkle in his eyes. "Below the sewer line. You should ask the City Maintenance Department."

"But I thought it was all a myth."

"Oh no," the woman said. "We always know we've found another one when the floor starts caving in."

·XXXII·

I stayed upstairs at the Royal, and my floor did not cave in. The walk from the cash-desk to my room was a little unnerving, however. Every second or third step produced a loud creak, and every creak seemed to produce the head of an old codger peering carefully around his door. I had a vision of a building full of grizzled men who spent their weeks waiting on the brink of their rooms for the excitement of a passer-by. The corridors and stairways were dimly lit, perhaps to obscure the green peeling paint, perhaps to increase the challenge for the codgers. I collapsed on my complaining bed wondering how Lady Godiva felt.

The hotel was once a brothel. In the Royal's heyday, the 1920s, Moose Jaw already had a chequered, pungent history and its residents still dreamed of wealth. A hamlet had grown around the turning where (it's said) a river bent in the shape of a moose's jawbone; when the CPR made it a regional headquarters, the hamlet ballooned into a city. Its population by 1912 was 25,000, three-quarters of its present level. With a sublime, erroneous confidence the city fathers sank a hundred thousand dollars in the subdivision of University

Heights; Saskatoon then harvested the provincial university, and the subdivision reverted to prairie. It was one of countless schemes where Moose Jaw ended up a loser. The city's history recalls the misadventures of one of Walt Disney's carnivores—a cat, a wolf, a coyote—whose gluttonous pounces produce nothing but a sore head and a laugh.

After a while, the laughs die out. Even when River Street had become a byword for sin, even when the city's police chief arrested his entire force for corruption, even when a member of the Ku Klux Klan ran for mayor and won, Moose Jaw held some thriving industries and some reasons for hope. Then the Depression bit. The industries closed down or pulled out, and the city skidded into a long bankruptcy. Soon its most famous institution was the provincial school for the mentally handicapped, which did not arise on University Heights.

A surveillance of the central core is enough to show that Moose Jaw has never recovered from the past. Its finest building is the Land Titles Office, an elegant, ornate affair from 1910. Within sight lurk half a dozen pieces of anonymous, vacant land, a silent mockery of the frizzled stonework. The truth is that Moose Jaw, like Portage la Prairie, is just a little too near a wealthy neighbour to flourish; Saskatchewan's capital, Regina, sprawls less than forty miles down the road. Moose Jaw has become, for those with a cruel or a detached frame of mind, a museum of western development. Its old brick walls preserve a collection of painted advertisements that the merchants in any prosperous city would have erased years ago. The Army and Navy still promises to be THE PLAIN STORE FOR PLAIN PEOPLE, and its business, at least, should be brisk.

I walked down Main Street, a thoroughfare that used to incarnate Moose Jaw's commercial virtue just as River Street embodied its vice. Nowadays the virtue is threadbare: store after store stands vacant. If the economy of the Canadian west tends towards the manic-depressive, Moose Jaw makes do without the mania. The Kinsmen International Band Festival and Choral Competition was underway (three posters and a banner announced it), and I expected a few international revellers from Malta, Glasgow, Havre or other Montana towns. No such luck: the Band Capital of North America wore a torpid, tranquillized air. I ducked into an old cinema and watched *The Company of Wolves*.

Half a century ago the cinema must have been massive and impressive; these days it functions in triplicate, and the new walls are thin. Screams and staccato gunfire kept impinging from some vengeful Hollywood trash on my right. On my left, a covey of cherubs sported in a creamy plasterwork. I sat alone with the cherubs and the wolves. Darkness had fallen when I emerged, and Main Street was devoid of life.

Sometime after midnight a three-way argument in an adjacent room broke my sleep. It intrigued me at first: each of the shouters was resorting to *fuck* a good three times per sentence. No other profanity arose. Was this the secret life of the codgers? The argument outlasted my intrigue.

"Nice day, eh?" an unshaven, cheery man of about sixty said to me next morning. I was leaving the hotel, a suitcase in hand, a shoulder bag over an arm.

"Beautiful!"

The man fell into step beside me. In his light-brown jacket and corduroy trousers, he looked like a teacher or a civil servant who was taking the blue day off.

"Can you spare some change for breakfast?"

I was amazed.

"Sorry," I lied through my teeth, "I don't have any change."

"Got a buck or two?" he asked shrewdly.

He had been standing in the lobby while I retrieved the two-dollar deposit for my key.

"No, sorry," I said, and broke away.

"Okay," he replied behind my back.

Was it sheer surprise, or powerlessness, or anger that my intuition had been wrong? What had made me a tightfisted liar? I was brooding on such sour questions while I drove along an alley behind the hotel, eased down the street, and passed Moon's Chinese Café as the jacketed man stepped in. A dollar might have paid for his egg and toast, two dollars would have added bacon . . . I was almost out of town before I noticed a scrap of paper flapping like a broken wing under a windshield wiper. Stopping by the side of the high-

130

way, I released the paper and read: YOU ARE PARKED ON PRIVATE PROPERTY. THE NOTE IS FREE. A TOW TRUCK IS NOT.

A short, swift drive took me to a city I wanted to like. Growing up in Saskatoon, I despised Regina with a teenage fervour: it was guilty, I decided after two brief visits, of bleakness, ugliness, materialism and manifold other evils. Secretly, I could not forgive Regina for being the provincial capital and for possessing the only professional sports team in Saskatchewan. It seemed a leap further than Saskatoon from the living death of the hinterland, a leap closer to wherever "it all happened." In short, I resented living in the second city of the province.

That morning the parking lot in downtown Regina pleased me. Although it was as ugly as anything I remembered, a morsel of graffiti redeemed it:

UNKNOWN PLEASURES
CLOSER STILL

The pleasures of Regina are not immediately obvious. Its centre fails to cohere, its buildings are a graceless jumble, and its topography could hardly be flatter. Allowances, however, must be made.

Much abused Regina! Of all the places in the North-West not one has come in for less praise or more abuse. . . . That Regina's position is not the most picturesque one in the world I freely acknowledge; that a better one might have been selected may be granted; but in spite of her lacking beauty of situation Regina is going ahead.

The words, which still hold true, appeared in the Regina *Leader* in 1883. A year earlier the site had been remarkable for nothing but a pile of buffalo bones beside a creek. But the creek lay near the CPR line, and the Lieutenant-Governor just happened to own 480 acres of land in the vicinity. Amid nothing, the town arose. When Louis Riel was hanged there in 1885, Regina contained one tree.

A century later it has trees by the thousand, as well as an extensive bird sanctuary beside its man-made lake. Its streets are as tidy and unsurprising as one might expect of a place whose fortunes

131

came to depend on civil servants and the RCMP. Swollen by juicy suburbs to accommodate the bureaucrats, policemen and displaced families from rural Saskatchewan, Regina has a prosperous air. When I wandered down a side street of shade trees and tulip beds, I noticed an old woman leaning against her door, watching the world pass by. She seemed a trifle alarmed by it. Her walls were lime green, and her door was elm green, and her roof was pine green. The world, apart from me, comprised a brown pickup truck with three Indian boys riding in the back.

The sight is commonplace in Regina. Indians too have swelled the city, drifting in from the southern reserves—Day Star and Star Blanket, Standing Buffalo and Poor Man—in search of jobs or opportunity or alcohol, and finding, too often, only the last. No one is certain what to do with them all. Many of Regina's whites wish they would somehow go away. In the middle of the afternoon three or four Indian girls in halter tops and laconic cutoffs teetered on their high heels outside the Sheraton Centre, waiting for men. Slow sedans cruised the kerb like metal scavengers.

> *Regina's night life is alive.*
>   There are 4 hospitals
>   9 indoor ice arenas
>   10 movie theatres
>   13 museums
>   15 art galleries
>   and,
>   1 water slide, which is not open just now.

Or so said *Focus Saskatchewan,* a free magazine in my hotel bedroom. Above this promising information stood a photograph of an empty cocktail lounge.

Yet whatever absurdities a thirst for glamour might provoke, Regina is truly a city. Sometime during the past century it ceased to be an overgrown little town and acquired a moneyed complexity. In the Sheraton coffee shop, amid a succulence of potted greenery, three men in tuxedos and a woman in a floor-length gown were discussing the intricacies of Paganini sonatas and the value of French immersion. Their costumes, their ostentations, even their accents were urban. They had a choice, after all, of twenty-eight galleries and museums.

I took the elevator late at night to the top floor of my hotel. Ten storeys high, what is most striking are not the city's buildings but the spaces between its buildings. Regina is a child of the plains, offering endless opportunities to the wind. And I realized, looking down at its flecks of scattered light, that I had been spending too much time in the cities of the west. I had been careening through the countryside too fast. It was time now to leave the tuxedos and the parking lots in favour of the greening land.

·XXXIII·

The first inhabitants of the prairies left no elaborate monuments behind them. Over time their traditional presence reverts from a memory to a rumour to a dream. White men saw the western landscape as empty and chaotic, and imposed on it a geometrical order: their surveyors preceded their police. The result, wherever wheat broke through the clay, was a chessboard division of the land by a mesh of roads. Angles of ninety degrees sprouted across thousands of miles. Nothing more alien, more flagrant to the Indian spirit could have happened to the surface of the earth. When I left Regina on a bright May morning, I followed a highway that stretched to the horizon without a hint of a turn. I was heading for unfamiliar country: Saskatchewan's underbelly, its far south.

To the white settlers, the land was a commodity to farm for

133

profit. It was something to respect, perhaps to fear, but in the end to *use*. The greatness of mankind, in their tradition, was a function of his independence from the earth. For centuries Christians believed that the world was made for mankind; the earth serves the interests of men and women just as they should serve the interests of God. "The man who finds his homeland sweet is still a tender beginner," a monk wrote early in the twelfth century. "He to whom every soil is as his native one is already strong; but he is perfect to whom the entire world is as a foreign land."

The monk taught for sixteen years at the Abbey of St. Victor on the Seine's left bank. Students from across Europe left their native soil and journeyed to Paris to hear him teach. History, the monk explained, was the gradual progress of the Word. But ironically, having preached man's liberty from the constraints of the physical world, the monk became known by a name—Hugh of St. Victor—that incorporates a place. Paris, admittedly, was not Hugh's native soil; he came from Saxony. And as a later German philosopher, Theodor Adorno, would suggest, "It is part of morality not to be at home in one's home."

In the worldview of North America's Indians, such a claim is incomprehensible. A detachment from the land is in their eyes a sickness. Home and morality, land and God are not concepts to be ripped apart at will; to love God and not to love the physical world is a contradiction in terms. The breath of the divine spirit infuses every antelope and river, every hill and duck and wind.

Even so, some places on the continent hold a special power: places where the spirit becomes manifest in a sign, a song, a dream; places where a young man's quest for a vision might find a strong reward. One such place is a sandstone outcrop high above the western plains.

To reach the outcrop, I slipped past the Dirt Hills in the wind's teeth. I veered westward to the town of Assiniboia, then left its Empire Road for a chain of dark, rising rectangles of farmland. A side road led me to a tiny village in the shadow of a steepled, white-painted church. The village's name happens to be St. Victor. Another side road breasts the farms on its ascent to the carvings of a vanished people: the St. Victor petroglyphs.

134

The gravel car-park was empty. A narrow path squeezed down from it into a rumpled valley, thick with poplars and chokecherry bushes, and loud with the animated monologue of a brown thrasher. The path curved and rose towards a cluster of tan, contorted rocks against the sky. As I climbed, the wind sharpened and the chokecherries gave way to juniper. A mountain bluebird, swaying on a twig, watched me nervously from the peak of the outcrop. I climbed some more, and turned, and my eyes went numb with possibility.

Below the rocks, grey-green ranchland followed the ancestral contours of the earth. A few miles farther, ploughed oblongs dominated the plain. The road seemed a silver needle stitching a geometrical quilt. Far beyond the village of St. Victor and its pale adjacent lake, Assiniboia's grain elevators quivered above the town. The horizon from such a vantage point is so remote that the land merges with its sky in some liquid shimmer of the mind, as though the air and the soil are one.

I began to search for the carvings. The intense sunlight was a handicap, for petroglyphs are clearest in a damp half-light. Scrambling off the path, I walked under the outcrop, dodging the mosquitoes in the green hollows and hoping to detect in the hidden reaches the hoofprints, the faces, the toothed mouth that seekers carved here long ago as tokens of power and grace. What I found inescapable were the scrapings of vandals: all the possessive initials, the contemptuous JACKs and JANICEs who had felt a burdensome itch to scratch their own identities in stone. Once, where a slim rock pawed the air, I saw (I think) an ancient hand disfigured by BOB and his chums. A forlorn rage came over me.

Yet perhaps the vengeance of the invaders concealed a deep uneasiness. Perhaps their mockery hid fear. For in that wind-ridden solitude, I felt the Indians' presence on the prairies as a force that lingers: a power that smallpox, alcohol, despair and their confinement on little reserves have not been able to expunge. A sense of holiness can outlast its makers. I collected a few candy wrappers and tufts of loose plastic, and stuffed them into my pockets. Regrettably, I could do nothing about the broken glass. I was clambering back towards the summit, having almost abandoned hope of a good

135

look at a carving, when a low table of rock at the corner of my eye presented a clear stick-figure man, a wayfarer in stone. The bluebird gave his quick alarm call and fled.

A blood-breasted hawk was hunting the pastureland, his shadow gliding rapidly over the spring grass. I sat cross-legged on the high prairie and wrote my name with a juniper stick in a smudge of sandy earth. The rocks received the sun, geologically patient. Below me was a foreign land. I found it sweet.

The day wore on. I got back into the car and drifted down the tall hill to the village. The province's guidebook gives its population as sixty-three and warns: "No Hotel Accommodation Available." I might have driven through without stopping except for a small sign that alerted me to the McGillis Museum.

It pointed, in fact, to a wire fence and a cabin with changing rooms. I was out of the driver's seat and baffled when Etienne appeared: a grizzled man of sixty, wearing jeans and a heavy green shirt. He escorted me through a gate and across a field to the one-roomed hut of a Métis pioneer.

"I should be able to open the place up," Etienne said, fumbling with keys. He tried a couple in the door, which refused to budge.

"Nope!" he added happily.

So I shaded my eyes and peered through a dirty pane at the chair, the table, the concave bed and the sparse remaining implements of Angus McGillis's home. It had grown from sod and timber in 1889; after eighty years in the hills, it had gained a second life in Jubilee Park. Under its eaves stood a milk-churn and a barrel. Even dingier were the tobacco-cutter, the jug and the carved stones inside a long glass case. The relics were unlabelled and disordered.

"We had some more things," Etienne said vaguely, gesturing at the glass, "but they were stolen."

"You know the village well," I said in French. It was one of those polite, fatuous remarks that leads, on occasion, to a tale or two.

"Well, I should know it, my friend," he replied expansively. "I used to be the mayor."

"So what's that sculpture over there near the changing rooms?"

"Oh, *that,*" he said with a slight reluctance. "Well, we had the provincial jubilee back in, when, 1980? And some of the farmers and ranchers got together and built the cowboy as a tribute to our pioneers."

The cowboy was made entirely of old machinery: scraps of a binder, a reaper and other lost metal had been welded into human shape under a tall hat. He stood like an industrial skeleton watching over the flesh of the village. I had seen worse art in expensive galleries.

Etienne preferred to talk about St. Victor's history.

"See that cross up there on a hill?" he said. "It was put there by a curé called Poirier. The war was on, and the curé wanted to protect the village. Well, you know, of all the young men who went overseas, every one returned safe!"

The Catholics, then, had also felt an urge to make these hills a sacred place.

"St. Victor must have been a lot bigger in those days," I said.

"But it wasn't the village that closed the church. It was the diocese that forced it on us. We still had a congregation, but they wouldn't give us a priest."

So the slender landmark of the rolling miles, the focal point of the village, had become a relic. The tongued bell beneath the spire would call no more. And I wondered what kind of spirit-death its silence implied for the town. Though it had a museum, it contained no school. St. Victor seemed to be fading like a petroglyph: modern times were erasing it from the map. Etienne yanked on his Assiniboia Credit Union cap and said, with an air of defiance: "But the post office is still here!"

In that sense, if no other, St. Victor had the edge on Forget.

"My father should never have come to the west," he added unexpectedly.

"He was from Quebec?"

"No, Massachusetts. He worked in the printing trade in a town called Holyoke. A skilled worker, eh? But he had an urge for land. When I was a boy, we lived way up in the hills in a house with two rooms. My father didn't know a thing about farming! But I have to give him credit: he succeeded. In the end, he succeeded."

Etienne's voice was bitter.

A shirtless boy passed by, dragging a hose.

137

"Well," Etienne said in English. "I guess I better get back to that swimming pool."

The pool was at present a sandy depression in the park. A diving platform and a lifeguard's tower loomed over the dry recess.

"Thanks for the information," I said.

"It's nothing. It was a pleasure. I don't have the chance very often to speak French to anybody new."

The shadows were growing. St. Victor's street became a gravel road travelling east through a bare valley. Brown cows and an occasional sudden horse grazed beneath the escarpments; on a drying slough, a hundred or more phalaropes span. For a moment I thought the water itself was tumbling in shallow waves.

At Willow Bunch—the birthplace of a bashful French-speaking giant who died, aged twenty-one, as a freak in an American world's fair—I turned south once more. The smooth paving of Highway 36 hides the Powder River Trail, which galloped from Moose Jaw down through Montana and Wyoming to the dust of El Paso and the waters of the Rio Grande. No monument marks the point near Willow Bunch where Sitting Bull gave himself up to the justice of the white man's law. Gave himself up, that is, to death. He and the remnants of his Sioux nation rode south from the famine of Queen Victoria's sanctuary towards the imprisonment, humiliation and murder they would meet on native soil. In defeat the plains Indians were, by Hugh of St. Victor's exacting standards, fast becoming perfect. They cherished the world. The world became a foreign land.

·XXXIV·

FRENZEL: PAUL

Paul Frenzel homesteaded in 1915 or so. He was born in Germany, where he was an accomplished concert pianist. However, with years of hard work and no instrument on which to practice he was so frustrated when he would sit down at the piano and try to play some of the beautiful music he remembered. "I no can do anymore," was always his sad remark. He passed away during the 1930s.

Western Canadian history, as I studied it in high school, was a tedious affair. Freight rates and tariffs were the seams; the evolution of a new grain or a new political party supplied the brightest threads. I occupied myself by dreaming of the foreign past. Somehow the simplest truth eluded me: history can be the daily record of women's and men's lives. History is not just a graph of taxes or a chart of votes; it is gossip and idealism, prejudice and jealousy.

Growing up in a prosperous city, I acquired a simplistic notion of progress: history, I came to believe, is the proof of advancement from the darkness of the past. We know more than ever about the physical world; therefore (I was taught) we also know more about our lives. My teachers never quite suggested that whatever is, is right. But I acquired a belief no less complacent: in Canada whatever is, is preferable to what has gone before.

It was hardly likely, of course, that *From the Turning of the Sod* — thrillingly subtitled "The story of the early settlers in the Rural Municipality of Hart Butte no. 11" — would find its way hundreds of miles northward to a classroom in Saskatoon. But if I had read it, and a few other local histories, I would have learned that the majority of pioneers left the mocking land never glimpsing the pot of gold they had expected prairie rainbows to bring. I would have seen that among the people of rural Saskatchewan, the commonest experiences are those endured by Paul Frenzel and Zid: failure and defeat.

> Zid . . . was a bachelor. Since times were hard and money was scarce, he . . . set up his still in an old coal mine. It was an excellent place as he had the fuel handy to heat up the brew. On a clear day the smoke could be seen drifting from the mine shaft. However, Zid could not outsmart the police for too long and finally he was caught. . . . After this adventure Zid returned to Syria.

Zid was bootlegging in the Big Muddy Badlands, a little-known border country between the grain empires of Saskatchewan and the U.S.A. Butch Cassidy and his cohorts used to retreat here when the chase heatened south of the imperceptible frontier. It is a region of grandeur and enigma: of a taut, carnivorous beauty. Some of its most rugged sod has never been turned.

The white man's history of the Big Muddy is brief and intense. Railways, and therefore towns, arrived in the region late. Buffalo Gap, for example, was born along the tracks in 1928. A year later a triad of grain elevators guarded the rails. Soon the place also had a post office, a pool room, a hardware store, a dance hall, a school, a bank, a barber shop, a butcher, a blacksmith, two gas stations, three restaurants (one of them Chinese), a stockyard, a lumberyard, a carpenter, a flourhouse, a laundry (also Chinese), a church, a doctor, a painter-decorator, an implement dealer, a shoe shop, an electrical plant, and a general store that sold whatever goods the specialized businesses of the callow town might have overlooked.

Some of the businessmen made a quick profit; many did not. All pulled out. Like one of those desert flowers that blooms and dies in a single day, Buffalo Gap sped from infancy to senility without ever experiencing the pleasures and compromises of a mature life. When the 1980s arrived, two families lived among the ghosts of what might have been.

"Out near Rockglen," Jill Hands told me, "there's an old man who farms twenty-four sections of land with his sons. That's more than fifteen thousand acres. But when he was growing up, twenty-six other families lived and worked in the space he's got to himself today."

"Is he happy about what's happened to the district?"

She shrugged. "Not particularly."

Jill works as the United Church minister in Coronach, a bland town southwest of the badlands. Every Sunday, regardless of the weather, she drives eighty miles along the border highway to lead worship in four communities. Her husband Ted leaves Coronach for a few months each year to fish for salmon off the British Columbia coast. The ways of the Lord are mysterious indeed. They seemed a happy couple.

One morning I borrowed their detailed map and set off to explore the Big Muddy. My first road faded to a dirt track, then a pair of dry ruts on a hill. I retreated delicately. But the false start had been lucky: a badger was on the same trail. Hearing the car, he turned to look: a big, muscular animal with ash-coloured fur that reddened on his tail. Black markings down his face gave him the air of a chunky bandit. He humped a little farther along the track and lumbered with surprising speed into the brush. I searched for his burrow without success. Three blue butterflies were flitting over the yellow flowers—locoweed and golden bean—where the badger had vanished.

A gravel road—the right one, this time—took me north into the heart of the Big Muddy valley. As late as the 1950s the road did not exist and the valley's seclusion was absolute. Its few residents would still find, on occasion, the remnants of Indian tree-burials in the berry trees under the buttes. Despite the fierceness of its weather, the land has not always seemed "bad." That day it rolled below the great sky like a breathing sculpture. Cattle grazed in a green distance. I stopped to eat a lunch of apples and Coronach muffins on a slope overlooking Big Muddy Lake.

The name misleads: most of the lake is an alkali plain devoid of water. When a breeze tugged, smoke drifted from the dry white lakebed and dispersed in the air. So dazzling was the whiteness that even with sunglasses, I had to avert my eyes. I scrambled down the sandy hill and walked onto the lake: soft underfoot, though pebbled with innumerable tiny stones. Upturning a rock beside the smoking shore, I disconcerted a beetle the size of a plump watchface, wearing luminous red spots on his black back. He scuttled for cover as though the light could kill.

The afternoon lengthened. I drove across a small dam and up into the ranched hills. Wire fences and a seeded field gave the only signs of human presence in a solitude that descended like repose. The car seemed no more than a blanket; my ceiling was the placid sky. A couple of inexplicable half-tons disturbed my reverie with the cut of rasping motors and the thrust of surprised eyes.

Over the grassy crest of a hill, the road dropped into the midst of twenty-three horses, dark-coated and glossy, grazing a wilderness of choice meadows. A spindly foal sniffed the wind. Although I considered lingering, I could think of no justification to remain in Eden. And the road fell back into the valley. It twisted among buttes, as bare as upturned hoofs, and skirted the bases of sandstone hoodoos. The landscape's geometry—cubic through much of southern Saskatchewan—turned Cubist. Cacti flanked the gravel. A wind played little games with the car. I was suddenly glad when the road intersected a highway, arrowing north to the dusty town of Bengough or south towards the U.S.A.

But I stopped once more. I'm not sure why. Beside the brown abandoned house, a persistent meadowlark and a parliament of insects made all the noise. I slipped under the inevitable barbed-wire fence, climbed the knoll into the late sunlight, and walked towards an open doorway. A hedge of feral caragana was afire with yellow blossom. Had this family, I wondered, like so many others, left no descendants near the land they broke and cursed and loved? A barn swallow chattered and zoomed.

The house was small: only five rooms. Swallow nests hung from the ceilings of the porch, a bedroom and the living room. The birds swerved, circled, cried and made tentative diving forays at me, frantic with rage. I opened the back door onto the long grass and stood for a few minutes watching the implacable sun as it fell to a grapefruit-coloured rumour in the west. The sky softened and hinted at mauve. And it occurred to me then that for a swallow, the

142

brevity of life may be summed up by a man who steps out of the vast light into a bird's territory, stands for the twinkling of an eye under a nest, and disappears.

·XXXV·

Folk wisdom from Walter, a barber in Assiniboia: "If Mother Nature had intended there to be a cure for baldness, you wouldn't have all these millionaires walking around with wigs on."

The rooms next to mine in a local hotel were occupied by a forlorn-looking rock group. "Plutonium" had left Regina two days early, and its musicians were lost for action in a small Saskatchewan town. All four of them were young, polite, long-haired (their manes looked a decade out of date) and bored stiff. I saw them walk up Centre Street in a blond cluster; when they reached the end of it, they waited at the traffic light, crossed and paced down the other side. In the coffee shop they crouched over their enamel cups, painfully aware that curious farmers were observing their every move.

"Yeah, the seeding's mostly done by now," said the teenager who checked the car's oil.

"Looks like it might be a good crop, eh?"

"Ah," he shook his head, "but we gotta wait for June and July!"

On the prairies a consciousness of hope deferred, an intimacy with disappointment, unites the generations like a common tongue.

I drove west to Limerick: three red railcars, six white elevators, and a low huddle of homes and trees in the immensity of a seeded plain. The land beats a continual retreat in the eye, leaving little for the mind to hold. Only the memory of a narrow highway rising to the Wood Mountain plateau, its turns oddly precipitous for Saskatchewan; the suggested speed around one sly bend was twelve miles an hour. I did a dangerous double take as the car passed fifteen or twenty buffalo.

"Oh sure," said a knitting woman in the basement of Wood Mountain's Co-op store. "That's the buffalo ranch."

Wood Mountain is a scrawny, dishevelled village. It hunches away from the railway line as though history, weather and an acrid economy have punished it without respite. The place is small enough to die: its official population is thirty-eight; its hotel bears the name "Trails End." But a local resilience, a rooted toughness, forestalls any prospect of abandonment. Some residents have even tried to start a theatre group.

"Yet we could easily turn the prairies into another Ethiopia."

"How?"

"By destroying the land," Charlotte Fitzhenry said. "By wasting the topsoil. There are hills around here that should never have been ploughed. But the men wanted to make a fast buck, so they farmed the hills for grain. And after a couple of years, the soil drifted away."

"You can't get much more shortsighted than that," I said.

"But it's not just happening around Wood Mountain. All over the prairies you come across farmers who dump huge amounts of chemicals onto their land. It's crazy. Some of them end up spending more money on their herbicides and their pesticides and their fertilizers than they gain from the extra yield."

Between farmers and ranchers in the west, not much love is lost. Charlotte is a rancher's wife; her son and husband run a vast range west and south of the village. Their farthest property, near the American border, lies forty miles from home. To shunt their herds of cattle to the southern range demands a journey of three days. Charlotte's son is the fourth generation to earn his living from the rippling land that Captain Palliser, the Irishman who first described the plains in detail, characterized as "this central desert."

Like so many women of the desert, Charlotte is both thoughtful and well read. Among her pupils at the local school were both of Wood Mountain's published writers, Thelma Poirier and Andrew Suknaski.

"Andy," she said wryly, "had to go and put real people into his *Wood Mountain Poems*. Under their real names, too."

"He didn't alter any of the details?"

"Only with the biggest scandals. And even then, not by much!"

Driving back into the village, I passed the architectural marvel where Charlotte used to teach. Two country schoolhouses, removed from their first fields, buttress the original four-room structure and a modernist extension. Tiny though it is, Wood Mountain flourishes more than most of its neighbouring communities. An adjoining rural municipality, full of big rocks and green deserted fields, has the apt name of Stonehenge.

Indians still inhabit a postage-stamp reserve in the hills south of town. Their ancestors gathered in desperation at Wood Mountain when the buffalo herds were gone.

I chose not to linger. The sun, still high, poured like gold dust through the window as I kept on westering through grazed land. After Mankota had vanished from the rearview mirror, it was a drive of forty miles to the next settlement, Val Marie. By the time I turned south at Pinto Butte I was lopsided: my left arm, reddish-brown, prickled with heat, yet my right arm remained pale.

The butte was steep enough to challenge the car. I stopped at the crest, thirty-two hundred feet above the level of the oceans, and sat beside the road. Not a vehicle passed, or was visible, or was audible. A gopher, an exalted vesper sparrow and some clumps of golden bean in the grass were my only company under the windy sky. I read the label of a Malted Milk bar and discovered that I was inserting into my stomach sodium hexametaphosphate, sodium aluminum sulphate, sodium lauryl sulphate, triethyl citrate, artificial flavour and the mysterious B.H.A. Below my chemical feet the continent divided: rain to the north would join Hudson Bay; rain to the south would swell Denniel Creek, the Frenchman River, the Milk

River, the Missouri River, the Mississippi River, and finally the Gulf of Mexico a lifetime away from Pinto Butte.

The Sioux set up camp near the butte in 1877. A year earlier, they had triumphed at the Little Big Horn. Game, if no longer plentiful, was available; the warriors, if not mighty, were in no mood to surrender. Their last culture of liberty was far from idyllic, except by comparison with the long squalor to come. Maybe those confused few years, when the unsettled territory overflowed with Indian refugees from the U.S.A., provide the source of a local legend: that a cairn of rocks near the summit of Pinto Butte, enveloped by wild roses, marks the grave of an Indian princess and her beloved pony.

Only in the pages of bad romantic poets do Indians have "princesses." The legend, nevertheless, may arise from truth: a bush, a horse, a dead girl.

The highway toppled into the arid, eroded valley of the Frenchman. In this country, the previous summer had been so dry that some farmers left their pitiable crop to wither on the stalk. A village with the sumptuous name of Coriander was now part of a field. I reached town like everybody else does: in a curry of dust.

Folk wisdom from Ethel, a cashier in Val Marie: "Even in the Great Flood of Noah, Val Marie only got an inch."

I ate in Rusty's Café and decided to live on fruit.

"Can I have a hot beef sandwich, please?"

"Got no beef."

"A hot pork sandwich, then?"

"Got no pork, either."

"What've you got?"

"Loaded burger."

So I suffered a loaded burger with fries, which made me comatose for an hour. Yet my cramped room at the Val Marie Hotel discouraged me from a solitary evening. It lacked an armchair, a shower, a toilet, a telephone, a radio and a TV. It did contain a desk, which boasted three Gideon Bibles and a pair of jokers.

A drowsy subsidence on the sagging bed left me ready for a drink. Downstairs the bar held a single customer, a jovial man in a green cap, watched from the walls by an antlered face and a shaggy buffalo head. The crow's-feet around the man's pale eyes were transforming his face into a chart of the valley.

"You go down to Montana much?" I asked.

The border is less than twenty miles south of Val Marie.

"I don't," he said, "but some people do their cotton-pickin' shopping down in Malta."

"That's a fair distance, eh?"

He shrugged.

"Same as Swift: round about seventy miles. A lot of folks go shopping up there, too. But I tell you one thing: there's a bar seventeen miles south of the line. No store. No gas station. Just a bar. And that's where Canada goes on Sunday!"

We lapsed into silence for a while. Then:

"You're a visitor, eh?"

For a second I considered an extravagant, unbelievable lie.

"That's right."

"Have you gone over to Perrault's?"

147

It was not far to walk. Val Marie's population has fallen below 250, despite an influx of farmers and ranchers who spend most of the year in town. Across from Rusty's Café, the Palais Royal Theatre is dark. The wide streets, populated by half-ton trucks, remain unpaved but for a thin, alkali-white band of sidewalk that separates the potholed gravel from the lawns. That evening a long twilight gentled the town and gave its struggling trees an almost gracious air. I found Lise Perrault putting a bowl of food outside her screen door for a cat.

"Come in!" she said at once. "Maybe you'd like to look at my paintings?"

Every spare scrap of wall in her kitchen was taken up by her oils; an unfinished canvas stood propped on the refrigerator. Most of the paintings showed yellow-brown or grey-green vistas of the Frenchman Valley—Shotgun Coulee and Pinto Butte, Lookout Point and Dogtown—accurate to the humped, sprawling topography. One scene was framed by a distressed wood: buffalo berry, twisted and red like a gnarled cedar.

The interminable hockey playoffs were still alight in the living room. On top of the TV set, overshadowing the violence below, stood a stuffed golden eagle. Heads of bighorn sheep loomed in a corner. Snoring on the couch was Fernand Perrault.

He woke up as grumpily as a bitten bull, insisting to his wife that he had been awake all the time, glaring at me from the depths of a creased, rocky face.

"I can't say anything good about your beard!"

"Have you ever had one?" I asked in slight alarm.

"Grow one every winter," he replied.

Fernand was getting ready for the open range, where he ranches, clean-shaven, through the broiling summer. His wife pointed out a knot of trophies on a coffee table.

"They're from son number three," Fernand said.

Son number three had been the arm-wrestling champion of Canada; I didn't even know there was such a thing. Lise showed me a snapshot of the man in action. He appeared to be in extreme pain.

"So are we watching this hockey game or not?"

"No," said Lise.

"Good," said Fernand, grinning. "The Flyers are losing any-way." Both of them, I noticed, spoke with a slight French accent.

"Would you like to see the basement?" Lise asked.

What kind of invitation was that?

"Definitely," I said with an effort at enthusiasm.

"Good," Fernand said again, opening the door that led down into the dark. "I hope you like snakes."

I followed the couple into a peculiar and wonderful space. Its oddments and clutter, its jumble of earthly delights, added up to a self-portrait of the Perraults in four dimensions and a surreal crowd of materials. The affection and the knowledge they bring to their "museum" defy anyone to classify some objects as valuable and others as old junk. Most of the collecting cost the pair nothing. Over the decades, the land offered up riches to their hands.

Riches such as three live rattlesnakes in a glass cage. I approached to within a few feet. The snakes flicked their forked tongues and flashed their tawny heads. Their rattles made a dry, brittle noise like a desiccated castanet.

"I haven't fed 'em for seven or eight months," Fernand said.

"Months?"

"Sure, I just give 'em a little water now and again. They won't eat meat, you know, even raw. Has to be something that's alive."

"And they don't go after you?"

"They might try it. But these ones are adults, eh? The young are more dangerous."

"And you'll keep the snakes till they die?"

"No, I'll let 'em go in a couple months. Then I might find a few more in the fall."

It seemed an odd way for a reptile to pass a winter: imprisoned in a dark room in the company of a bear trap, a vintage sewing ma-chine, four oxshoes, a couple of tomahawks, the first typewriter to arrive in Val Marie (a black Underwood very like my wife's), and a *Bob's* soft-drink bottle from about 1939.

"This is where my grandmother got her arm muscles from," Fernand said, passing me a rusting kettle. I nearly dropped it on the floor.

"I don't like this trap," Lise said. "We should get rid of it."

"Crazy woman," Fernand said shortly. "Look at those jars, will you?"

WIDEMOUTH ADJUSTABLE was sitting on a shelf. A twin beside it read WIDEMUTH ADJUTABLE.

"And this is how it all began," Fernand said, passing me an inscrutable object the size of a fist. "What is it?"

I had no idea.

"Well, what does it look like?"

It looked like a heart of stone: corded veins were standing out against the grey rock.

"Right!!!"

I wasn't sure if he was pleased or sarcastic.

"Plains grizzly, maybe?" he said, slipping the object into a wooden case and fastening the lock. "I'm not sure. But you know what *this* is?"

The long stone had protuberances at one end.

"?"

"It's the footprint of a sasquatch."

Lise and Fernand burst out laughing. It struck me that broad, spontaneous laughter from old people seems as rare as petrified hearts.

"Here's a real treasure," he said, pointing at a pair of skates behind glass.

"?"

"Bryan Trottier's skates! From 1976! The year he won the Calder Trophy!"

Val Marie's highway sign used to say: PRAIRIE DOG CAPITAL OF CANADA. Then one of the Trottier brothers attained a chippy heroism with the New York Islanders. A sign now announces HOME OF BRYAN TROTTIER. The most prominent building in town is the forbidding Bryan Trottier Arena, shaped like an upturned bath.

"Does he ever come back?"

I knew that Trottier had taken out American citizenship.

"Nearly every summer," Lise said, "for a few days. You know he has one of my paintings?"

A scatter of her early works, stiff and lifeless, weighed on the basement walls. Lise was past fifty when she began to paint. The failure of these preliminary oils pointed up the sweet competence, even the grace, of her recent art.

"Look at those guns," Fernand commanded. "That one's a Russian rifle from 1942. And this—how old do you think it is?"

"First World War, maybe?"

He looked disgusted.

"It's American, dated 1873," he said with pride. "And I think—I think—"

"Oh, come on, Fernand," said Lise.

"*I* think it was brought up here by Sitting Bull's warriors. An old bachelor found it years ago out in Shotgun Coulee. My guess would be that an Indian took it from one of Custer's soldiers and carried it up with him north of the line."

"And then left it lying in a coulee?"

Fernand glared. Lise crowed.

"Well, have you got any better ideas?"

"No!"

Fernand beamed.

"And that's about it," Lise said.

"You got to see the picture of Kavik," Fernand said. He vanished for a minute, and reappeared clutching a framed photograph of a bobcat.

"You kept a bobcat in the house?"

"For nine and a half years," Lise replied. "He was so tame with the family! He'd even sleep on the children's beds. But oh God, he was a terror to the cats of Val Marie."

"And the dogs!" Fernand said, chortling.

I bought a copy of *The First White Woman in the West,* Lise's translation of an old, curt biography of Marie-Anne Lajimonière. She emigrated from Quebec in 1807, a young bride accompanied by her voyageur husband, to spend her life among the Métis and the plains Indians who "took undescribable pleasure in looking at her." They had plenty of time to look: Marie-Anne reached the age of ninety-six. One of her grandsons was Louis Riel. The moral of her story seemed to be that "the desert we cross is filled with mirages and we ever walk encouraged by the sight of an oasis where we will find repose."

"I got to slow down," Fernand admitted at the top of the basement stairs.

"He had a heart attack," Lise told me. "I wish he didn't have to spend another summer ranching."

It dawned on me finally that none of their sons lives anywhere near Val Marie.

"Yeah," Fernand said. "That park better happen fast."

"If the park doesn't come," Lise said, "Val Marie is gone for the bun."

·XXXVII·

The prairie dogs adore dry heat. A hundred years ago these chunky rodents foraged throughout the sun-charred realm of short-grass prairie. But unlike their tough cousins the gophers, they proved unable to adapt to ploughed land. For many years the animals' Canadian range has consisted of a few scarred miles along the Frenchman valley. There they inhabit colonial burrows that stretch as deep as fourteen feet below the threadbare, sage-scented earth. Appealing, accessible, endangered, the prairie dogs are the prime symbol, the liquid-eyed image, of the Grasslands National Park.

Other animals need protection too—burrowing owls and short-horned toads, ferruginous hawks and wind scorpions—not to mention a regiment of plants. They are relics, nature's old-timers on a plain that has become, as Adrian Forsyth and other biologists realize, "the most altered habitat in this country and one of the most disturbed, ecologically simplified and overexploited regions in the world." This knowledge and its sour implications have made next to no impact on the citizens of the west. To most, the land is nothing more than a vast commodity for human use. In the 1960s and

152

'70s Saskatchewan's government agreed in principle that a Grasslands National Park should be established; yet it has stalled or undercut every initiative to turn the principle into a living fact. To politicians, the slim chance of an oil or gas discovery has far outweighed the value of saving a rare, ancient environment. In consequence the park remains a kind of legal fiction, a dryland sanctuary in limbo.

While the governments dawdle and endlessly ponder, much of the semiarid territory around Val Marie has been converted from ranchland to grain fields, which bring their owners a fast, short-term return provided an occasional spasm of rain dampens the blowing soil. Ranchers who want to sell their land to Parks Canada are seldom able to complete the deal. When I drove south one morning past the town's false-fronted Main Street and its tire-spangled playground, the high gravel road cut through a mile of cultivated earth.

From the gravel I turned onto a dirt track. Soon it became a sandy trail. The ruts led into a rancher's yard and out again; opening a barbed-wire gate, I made a clumsy gash in a palm. A lower world began to open up on my left. Finally, the trail bent that way and hauled me down a precipitous butte. In a field at the hill's foot lay what the residents of Val Marie call "Dogtown."

Fifty or sixty tawny animals were visible as I eased to a stop. Cat-size, they peered on their hind legs like sentinels guarding the mounds of pallid soil that protrude from the scant grass. Or they nosed for food nearby; or they scuttled, in a curious scurrying shuffle, between burrows. The presence of the car made no apparent difference to this scene of communal, sun-drenched foraging. I was close enough to see the animals' small ears and the black points to their tails. They preened and glanced and basked.

Heat poured off the tableland and into the car: the day balanced on the brink of the dry brutality of summer. Shutting the car door as gently as possible, I walked with an apple and a water bottle to a tussock overlooking the valley and its small, remote river. But the rodents were annoyed. All but the farthest, a quarter-mile along the slope, dived for earth. A racket of shrill alarm calls bounced through the air. I munched surrounded by earth and sage, a dome of scarifying light, and the high-pitched complaints of the prairie dogs. They sounded like a crowd of Russian hockey fans protesting a Canadian high stick. Once I stepped back into the car, peace reigned and the animals emerged.

After a while I drove in first gear up the fearsome hill and out along a rough chain of roads across the plateau. Its wheat fields were barren rectangles. But a medley of birds brightened the grassland: lark buntings, a black-and-white flash against the pastures; longspurs masked like desperadoes; and, to my delight, four curlews, their long curved beaks seeming an impossible handicap, a Pinocchio's curse of the air. I stopped above the valley's curving rim. Before the car slid again, I wanted to explore the bushed, fragrant coulees by the edge of the buttes.

They deceived me. I lost my way in a tangle of willows and saskatoon-brush that dwindled into a forest of ankle-high cactus. Because I had to watch every step or suffer, I noticed the first cactus flower of the year: a pincushion had opened up to a precocious, intense scarlet, as though its spikes had drawn a ball of blood. The piercing cry of an unseen bird fell twice from the rocks above.

I turned back and scrambled up a ridge. In a sloping tussle of shrubs I found a natural sculpture, scuffed white against a backdrop of silvery green. When I blew away the dust, I saw that I was holding a perfect set of antelope horns. They rose from a central knot and divided to a pair of incurving symmetrical tips. I clambered again, gripping the horns like a talisman or a banner, and regained the line of gravel a good ten minutes' walk from the car.

On the back seat, I knew, was a bottle of water. As I walked, the car keys in my pocket jangled like jewellery. I would not have traded them at that moment for a cupful of diamonds.

Strengthened by a long swig, I followed the road as it snaked down the hill, met and crossed the Frenchman, and twined back towards Val Marie. Poplars, swallows, a pair of placid mallards: the river heaved a mild domestic breath into the wild breeze. But the valley unnerved me now. Its rocks wore a grey, lichenlike colour with the merest tinge of green. The sun beat down. The high hawks drifted. Odd herds of cattle and horses browsed the earth. I felt unwelcome, an intruder, a little afraid. The valley suggested an existence on the far side of change, beyond cruelty and tenderness alike, as though a landscape from a sister planet had been surgically moulded to our own. Or else: a mute underworld below the surface of the plain, haunted by the sunken spirits of what the plain had been. The prairie dogs scuttled (I passed two more colonies), and I kept driving. As the car climbed back onto the tableland, I felt a brief strange sadness and a stranger relief.

·XXXVIII·

The next day began ever hotter. I loitered in Val Marie, visiting the Parks Canada office (an ignominious trailer) and chatting with the warden, a pleasant, frustrated man.

"So at the moment your job is basically to be a diplomat?"

"I guess that's right."

Eventually I drove west, away from diplomacy towards a kind of desolation. The first village along the highway, Masefield, was all but forsaken; having lost its grain elevators, it consisted mainly of drooping shacks. The provincial highway map has given it up for dead. Orkney, slightly less derelict, came next. It was succeeded by Bracken, whose handpainted road sign boasted: THE BEST WHEAT IN THE WORLD GROWN HERE! POP. 65. Under the boast was a green sky; under the sky, a portrait of the community. It showed Bracken with a trio of grain elevators. Nowadays the village has but one.

The real sky was growing theatrical: a black cloud ate blue light before my eyes. I decided to let the storm pass over me in Bracken, and humped across the railway tracks into the village. Even in May, a clutch of signs forbade the residents to sprinkle water over their gardens. Most of the stores were boarded or empty. The station was now a museum; an antique tractor gathered rust on the platform; I knocked and received no answer. My alternatives came down to the Evangelical Free Church or the bar. For once I resisted temptation and elected, after all, to tough out the storm in motion.

Rain hit within five minutes. I slowed the car and added head-lights when fat smudges of water started to attack the windshield; I stopped on the highway's shoulder when raindrops as big as birds' eggs broke against the car. The wipers, even at their quickest, could barely keep a view clear. The temperature had skidded. Forks of lightning shattered fault lines in the sky. I could still discern, far to the south, splashes of bright blue—but the highway resembled a river undergoing a flash flood.

Abruptly, the storm vanished. For a minute the sunlight and the hard rain were partners, and the young winter wheat shone a brilliant green in the teeth of grey-black air; then the light dried. When I looked back, Bracken's elevator shimmered beneath a wet, misty sun, trapped by an arch of rainbow against a reluctant mass of cloud. I turned the key in the ignition.

Ten minutes later the road was dry, the ground bony and the sky a lambent blue. In a field near some corrugated iron pipes:

ICE   SOFT ICE-CREAM

WELCOME TO THE

CLIMAX HOTEL

BORDER ROOM AND RESTAURANT
GOOD TIMES — GOOD FOOD

The place names of this demented province! I had already raised an Eyebrow, by-passed an Elbow and driven far beyond Forget: now, at last, I reached Climax. Unfortunately, Love was out of the question. The village lurked too far in the northeast for me to turn and stay in its Hillbilly Haven ("2 Non-Modern Rooms—Occasional Entertainment"). Climax, in any case, is twice the size of Love.

I replenished my tank at Albert's Esso. A slender man in a green

156

cap, green workshirt and green trousers appeared when I pulled in.

"Fill her up with unleaded, please."

"You betcha."

"That was quite a storm we just had!"

"Could'a done with a lot more of it here. What we got in Climax was mostly wind."

"No kidding . . . I'd like a receipt, by the way."

"You betcha."

Inside his grimy little office, Albert had pinned a typed page: "Psalm For Today." It began: "The government is my shepherd, Therefore I need not work." It mined the vein for six verses until: "I shall dwell in a fool's paradise forever."

"Thanks a lot," I said.

"You betcha."

I didn't stay to sample the times or the food. At the next town, Frontier, I wanted to meet up with Paul Kundera, a middle-aged, ruddy-faced rancher whose family has owned land on the Boundary Plateau since before the First World War. These days he lives on a hay farm forty miles away. When I climbed into the cabin of his half-ton, the view tripled.

We travelled for half an hour, saying little: Paul hides his intelligence behind terseness and a cowboy hat. Before we reached his land, which rises away from the road on a series of sweeping ridges, his small talk was used up.

Much of his property has never felt the plough. If he has his way, it never will. He drove scrupulously along a network of slim tracks, disturbing a dozen cattle and a herd of six antelope. They bounded over a sunglazed hill, white rumps flaring.

In the rare places where it deserted the tracks, the half-ton created wheel-ruts that will remain discernible after fifty years. "Wearing any such path in the earth's rind is an intimate act," Wallace Stegner wrote in *Wolf Willow*, probably the finest book of nonfiction about the prairie west, "an act like love." The rind is, in truth, a fragile skin. While prairie buildings fade into an insubstantial pageant, wounds to the earth endure. After a couple of generations, when a wagon seems as impermanent as an ambition or a desire, wagon-ruts linger like tattoos.

157

Paul stopped the truck on the side of a low ridge. Along its crest, five or six circles of stones displaced the wiry clumps of grass and cactus. These stones, a century or more ago, anchored the tents of Indians against the powers of air. In the ring of land between the Cypress Hills, the Sweetgrass Hills and the Bear Paw Mountains, buffalo grazed in abundance and tipis sprouted like sunflowers. Then the power of the white men grew irresistible. "I would not seriously regret the total disappearance of the buffalo from our western prairies," the American Secretary of the Interior observed in his annual report for 1874, "in its effect upon the Indians. I would regard it rather as a means of hastening their dependence upon the products of the soil . . ."

Near an empty circle's rim a yard from my shoes, a blackbird flew up in dismay. I bent down and discovered, inconspicuous inside a nest of woven grass, four eggs the colour of the sky.

Because its grasses are native to the west, Paul's ranch suffers little hardship from grasshoppers—so virulent elsewhere on the prairies against grain and imported grass. All it needs, and all it lacks, is moisture. The winter's snowfall had failed once again to foster lush grass in the spring; spring had brought dust; and Paul decided that this year most of his range would have to remain ungrazed.

We stopped by the barns and the wooden house where he had grown to manhood. Now it was occupied only when he and his wife found reason or excuse to visit. A tortoise-shell cat scampered up, desperate with joy that her master had returned at last. The horses were equally delighted. But Paul stayed only to correct the angle of their trough, which was dribbling water onto the ground. He drove off to inspect a cattle pond. The animals looked desolate.

His first home, at least, was in good repair. Otherwise, a laconic catalogue:

"This was my uncle's land" (a shack, some wheel-ruts). "Another uncle lived over here" (a fence). "That was my cousin's place" (an antelope pawing in the dry heat) . . .

A few miles to the south, Wallace Stegner's father tried to farm the Boundary Plateau during the First World War. Stegner passed five summers in a shack before his defeated family tumbled back to the U.S.A. When he visited Saskatchewan more than thirty years later, he was pleased to see the town of Eastend, where he had attended a square brick prison of a school and had shot stray cats. Yet he refused to look for the homestead. "That dehumanized waste" was his phrase for the plateau: "I don't want to find, as I know I will if I go down there, that we have vanished without trace like a boat sunk in mid-ocean."

Even though the buffalo, the swift foxes and other grassland animals are gone, "waste" seems a harsh term for a chunk of earth teeming with antelope and songbirds, coyotes and hawks. It is true, however, that nothing keeps this morsel of plateau from becoming "dehumanized" except the fierce and loving will of Paul.

I never bothered to ask him about his love of the land: nothing could have been more obvious, nothing harder to fabricate an eloquence for. He knew every fence and track, every curvature of the bare hills, as intimately as a body. It was the closest resemblance to a hunting Indian's awareness of the plains that I will, perhaps, ever see.

"Right here must be about the worst location," he said with an ambiguous smile. "Any rain that makes it over Alberta gets dumped on the Cypress Hills. So that nothing falls here."

The cattle pond, created by a miniature dam that backed the trickle of a creek, looked full to me; the nesting pintails agreed. Some cattle were dining on a grey-green pasture beyond the water. Paul shook his head:

"Be dried up by July."

His grief hid its power in a more powerful calmness: his anger was slow to burn. In the end, he accepted the drought. The land had endured its like before.

"You'll sell your cattle, then?"

"Most of them. Next week."

"What'll you keep?"

"Just the horses." (He didn't trouble himself to add: "The land.")

"And if the drought goes on?"

He shrugged and smiled again.

"Just wait it out, I guess."

·XXXIX·

I drove northwest from Frontier to reach a prosperous ranch that nestles in a zone of long-grass prairie nourished by the rains of the Cypress Hills. The creek that slips through its yard was furred with wild white violets. I slept between a stuffed burrowing owl and a brass-rubbing of a burnished knight; when I woke in a pure darkness, I heard the yips and howls of coyotes at play in the invisible hills.

Sunday dawned grey and cool. I was fondling a cat by the name of Beethoven—she loved to roll over—when Don Carnaby appeared from a shed. Beethoven abandoned me. Before he took control of his father's farm and ranch, Don had studied architecture at a distant university. He was, for a rural westerner, typically thoughtful and untypically watchful.

"Would you like to come along to a cattle branding?" he asked a little diffidently.

"When?"

"Now."

"It's about the last of the communal activities round here," he remarked ten minutes later with what may or may not have been sadness. I had to strain to hear him above the rattles of the inevitable half-ton as it heaved uphill.

"You don't need a lot of help at harvest-time anymore," his wife added. Jo-Ann was an athletic woman, slightly taller than Don, with black hair that streamed below her shoulders. "And the big roundups are a thing of the past."

Seven weeks earlier, when I was a stranger to the rural west, the ride from the Carnaby yard to the Patten house would have shocked me. Don steered for twenty minutes through grassland and megafields of wheat, pinpricked by derelict farms, never passing a home. By now, though, the emptiness seemed normal. When the dirt road declined into a broad bowl of land with a ranch house at its centre, I was almost surprised that the ride had been so short.

"Brent Patten's a painter," Don said as a profusion of lilac gave

160

way to the door. "Don't say I didn't warn you."

Brent greeted us firmly and made space in a luminous breakfast-nook overseeing the valley. While his girlfriend fed us coffee and toast, a couple of vans and a small herd of half-tons drew up outside the garden. Soon about thirty men, women and children had trick-led into the house. The men flaunted a mixture of caps and widebrimmed hats; the women's heads were either cowboy-hatted or bare. Over the banter of coffee, the caps were removed. The hats stayed on. Wisely, nobody broached the host's oil paintings, which inhabited most of his walls. They were in the abstract expressionist mode. They expressed very little.

On the company's fringes lurked the children, quiet with anticipation and, perhaps, shyness at the sprinkling of unfamiliar adults. A boy of about eight wore the costume of prairie ceremony: a patterned white shirt and Levi Strauss jeans, fastened by a hefty leather belt and tucked into tooled boots. The only adult over forty was, in fact, well over sixty and as bald as porcelain.

"Been to the barber lately, Ben?"

Caps slid back onto heads, cups onto the crowded table. Without discussion or a hint of a command, the women and men drifted out-side and the half-tons bumped over a stony trail to the corral, half a mile from the house. The children followed impatiently on foot.

"It's the first big branding of the year," Jo-Ann told me as we joined the procession. A couple of horse-trailers, I noticed, were al-ready parked by the corral.

"Does that mean the calves are pretty young?"

"Yeah," Don said with what may or may not have been regret. "Seven weeks at the most. Some of them might be less than a month old."

"Why does Brent want them branded now?"

"Oh, he's going to move a herd up onto Hutterite pastureland thirty, maybe forty miles from here. And he's got to brand the calves before they can leave the ranch."

The calves were Herefords, destined to be cooked. Nearly a hun-dred had been packed into the corral—a kind of wooden stockade held fast by wire that stretched five feet high between the posts. A similar number of cows pressed against the calves, some of which were suckling. Scarcely able to move in the melee of their own bodies, the animals eyed the world and bellowed with unease. And so the ritual began.

The first work was to evict the majority of cows. A narrow gate opened in the stockade; two men and two women entered, and their intricate body language encouraged the cows to leave. Through an assortment of shouts, runs, arm waves and occasional dives, a couple of people detached a mistrustful cow from the herd. A third then drove her through the gate. Any calf that scampered past the guards found the gate shut in its face. The anxiety of the prisoners grew.

Once the cows had left the corral, some meandered away to browse on the hills' fresh grass. But others—the younger, excitable mothers—declined to leave. They pushed at the fence, mooing a lament or a reassurance through the wire. Still others wandered aimlessly among the trucks, as though they were trying to recall some lost desire or power.

One calf achieved a brief escape. Tucked beside its bolting mother, it dashed into the pasture, paused and gaped in bewilderment. It made no effort to escape the cowboy who rode up beside it on an elegant chestnut gelding, lassoed it, and dragged it on its side to the corral. Its mother ran for the hills.

The exodus ceased when about twenty cows remained inside: the corral was empty enough by now for the day's work to proceed. Old Ben entered the stockade and took charge of a small tank of propane. He heated half a dozen irons in its tongues of flame. The chestnut gelding and a darker, smaller horse invaded the ring. Their riders would stay in the saddle for the next two hours, taking turns to bring the calves to the fire. Fourteen men and women were now inside the corral. The children, alert as apprentices, observed.

Ben gave a signal. A scurry of hooves: a rider lassoed a calf by a brown-and-white hind leg and tugged it across the earth. Four hands pulled away the rope and wrestled the calf into submission. It squirmed, helpless and shouting, a woman astride its shoulders, another on its thighs. So far, all had been indignity; now came the pain.

A third woman ran up with a needle and shot the animal full of growth hormones; a fourth injected it with vaccines. But it was a man, using a knife as sharp as a whetted razor, who clipped off part of the calf's ear: the V of its amputation serves as identification on the open range, especially when a growth of winter hair obscures the brand. And it was another man, having accepted the iron from Ben, who planted it for a couple of seconds against the animal's skin.

It sizzled. The calf screamed. A long, curling tongue unfurled from its wide-open mouth. The man returned with a different iron and branded the calf again. Brent's cattle receive their identity scars above their left hind legs; other ranchers set a mark on the calves' flanks or shoulders. A brand endures for a lifetime.

Painful though the experience was, these calves were fortunate: nothing worse would ensue for many weeks. Elsewhere in the west, the branding of calves often accompanies their castration and dehorning. Castration enables the branding crew to share a meal of pan-fried testicles — the "prairie oysters" that consummate a day's hard work. Dehorning causes agony, as well as a fountain of blood.

When it was branded, each calf staggered up and lurched blindly off, as though its mind could no longer register what its eyes perceived. Two animals ran into the fence so hard that their heads got stuck between the wires. They had to be extricated fast. Although most of the calves rejoined the nervous herd within a minute, none tried to suckle.

I watched eighteen or twenty animals suffer their trial by fire. Sometimes two calves lay on the ground at once, being needled, clipped and branded by different teams. Most of the children drifted away. The work was unpleasant to behold, despite the efficiency and good humour of the branders. They even showed occasional compassion: Jo-Ann Carnaby rubbed the chin and throat of one terrified calf in a quick act of tenderness. Yet I grew weary of the singe of burning flesh and troubled by the calves' rolling eyes. I was cold. I had to leave.

A large cow hurried before me; a meadowlark sounded ridiculously joyful; I jumped across a narrow creek. For a long time the cries of the calves were vivid, neighbourly. A wandering dog joined me as I climbed the crumpled, cow-speckled hills; then he shot after a couple of jack rabbits whose muscular hind legs propelled them over a ridge and out of sight. By rounding sufficient folds of the

163

hills, I retrieved wildness and silence. The damp, bushy hollows and the undulating slopes bristled with flowers. Near a blue knot of lupines, I met a few of the lily-shaped, translucent plants that go by the name "death camas." A lunch of them can kill a calf. The sage and cactus of the drylands were nowhere to be touched or smelt.

The air above the flowers was still: the north wind that had reddened the branders' ears sank beneath a murmur. Most prairie literature, good or bad, celebrates the power of the wind: its ageless, implacable capacity to sweep or shrivel everything in its path. "The wind our enemy" is a perennial western theme. Only the Cypress Hills, perhaps, have inspired a counterpoem in honour of the wind's failure. A local writer called James M. Moir—"Mac" Moir throughout his home territory—has described how the hills succeed in wrestling a bullying wind to surrender:

> and it was the wind that night
> the beaten wind
>   who fell back.

The Cypress Hills are accustomed to challenges. They defeated the glaciers too.

By the time I strolled back to the corral, regaining the dog along the way, the branding was nearly complete. The final animals shrieked, writhed and fled, all consciousness shrunken to their dry burn. Three or four of the branded calves, I was happy to see, were suckling again. A couple of cases of beer emerged from a convenient half-ton as the irons cooled. The bellowing of the cattle diminished. But the day was still young; energy was high; lunch was unready.

"So let's ride a few cows?"

I don't know if the cow-riding was planned or spontaneous, predictable or surprising. Certainly the idea of it spread like a rumour of treasure. For while I watched with some astonishment, an amateur, homemade rodeo was born.

Six or eight volunteers pitched in to clear the corral of cobblestones. Meanwhile, a rider and two shouting, hand-slapping pedestrians cleared most of the bemused cattle out to the valley. They herded the remainder into a chute at one end of the corral.

164

Don Carnaby and a colleague, improvising a system of gates from long slats of wood, manoeuvred the first cow into a pose of immobility. They wound a piece of rope around her chest and upper back; a rider, by controlling the rope, could hope to stay in place. The cow waited, apparently calm even when a rider—who proved to be Jo-Ann—vaulted the fence and slid onto its bare warm hide. An inexplicable minute passed. The chute opened.

The cow charged out. She reared and kicked and shook, depositing the rider's cap in the muck; but Jo-Ann clung on across the corral. At last, to avoid a collision with the fence, she fell sharply to her right. The cow continued to race round the enclosure, kicking up her hind legs and letting out yells of disgust. The spectators hollered with delight. Jo-Ann stood, grimacing.

Nobody else that afternoon would ride as far: for their pain and indignity, the animals took some innocent revenge. The master of the revels, Brent Patten, was evicted from his plump mount on the second leap. The fun was brief; the falls were hard. Only one child asked to ride: the thin boy of eight in the patterned shirt. He gained an earful of instruction from the men, and tumbled off his calf at once. The fall bruised the boy's right knee. I saw him limping a minute later around the parked trucks, calling OW-OW-OW-OW-OW in a brave silence, and battling at all costs not to cry.

Seven adults rode and dropped. No further candidates stepped forward. The boy demanded a second chance.

"Well, I don't know, Darryl. You fell mighty hard last time."

"Dad, come on; Dad; Dad; Dad, *please?*"

So Darryl was hoisted aboard a second frightened calf. It leapt from the chute as wildly as a flame, hurling the boy to earth like a singed stone. After a terrible couple of seconds he came up bleary, crying hard. Cow manure stained his shirt. Three men rallied to his aid, patting and hugging the child; the ritual of his comfort was male. Although the women looked on with sympathy—mingled with anxiety and, I suspect, a tinge of shame—none dared to intervene.

"You done good, cowboy," a brander told the boy. His tears were drying into short, fierce gulps. "Cowboy," in these conditions, was a word of honour.

The rodeo was over. While most of the branders slowly drifted back to the house, three horsemen rounded up the cows and calves that had spread to graze throughout the sleek hills. The horses galloped, stopped and swerved like extensions of their riders' minds. When the herd was assembled, the riders began to drive it north along the green edge of the valley: a line of lives on the move under the line of the horizon; a sweet and mythic sight.

"Come on," Don said. "Don't you want some food after all that?"

Lunch was a buffet of wieners, chili and homemade pies. The mood was quiet, almost tense. I had expected more signs of release.

"My arm has swelled up pretty bad," I overheard Jo-Ann tell her husband. "Think maybe I broke my wrist when I fell."

In the living room, enveloped by more of the host's furious abstractions and a polite selection of his cattle-breeding journals, I talked to a ranch hand called Schwartz.

"Ever hear about that rodeo rider from up Rosetown way? The one whose bronc kicked him in the head?"

"No," I said.

"Oh. Is that right? Well, anyway, he's a vegetable now."

Schwartz grinned. I shook my face and munched my apple pie.

·XL·

I skimmed a portly book of local history, *Between and Beyond the Benches,* and took the Skyhawk east along a gravel road that tears the Frenchman valley. Upstream from Val Marie the valley was thinner than I remembered, steeper, and some of the exposed hills were vertical enough to justify the name of "cliff." Pale deposits of clay stood out like ghost rocks at the hilltops. The clay gave the Frenchman River its first and local name: the Whitemud.

The first function of history is remembering: a people without memory is a people without self-awareness. To remember accurately is to be immunized against a vicious strain of stupidity.

I tried to remember the entry in the history tome for Guy Armand Thomas Marie de Cargouet:

> About 1902, a Frenchman with this long name, who claimed to be a Viscount from France, settled on the Whitemud two miles north-west of where Ravenscrag is now. When the land was officially sur-veyed in 1908 he received a grant, or squatter's right, of forty acres. His main occupation was raising fine horses and consuming huge amounts of whiskey, being assisted in the latter by many drinking friends. He left the district in 1908, no one seems to know where he went.

At their simplest, the local histories of the west celebrate or mourn those settlers who disappeared into an heirless oblivion. Every village has its equivalents to de Cargouet or Michael Oxarat, the Basque rancher who raised thoroughbreds in the Cypress Hills: his finest animal, Blair Athol, was destroyed when a rival poured sulphuric acid over the horse's shoulders. Oxarat and de Cargouet made a reputation and vanished like smoke. Behind them they left nothing but an occasional debt and the memory of burnt glamour, filtered through jealousy and awe.

But when history impinges on the present, hard choices arise. Forgetfulness can become convenient. *Between and Beyond the Benches* recounts, briefly and neutrally, the extraordinary life of Mrs. Belle Dale, a.k.a. Mrs. Bill Kinnick, a.k.a. Mrs. Willard. The daughter of a saloonkeeper in the American west, she moved alone to the Cypress Hills; there she homesteaded around 1914 and taught school in her home. Later "she ranched and farmed some." Later still she cooked for the lumbermen of British Columbia and spent a mild old age reading tea leaves in the Okanagan Valley. "She was also a good artist," the entry observes, "and did very nice crochet work." What set her apart from the women of the hills was not her knitting, her teaching or her tea leaves, but her leadership of a gang of thieves.

The local "Ballad of Robbers' Roost" tells much of the tale: how a team of rustlers, working by night, would herd the stolen horses and cattle onto her land. The police, they were confident, would never suspect a charming teacher of involvement with animal thieves. Their confidence was, at first, well founded.

> A hobo came to the rancher's gate
> "I need a job," he said.
> The maid was kind as she was fair
> She gave him bed and bread.

The hobo was a mountie. In the next weeks, while he did odd jobs around the ranch, he recorded brands, numbers and dates. His observations filled a small black book like the raw material for a theorem. When the evidence coalesced into proof, the gang was broken.

> The rustlers had to face the judge
> For them he had no pity
> To jail they went to pay for sin
> And with them went the lady.

So much is common knowledge: part of the folk history of the hills. The unsung, unprinted history of Robbers' Roost recalls that the hobo/policeman fell in love with the daughter of a prominent thief. To declare the man's guilt would have been to abandon the courtship. In the end, desire conquered justice: one of the rustlers never faced the judge. As a reward, the mountie got his woman.

Some of the thief's descendants inhabit the Cypress Hills, and for their benefit the writers of the local history omitted the embarrassing truth. Where history is warm and oral, many people revere cold print. A few words of print, in the case of Robbers' Roost, might have broken friendships. The gossip in the grasslands is ferocious, and a scandal thirty miles away can seem closer than a scandal down the third street of a city.

History, beyond memory, is speculation: the play of a mind with facts. Approaching the little town of Eastend, I also approached Anxiety Butte. The surveyors who christened the hill had camped near the ranch of a certain Dan Pollock, who was so notorious a worrier that behind his back the early settlers called him "Old Anxiety." He had taken up land near the Whitemud River after serving with the North-West Mounted Police: so much is common knowledge. The news may not be so familiar that Pollock was the sergeant in command of the guard at Regina when Louis Riel was hanged.

I can't know that the man's anxiety had the remotest connection with his memories of Riel's death. He may have suffered from permanent indigestion or a faithless wife. But I choose to speculate that a past hounded Dan Pollock: the image of a corpse dangling in the air; of a rope that kept swinging back and forth under the brim of his hat.

Its spectacular setting—a river, strong hills, some tucked surprising forests of conifers nearby—gives Eastend an air of expectancy. Great things, if you will only wait forever, seem certain to materialize. The big streets dwarf the shops. I bought some provisions at a Co-op and ate a horrendous lemon square in the kitchen of a local folk singer. Her repertoire of songs in French and English (mostly, to be honest, American) reckons well into the hundreds. Old age and a lack of fresh occasions mean that nowadays her performances are rare; by way of compensation, she has taken up landscape painting. It began to seem to me that the older a woman grows on the prairies, the more she experiments.

From the standpoint of literature, the greatest thing that happened to Eastend was the temporary return, in the 1950s, of the middle-aged Wallace Stegner. The visit inspired him to write *Wolf Willow,* in which he called the town "Whitemud" and analyzed it with a merciless love. Stegner had none of the milktoast sentimentality that so often afflicts city dwellers when they set out to evoke a rural past. "Where the summer sun is shining / No-one sits down there a-pining"—according to an irksome ditty—"Each day has its silver lining / Where the Whitemud River flows." Stegner remembered accurately; he knew that the summer sun can roast a field into a waste patch and drive a farmer beyond pining to despair. Nonetheless, his strictures against Eastend—and, by implication, all the little towns in the west—strike me as sometimes cruel and unjust.

"Unless a town like this," he suggests, "acquires an academy or college—which by definition would have to be second or third-rate—it is certain to remain a stagnant peasant society whose transplants will have to mature elsewhere." The trouble is, throughout the prairie provinces I had yet to meet any stagnant peasants. Men and women whose isolation from the main currents of society, and from each other, embitters and frustrates them: the west is full of these. But men and women whose minds have stagnated? Eighteen years of formal education have given me somewhat less reverence for academies and colleges than Wallace Stegner possessed: less confidence in their ability to draw the best out of the brightest; less faith in their definition of "maturity."

Over the decades the human seedbed of the rural west has proved amazingly fertile. Somehow a distinction of character continues to germinate in the dusty sunlight and the snow. The solitude which Stegner laments, which he is joyful to have escaped, can act as both a spring of strength and an incentive to co-operate.

Isolation gave Eastend a rough, unpredictable folk culture that was more valuable than he chose to admit. He saw the unruly pettiness, the recurrent desperation, the dis-ease; and he interpreted them, wrongly, as evidence of failure. Eastend in the 1950s looked and smelt to him like "a dead little country town." Yet Stegner knew the dinosaur hunter who crafted violins; he knew the town's observatory-builder; probably he was acquainted with the local balladeer who had also been a miner, barber and politician; he may even have met the folk singer with a yen for sickly desserts. They (and many others) provided Eastend with a private vitality. Give the place a third-rate academy, and you drag it closer to the indistinguishable mass culture of the continent. You pasteurize it, homogenize it, irradiate it; you make it safe for consumers; you also begin to drain its flavour. There, to my mind, true stagnation lies.

"Whitemud," in Stegner's sour opinion, "demonstrates all over again how much of amenity and the refined intelligence is lost when civilized men are transplanted to a wilderness." I used to agree: I even looked on Saskatoon as a backward outpost. But now my prejudices are different. Now I suspect that when the refinements are hard to win, passion and shrewdness and a depth of practical imagination trickle to the fore. The small towns of the west display little or no sense of the exquisite; but a distillation of aesthetic taste is very different from power of character. Stegner can keep most of his amenities, as long as he avoids equating them with civilization.

The truth is, I'm jealous. "I may not know who I am," he could write, "but I know where I am from." That easy confidence evades me; those smoky, sensuous memories elude me. Six years of Eastend and the Boundary Plateau were enough to brand him forever as a child of southwestern Saskatchewan. As for me, six years in southern Alberta and eight in Saskatoon left my hide unburnt.

Yet I think, by now, I know who I am. Whether or not my tumbleweed character makes sense to others, I understand it pretty well. And perhaps I should rest content with that rootless awareness. In the past couple of weeks the deep south of Saskatchewan had fired my imagination; but I cherished it as a foreigner. I didn't see that I had any right to gaze on its buttes and coulees, its cobblestones and tipi-rings, and say: "This magnificent piece of the continent, this part of the prairie main, these clods washed away by the wind might be where I belong."

If, by chance, I was mistaken, then a scrap of my history was going up in flames. Eastend was but a fallen rumour to the south when I noticed, in the distance up towards Bone Creek, a black feather of smoke. I speeded for a couple of minutes in case somebody needed help. But no: a man in a blue cap was content to stand beside the road and watch a large brown barn turn to fire.

"Property was abandoned," he told me above the hiss and crackle of wood. "We bought it cheap last year."

"You mean the owners just left the place?"

"No one knows where they went."

171

"So you . . . torched the barn?"

Decades of shelter and harvest dust were fluttering as ash across Saskatchewan.

"That's right," he said proudly. "Matches and diesel fuel. Strange thing, though."

"What's that?"

"Took me three tries to get it goin' ! "

The orange quills of the burning past shot up behind the man's head before they coiled into smoke. History is a trail of choices: it includes the choice to forget. My eyes prickled and my mind ached. I drove away from the acrid heat without asking the question on my tongue: "And what are you going to do with that elegant white house over near the shelterbelt?"

"None of your damned business! " he might have told me. Or: "I'll be burning it as well." Or: "Keep her. Maybe move her. Isn't she a beauty?"

I don't know what to choose to believe.

·XLI·

When did spring blow away? In a campground beside the Trans-Canada Highway I munched a solitary picnic, and realized over a sandwich of sultry cheese that summer had arrived before June. The lawns whirred with grasshoppers. Only the work of giant, revolving sprinklers kept the campground green and lush. The dandelion flowers among the grass stalks had already burst into seed.

West loves me; west loves me not; west loves me . . .

172

A white-haired lady in an orange halter-top and pink shorts wandered from one barbecue grill to the next. A catbird added his amused, sardonic song to the *fitz-bew* of a monotonous flycatcher somewhere in the planted trees. Though the shelterbelt made a poor imitation of a forest, I still needed to butter myself with Deep Woods Off. The campground is a manufactured oasis, a park cut from a mould; it could be anywhere; it hides its guests from the consciousness that around them grows a world of wheat.

The McMahon farm lies a few miles off the highway. The larks flitted and the dust flew. I left my car in the big yard and knocked on the kitchen door. After a minute a slow-moving man with a paunch and a stubble emerged to greet me. Tim was wearing a pair of ancient overalls, their blue having leached to a murky white that was blotched by a variety of stains.

"May as well keep these things on," he remarked, "so long as I'm workin' that pump."

His son followed: capped and bearded, friendly and enormously fat. We stood around and smiled and discussed the weather.

"Yessir," Mel said. "The one thing we're never short of in this country is wind."

The McMahons run a family farm in a traditional sense. How much of the land belongs to Tim, how much to Mel, and how much (if any) to Mel's younger brother Jim was something I never understood. Five generations flourish within a few miles. Tim keeps a few cattle, his wife looks after the chickens, and Jim takes care of some pigs—but these are hobbies. The work is wheat. Prairie farmers grow more than twenty million tons of it a year.

"Would you want to come on out," Tim said, "and take a look at the field we're draining?"

So I squeezed into the cabin of the pickup truck, flanked by McMahon men. A black-and-white farmdog leapt of his own accord into the back. After driving for a few minutes along a gravel road, Tim eased the truck onto a dirt trail that bisected massive plots.

The "field" was, to my eyes, a slough. Days ago Tim had set up a 180-horsepower pump to suck the water into a pipe, through a culvert underneath the trail, and out to a slim creek that would carry the slough to Antelope Lake. But the first force had proved insuffi-

173

cient, and that morning the men had hooked up a 250-horsepower pump. The machines had sucked enough water for the land to have the texture of a rotting facecloth. I stood and looked without pleasure, wondering how many pairs of water birds were out of food and home at the height of the nesting season. To drain the slough during a drought did not seem the wisest idea.

"Had much rain these last few weeks?" I inquired slyly.

"Oh, a fair amount," Tim said to my surprise. "But up until last August we went a whole twelve months with no more than three inches of moisture."

To him, the slough was unproductive land: in the crudest terms, it was money out of his pocket. Unless he could seed them fast, these soggy acres would bring no profit this year. And prairie farmers—rich though a majority has grown, in terms of equipment and property—are often poor in cash. Every year, hundreds go bankrupt. Many more give up the fight rather than endure the forced abandonment of a bankruptcy; between 1976 and 1981, more than 100,000 farmers across Canada left the land. Economic and political forces are driving farmers to press every possible dollar out of the hurting earth—even when they sense that their actions are, in a long term, foolish. "What would you do if you won the lottery?" one farmer says to another in a favourite provincial joke. "Well," the reply comes, "I guess I'd keep on farming till the money was gone."

Tim and Mel had seen all they wanted. They made a couple of adjustments to the pump and climbed heavily back into the truck. I threw a last stick into the creek for the wet dog to retrieve and jumped aboard, wishing I had joined him in the water.

"Yessir," Mel said as though reading my mind, "she's up above eighty degrees."

We drove back to inspect the concrete foundation for Jim's new home, which would rise across the farmyard from his parents' place. I was more interested in the carpentry shop, a tall wooden house from the 1920s that Tim McMahon had bought for a song and moved onto his land; but dutifully I contemplated an L-shaped hole in the earth. A middle-aged neighbour appeared and regarded the

174

same foundation from a different angle.

"Mother and me," he confided to Tim, "will be the only ones at the wedding. The wife has to go on up to Saskatoon to hear Sally in the music festival."

"Is that the Provincial Festival?" I asked.

"I believe it is. Sally's a *fluentist*."

I was lost for words. The neighbour chose a plug of tobacco, munched and spat.

Tim and I moseyed back to the farmhouse and drank a considerable amount of tea. His sense of humour, like the wind across his wheat fields, had a warm, dry strength. The aftereffects of a stroke were responsible, I finally realized, for his slowness of speech.

"Gets worse when I'm tired," he said. "It's one way to shut me up."

A car grew audible; abruptly, the sound of its engine died. A door slammed.

Tim winked at me: "That'll be the wife. At least, I hope not."

But it was. Dee rushed in like a plump tornado in a sleeveless dress. Her upper arms were bigger than some thighs of men. She was, I felt at once, a force of human nature: probably admirable, certainly tough.

"Ever been on a wagon train?" she asked me promptly.

"No."

"No? I went on a wagon train weekend last year. This year I'll be going for a whole week. Into the Great Sand Hills. There aren't any roads through there. But I guess you know that. Ever run into Allan Murdoch?"

"No."

"No? Wonderful old guy from Birsay. Very ill with heart trouble, unfortunately. But he went out on a wagon last year and he intends to do the same again. The poems that man can recite! He'd start to say a poem in front of a campfire and the noise would be something awful. But by the time he finished, you couldn't hear a pin drop. Even from the teenagers, and that's saying something. Ever hear of Jack Hitchcock?"

"Well, yes," I said, "yes, I have."

175

"Have you?" Dee looked pleased. "Allan Murdoch was a good friend of his. Do you remember a poem called 'The Prairie Heroine' ?"

All this time she had been bustling around the kitchen, unloading a shopping bag, pulling knives out of drawers and pots out of cupboards at speed. Tim winked at me again, a mixture of affection and amusement in his glance.

"I'm so mad at that community college," Dee said apropos of nothing. "You know, they might even have to cancel the Cypress Hills summer school this year? Just plain bad planning and lack of effort, that's what it is. Have you looked at my photographs?"

Prints of local landscapes, weathers and flowers hung on the dining room walls. Some of the pictures were both sensitive and dramatic.

"I think they're excellent," I said honestly.

"Do you? Thank you! Do you like beef?"

The farm adhered to a pattern I had come to recognize. Dee's kitchen, where great potfuls of tea were imbibed at a long table, overlooked a cluttered farmyard. The living room, with its deep chairs, its family photographs and its television, held a prospect of lawn and trees. Like the front door, the dining table was used infrequently. The sober meals featured ample helpings of meat, vegetables and homemade preserves. It struck me that the farms I had seen in other parts of the world conformed to a similar regime.

"So why," I asked, "did you join the bed-and-breakfast association?"

The beef was, of course, delicious.

"I always wanted to travel," Dee said. As she slowed, she gentled. "But when we were young and raising a family, we just didn't have the money. And by the time we had some money, Tim's health was becoming a problem. He was brought up on this farm. It's his life! So I decided that if I couldn't ever see the world, I'd have to bring the world to my farm."

"You're doing well, then. Financially. I mean, despite the drought?"

"We're doing all right."

Other farmers are not.

176

Showers of blessing, showers of blessing we need,
Mercy drops round us are falling,
But for the showers we plead.

In the 1930s churches across the prairies rang with the thin voices of children imploring the Lord with that hymn. The drought half a century later has not proven so fierce; its effects have been more local and less spectacular. Nonetheless, the present crisis in prairie agriculture matches, in certain ways, the severity of the Great Depression.

A basic cause is the sheer fragility of the land. Resilient under grass, the soil of the plains shies from the continual perpetrations of grain. Since the first amazing crops shot up less than a century ago, half the organic content of prairie soil has disappeared. Drought, economic pressure and (in many cases) a blatant lack of respect for the earth have led to soil erosion on a scale now "valued" at as much as $1,000,000,000 a year. In some parts of southern Alberta, more than a fifth of the topsoil blew away in the winter of 1985.

To make up for the gradual infertility of the land, prairie farmers are heaving onto it greater and greater amounts of chemicals. Annually, they use well over a million tons (a figure incomprehensible to me) of phosphates and nitrogenous fertilizers. But the herbicides and fertilizers need intensive cultivation, which in turn makes the soil more likely to emigrate at the first strong wind. Only by adding to the planet's glut of wheat can farmers pay for their pesticides, their fuel, their big equipment or their interest on Canada's $21,000,000,000 farm debt. The country's agricultural planners and bankers—and, it must be said, the farmers' own greed—have trapped the prairies into a system that defines success only in terms of export sales. On the dubious grounds of "inefficiency," diversity, small holdings and regional self-sufficiency are actively discouraged.

In the long run, western agriculture is headed for disaster. In the short run, its latest respite may come from a semidwarf strain of wheat called HY 320. Its low stalks produce an undistinguished kernel that may, despite a lack of protein, prove adequate for pitas, pastas and chapatis. If the Canadian Wheat Board can pour the stuff abroad, farmers will no doubt cherish it as though it held the seed of salvation.

"I filled my tractor tank the other day," Tim remarked over yet more tea. "The bill came to $414."

"How long will that much fuel last you?" I asked.

"About a week."

"And do you use a lot of herbicide?"

"Not as much as most of the guys. I only use it when I have to. You take some farmers round here, they just pour on the herbicide like it was some kind of medicine."

Night fell. A wind began to bother the trees in the windbreak and rattle the glass in the loft. At ten o'clock Dee strode out of the kitchen to lock the chickens in their coop. The previous night she had forgotten, and the chickens diminished by one. Tim and I smelled the rank odour before we heard Dee's call.

I grabbed a flashlight; he grabbed a shotgun. We walked quickly across the black yard. The air surprised me by its coolness. The smell grew fierce.

"I got him trapped!" Dee said in triumph. As an afterthought she added: "He squirted right at my face."

Warily I shone the light through the wire, searching for any movement that would reveal the skunk. All I could detect was a flurry of white feathers seething from the direction of some anxious squawks.

"Just in time," Dee said. "He was about to walk off with another one of my chickens!"

Nothing. Dee took the flashlight: nothing again. Tim lowered the gun and started to laugh.

"Don't tell me he's got an escape route!" Dee cried in dismay.

Tim went on laughing.

The odour penetrated the farmhouse loft, where I lay half an hour later looking out towards a toenail of moon. Dee's voice drifted up from the darkness below: "I'll have to tell the Hutterites about that skunk."

A cloud swept the moon away.

·XLII·

Icelandic or English, Mennonite or French, the vast majority of settlers to the west finally adopted a North American vernacular. Their clothes, their sports, their language cohered into a recognizable prairie idiom. Even the shunned Métis and Indians made their accommodations to the dominant culture. Yet one group of people elected to remain apart: outsiders, closely watched and ever watchful. One group of people chose to maintain an alien way of life.

As a child, I used to see them standing in clusters around Lethbridge's central park, looking (or was this my nervous imagination?) ill at ease. Many citizens gave them a wide berth on the sidewalk, as if the long black coats of the men, or the black scarves and ankle-length dresses of the women, might carry some shameful bacteria. The members of the Hutterian Brotherhood—Hutterites, to use the common parlance—had come to town, I imagine, to sell their produce and to buy new wares. They walked among us like escaped creatures from a zoo. We knew, at heart, they were harmless. But we had no desire to test our knowledge, and we were pleased when they returned to their enclosure.

Somehow, for no reason, I had absorbed the local distrust, even hostility. If I thought about the Hutterites in later years, I ascribed that hostility to an intolerance of strangers and a sour jealousy of the brotherhood's success. Hutterite colonies, according to popular legend, are spreading like a cancer across the body of the plains. The truth is that Saskatchewan's forty-odd colonies occupy a tenth of one per cent of the province's arable land. The rare bankruptcies of a colony have become famous throughout the west, giving a chuckle of malicious pleasure to thousands. By contrast, the frequent bankruptcies of a family farm delight no one.

"But they're just normal people!" Dee said. Her blue dress, I noticed, was more demure than her costume of the previous day. "Turn left at the next grid."

"You've become friendly with them pretty fast."

179

"What makes you say that?"

I had touched a sensitive point. The reeve of a local municipality was, she had told me already, an enemy of the colony. No doubt some of Dee's neighbours resented her friendship with the Hutterites: the ease with which she could phone the bossman's wife in a morning and arrange to pay a visit that evening.

"I mean the people have only been here since January," I said. "And you know them well."

"Oh sure," she said. "They're a lot of fun. You know, they don't have any TV, eh? But when Bobby Ewing got killed on "Dallas," about ten mothers and daughters just happened to come round to the farm on some errand. It was so funny, I couldn't help laughing. They knew *exactly* when the show would be on. So they crowded all round the set, and when Bobby was dying in hospital you should've seen them cry!"

"That's amazing," I replied. "I always thought they were isolated from the world."

"Well, there's still a few who are. Back in April I took a Dutch visitor out to the colony, and she met the old minister. He must be eighty if he's a day. And you know what the minister said to her?"

"?"

" 'Tell me, madam, is the war over yet?' "

A minute later Dee was saying: "Just park alongside one of these buildings. Look, they're coming out to watch!"

It was true: half a dozen women and a couple of men had stepped onto their wooden sidewalks. They greeted Dee with unaffected warmth and took us into the home of the colony's bossman, Jacob Entz.

Jacob lives in one compartment of a long, low cement building that also shelters four or five other families, each with the name of Entz. The colony is small. About sixty-five people live here; many of them are children, a few are celibate adults. A mile behind their concrete homes and sheds, the Cypress Hills rise enticingly; the commune stands at the frontier of the flat grain fields and the slopes.

We sat in Jacob's square living room. Its furniture was sparse.

"You are from Montreal?" he asked.

"That's right," I simplified.

"What a long way to come to us!"

Though he wore a sandy beard below his sandy vanishing hair, Jacob's upper lip was bare. The style gave him a wry, surprised appearance, like a philosophy professor who had argued himself back to the land.

"And what do you do for a living?" his wife inquired. A lively intelligence shone from Martha's creased, moon-shaped face. She might well, I thought, be the power behind this particular throne.

"I work as a writer."

"Ah."

Dee settled down in a comfortable disarray and asked about Martha's family. Jacob, watching me attentively, suggested that I should tour the colony with a few of its younger members.

"This is Michael," he said, gesturing at a handsome boy of about seventeen who wore a plaid shirt, black trousers and a rakish cowboy hat. "He will show you around. Ask him any questions you like. And this is Lisa, she also will come. With a friend or two?"

By the time we stepped into the long compound, Michael and I had accumulated five young women, all of them wearing long, dark dresses delicately embroidered with floral patterns. The girls were perhaps between sixteen and twenty-one; I found their ages hard to discern. They began to speak to each other in German as we trod the cracked earth towards a flat-roofed hut. I thought they were shy. I was wrong.

We entered the chapel: a bare, calm room containing pews for men on one side and women on the other. At the front, a low table held a prominent Bible. Every day in the late afternoon, the members of the colony gather here for worship. They have followed the same mode of life since the sixteenth century, when their ancestors, along with the first Mennonites and Amish, were radical Anabaptists. Like the Mennonites, the Hutterites migrated eastward; in the 1860s they lived entirely in Ukraine. Then, over a span of five years, they moved as a body to the U.S.A. Harassment during the First World War caused the majority to flee again, this time into western Canada. About two-thirds of all Hutterites now inhabit the prairie provinces.

The chapel adjoins an austere dining room, where the brotherhood takes communal meals three times a day.

"Are you a relative of Dee?" one of the girls asked, and giggled. Her voice was flavoured lightly by the spice of German.

We moved on to the colony's garage, the haunt of a few enormous tractors, their wheels far higher than my head.

"Are you married?"

"Yes, I am."

"Why didn't you bring your wife?" The voice below the polka-dotted scarf sounded, I thought, chastened.

The "blacksmith's" turned out to be an ironworking shop. Unlike the Amish, Hutterites take pleasure in some new technologies. Their machines gleamed as though mud and dust were mortal sins, and rust downright demonic. The colony's blacksmith may never have shod a horse. Nor does anyone keep a private pet, although the colony owns a dog and a few utilitarian cats.

"You should see our plumber!" Lisa suggested, drawing out her syllables into a sensuous croon.

"Why?"

I never did find out. The plumber was absent from his spick-and-span toolroom, but Peter the electrician sat at work in a concrete shed, fiddling with some wires. A middle-aged man with wispy brown hair, Peter takes care of the colony's power and light. He also serves as its jeweller, fashioning rings out of copper wire.

"And just imagine, he's not married!" a grey-eyed girl said with regret.

"Oh, Katherine!"

"Why isn't he married?"

"I don't know why. He's so handsome!"

I detected no sarcasm in Katherine's plaintive contralto voice.

We peered into another workshop. The spartan functionalism and the sour, antiseptic odour of the buildings were beginning to depress me; such qualities also seemed at odds with the jokiness and knowing sparkle of the girls. They were adept at removing young Michael from their company, banishing him to a far corner in order to flick an unnecessary light switch or open a door. He would hasten back and have time to say only "cement-mixer" or "combine-har-

182

vester" in a soft, earnest voice before one of the imperious girls would ask him to darken the building again or to close the door. He always complied. He was, I suspect, in a hopeless, unspoken love.

The next door opened onto a commotion and a harsh smell. In a windowless hangar, hundreds of chickens were crammed into a few rows of wire cages, the feathers of one squawking body thrust against the feathers of the next. The purpose of the birds' grim existence is to lay eggs, which the colony sells to supermarkets. Slightly luckier are the chickens whose fate is an oven or a frying pan: they can at least walk on the building's cement floor. The same is true of the turkeys and the geese. None of these birds ever sees natural light, hears the wind or feels the earth. Somewhat to my relief, the prison of the colony's pigs was locked, and Michael lacked the key. But I did pass the three dairy cows. They were hunched outside the poultry hangar, fastened into a contraption that reminded me of medieval stocks. The cows' heads and shoulders protruded through a grate that trapped their faces above a trough of fodder. The creatures were unable to turn around. They were milk factories on immobile legs: all they could do was feed. The Hutterites had reduced their animals to machines.

Slaughtering is women's work. In the spotless abattoir I confessed to a dislike of the killings, an attitude that puzzled and amused the girls.

"You see here?" Katherine said with gusto. "This is where the chickens hang."

"*This* is where the pigs bleed."

"And *this* is where we take off their skin!"

A few hundred yards away lay the communal garden—the only land in sight that was surrounded by trees. It had, perhaps, been the site of the dead farm that preceded the colony. Already the brotherhood was eating radishes and onions from this year's planting.

We walked towards the two schoolrooms. "Do you read much?" I asked.

The answers were shifty: "That depends." "We go to the library in Swift Current sometimes." "What is 'much'?" I didn't press the point. A librarian in Saskatoon had told me that the Hutterite

183

women who sell vegetables at the city's Farmers' Market also borrow Harlequin Romances as though they were going out of style. "Some of these girls," Dee said later, "buy paperback novels secondhand in Swift Current and read them under the bedclothes at night."

The schoolrooms adhered to different worlds. The kindergarten, taught by a Hutterite woman, was bare. A couple of swings beside a residence hut gave the only hint of a playground. At kindergarten children from two and a half up to six years of age are instilled with the German language and the first principles of the brotherhood. Yet provincial laws insist on a secular education in English, and so a teacher commutes daily from the town of Gull Lake. She teaches nine grades in a room. Maps, posters and children's paintings splashed her walls with an almost shocking brightness. No Hutterite teenagers reach high school, let alone university.

Among the women of the colony, the kindergarten teacher and the head cook are the only specialists. Unlike the men, each of whom trains an apprentice to his craft, the women labour at a multitude of chores in the garden and the kitchen, the laundry and the slaughterhouse.

Or so I was told. "Our system is very unfair," one of the girls said when Michael was out of earshot.

"Why?"

"It is the men who decide everything. We are supposed to do what they tell us."

"For example," another burst in, "when Jacob was elected bossman, the women could not vote. Do you think that is fair?"

"Well, perhaps not," I said cautiously.

"And when we marry, a girl has to say goodbye to all her friends and live on the boy's colony. Is *that* fair?"

Michael hurried back before I could express an opinion. His shy presence stifled their dissent.

The last domains I visited were the kitchens and the storerooms. The girls were growing more and more brazen. It was as if their chaste dresses and their knowledge of the visit's rules (I would be leaving soon with Dee) made possible a kind of ribaldry that most teenage girls in the outside world would shrink from conducting with a stranger. Hiding their desires in their ample garments, the girls could speak their fantasies aloud.

184

"I will be making bread early tomorrow morning," said Rosa, a round-headed girl with spectacles and ash-blond hair. A few strands crept out from her protective scarf. "You want to come and join me? Please?"

"She'll be all alone in there at four o'clock!"

"Just the two of you for an hour together!"

"It's a great idea," I said, "but I never get up that early."

Five girls groaned as one.

"Michael," Lisa said to the trailing boy, "will you see if we remembered to lock the school?"

He looked unwilling, he even lingered, but he went.

"Come and see the potato-cooler," Rosa said, stepping into a metal cellar.

"Are you afraid to join her?" Lisa asked.

I walked in, and she or another girl shut the door. Rosa and I were trapped in a pitch-darkness, surrounded by cold potatoes. The giggles turned to roars of laughter. Rosa said nothing; I was not even sure where she stood.

"Come on," I yelled, "let us out of here!"

The door opened on a quartet of delighted faces. Rosa was blushing. Michael ran down the stairs, a frown of suspicion between his eyes.

"Yes," he reported. "It was locked."

We strolled back across the compound to Jacob's home. No one else seemed to notice the crocus-coloured clouds that shone from a darkening sky against the green hills to the southwest. The sunset made the cement huts look as bleak as a prison camp.

Or so I thought for a moment, and felt angry at myself for the thought. However graceless their buildings might be, however hostile to decoration, Rosa and her friends bore no similarity to prisoners. They showed a confidence about the future that was untainted by cynicism, guilt or despair. The tour of the colony had suggested to me some reasons why Hutterites continue to be the victims of so much uneasy scorn: causes that may go deeper than simple intolerance or jealousy.

Their ways of life challenge and defy the society beyond. By their loving maintenance of an old language and costume, the Hutterites seem to spurn the New World. A European past is woven into the

185

fabric of their days. Because pacifism forms part of their beliefs, the men have declined to serve in any Canadian war, no matter how righteous the rest of the nation finds it. Even more outrageous, their economic system is communist (as distinct, of course, from Marxist); it forbids the accumulation of private wealth. Most Canadians, like their neighbours to the south, prove their liberty by the pursuit of happiness and money. For the Hutterites, happiness is but the by-product of a devotion to their community and to God, whose service offers as much freedom as most of them appear to desire.

Their particular brand of communism frees the brotherhood from dependence on commercial networks; their involvement with neighbouring towns is partial and provisional. Hutterites need to buy few goods and fewer services. Motel owners, jewellers, plumbers never see them. As a result they lay themselves open to the false charge of meanness. By their very success, they continue to prove that rural self-sufficiency is possible in the Canadian west—regardless of the dismal forecasts of economists. Instead of making greed into a commandment and consumption into a sacrament, the Hutterites flourish by austere co-operation.

I re-entered Jacob's home to find Dee holding court about her health. The tiled floor had no carpet. Except for a calendar and a couple of greeting cards, the walls were naked. I sat on a hard chair across the room from Jacob and Martha. The girls crowded the entranceway; Michael and two of his friends or brothers squatted on the floor.

"So how was the tour?" Jacob asked.

"Fine," I said. Rosa and Lisa were looking worried. "Very informative."

"Will you have a glass of wine?"

"With pleasure," I replied. Jacob rose and fetched a forty-ounce whisky bottle. He poured pale glassfuls for himself and me, offering nothing to any woman nor to the young men. My glass held a dry, fragrant, subtle rhubarb wine. I proposed a toast to the colony.

"At times," Dee resumed, "I still have a little trouble sleeping. But I don't like to take all those pills."

"Oh, I've had terrible trouble with my ulcers," Jacob said. "And

186

my sleep. I find it's when I wake up about two in the morning that my mind works best."

This too surprised me. In my simplistic scheme of things, Hutterites were not supposed to suffer from the ills of the twentieth century. But although the ancient brotherhood remains intact, it does not remain immune. Christian names of glamour are becoming normal. The young children of the colony include a Jason and a Tabitha—a legacy from, of all things, "Bewitched."

"A lot of English words have been coming into our language," Jacob admitted with regret. "In Medicine Hat, I have met some people from Germany. I find it hard though to understand all they say."

For Jacob and his brethren, the entire world is a foreign land. The Hutterites have succeeded in preserving themselves from the soft corruptions of western Europe, eastern Europe, the United States and Canada. But their peaceful simplicity has been bought at a price. Like the Hasidic Jews—another people whose religion, language and black clothing set them apart from their suspicious neighbours; another people, too, who value family life more highly than secular achievement—they seem perpetually out of place. Their own place is any bare room with a Book.

The lives of strangers therefore belong to a shadow realm of torment and temptation. Ordinary prairie towns like Swift Current and Medicine Hat acquire, in the eyes of young Hutterites, a little of the allure that Hollywood or Paris holds for other Canadians. Visiting the colony, I had, for the first and possibly the last time in my life, star quality. Like Bobby Ewing, I flowed through the outside world. I was, in the end, unreal.

In the end, I refused a third glass of rhubarb wine and exchanged a meaningful glance with Dee. Martha, sharp-eyed, saw.

"So," she said, "will you sing us a song? Or tell us a story?"

Panic hit my brain like amnesia.

"Give us something to remember you by."

I wish I could write that I proved heroic. In fact, I fell far below the occasion. I could think of nothing to recite, no witty tale to tell. Probably my cheeks turned russet. Faced with a similar request in the heart of Borneo, the poet James Fenton is said to have "launched

187

into a rhyming ballad, a long spontaneous poem about our coming from a far country, about our entering the Rajang from the sea, about the pleasures of the Baleh and the danger of the rapids and the hospitality of the strongest, the most beautiful people in all the world . . ."

In southwestern Saskatchewan I launched into silence. All that crept to mind was a proverb from the Welsh borderland of my mother's childhood: "A donkey doesn't bray to order."

"I beg your pardon?"

"I'm the donkey, you see. I can't make the right noise when people ask me to."

A roomful of disappointed faces: the coughs and glances of embarrassment.

"I'm sorry."

Nevertheless, Martha, Jacob, Michael, Rosa and a dozen other members of the brotherhood came into the dwindling twilight to wave a long goodbye.

·XLIII·

I watched the bucking-horse sale that prefaced the Cowtown Rodeo. The animals bucked and were sold in a corral on the outskirts of Maple Creek. Barbecued beef-on-a-bun in hand, I clambered into the dusty bleachers above the old arena and sat behind a pair of ladies, furnished with cardigans and floral hats, who seemed to have strayed from an Oxfordshire flower show. Some boys were wandering in formal gear, all boots and radiant buckles and broad-brimmed hats, striving to look important, or at least useful, or at any rate impressive to their girl friends, or at least their brothers, or at any rate their mothers. A herd of calm horses grazed a field between the corral and the railway tracks. Time slowed to a hobnailed amble.

But the amplified patter of the auctioneer I found incomprehensible. It sounded at first like some guttural language which happened to share its numerals and its currency with English: "Gobblegobblegobble320dollarsgobblegobblegobblegobble320 gobble . . ." The man perched in a little booth above the hard-eyed bidders. They observed each horse slip into a chute, where some intrepid cowboy scrambled onto its back; when the gate opened, the horse sprang out and tried to jerk, jump, lunge free of the harsh weight of a man.

After the horse had bucked for a few seconds, the auctioneer began his pitch. He would ask, if an animal looked large, young and mean, for a bid of $1000; more often he started at $500; in a few cases, when a horse was small and docile, he regretfully called for $200. By the time the bidding was settled, the riderless horse was out of sight, herded from the arena by two pickup men. Racing, feinting, gracefully blocking and (if all else failed) lassoing, the men and their sweaty horses guided the merchandise away from the wide, scuffed corral where its fate was decided.

I began to decipher the patter. Like Anglo-Saxon poetry, it was loaded with stock phrases—"Who'll make a bid?" "Let's have a ten!" "Need another ten!"—of a fixed, rapid-fire rhythm. When the bids would rise no higher, the auctioneer reined his galloping syllables to an almost normal pace: "Four hundred dollars now—let's have a 400—it's 400—400 even—All bids in" (pause) "—Sold to Harvey S. Peters for $380! Ladies, we sure would be grateful for a few cold drinks up here." The bidding was adjourned on a frisky mare who, not content with throwing her rider, jumped the wooden fence of the corral and trotted to the grazing herd. Other horses converged on her with interest, like neighbours gathering to meet a veteran returned from the foreign wars.

The spectators livened at the mare's escape. They gave her the loudest ovation of the afternoon. For the most part they were content to sit, gossip, nibble and offer tepid, brief applause. I could rarely tell whether they were clapping the rider or the horse. "—Sold to the Tigertown Rodeo for $600! Good eye, Len."

"How come he never says, 'Good eye, Harvey'?"

I had bumped into Don Carnaby at the soft-drink stall of the Rotarians' wives. The sun lit up a grove of cotton candy like pink electric wool.

"Harvey's buying them up for the knacker's," he said. He looked embarrassed. "It's only the best horses that get taken by the major rodeos."

"You mean . . ."

"Yeah, most of these horses will be pet food pretty soon."

It seemed a trifle macabre, I thought, that Harvey S. Peters had donated a prize buckle. It would go at the day's end to the local hero who had ridden the highest number of animals.

My pleasure in the spectacle diminished. Even the twisting leaps of a fierce black gelding, which the Calgary Stampede purchased for $1500, failed to excite me. It was followed by a chestnut mare with a scrawny build and a gentle disposition; Harvey S. Peters accumulated her meat for $175. I looked away then, far to the south where fields and pastures rolled to touch the granular clouds of the horizon. A CPR train was passing slowly by: two engines, eighty-three freight cars, a caboose . . . "Come on, ladies, I'm getting mighty thirsty up here in the booth . . ."

I quit the sale and looked round Maple Creek, a shady, curious town that seemed to teeter between an aging gentility and a desire to sustain a frontier myth. Perhaps the place had never recovered from its first doctor, who owned the instruments that had (he claimed) amputated Horatio Nelson's arm. I saw more cowboy hats on the checkerboard streets of Maple Creek than in any other prairie town. Some of them, of course, screened the heads of cowboys.

When I returned to the arena, decibels of country music were pouring out from speakers in front of the sunbaked seats: "Don't call him a cowboy / Until you've seen him ride . . ."

The auctioneer had changed his job and dropped his scattergun velocity. No longer was he working on commission and perspiring to swell each price. Yet as the master of the opening ceremonies and the drummer-up of enthusiasm, he still had a hard task. Although the Cowtown Rodeo began nearly thirty minutes late, its spectators were happy chatting to old friends and rivals. Festivals and competitions have, among the isolated ranch families of southwestern Saskatchewan, a signal importance.

"How's your arm?" I asked Jo-Ann Carnaby.

She pulled a face and stretched out a cast.

Well-dressed horses cantered into the ring at last, and their riders waved hats at the crowd. The flags of Saskatchewan, Alberta and the U.S.A. appeared in the hands of women. The announcer whipped himself into an unctuous frenzy: "Let's have a mighty big hand, ladies and gentlemen, for the lovely Miss Lesley Ann Warner of Picture Butte, Alberta, carrying the flag of the United States of America!"

Dead silence. The announcer tried again: "I know you all want to give a warm Maple Creek welcome to this year's three contestants for Rodeo Queen!"

Three spangled girls on horseback plodded around the corral to a further bout of silence. Finally the flag of Canada trotted in and drew a few dutiful claps.

And then an odd thing happened. While the banner-laden riders were forming an irregular line in front of the bleachers, a flock of birds became visible in the eastern sky. It was five o'clock, still a good three hours from nightfall. Within the first three bars of "O Canada," the crowd rose to its feet; I was just about the last man to doff my cap. The birds flapped steadily onwards, manifest now as pelicans, their black wings waving like slow sleeves beside their salt-white bodies. To my surprise, some of the men clasped hats over their hearts; I had thought the gesture was limited to Americans. By the third time we all promised to "stand on guard for thee," sixty-five pelicans were flying over the corral, taking a good look at the peculiar proceedings on the ground: herds of cars, people, trucks and horses, all of them motionless amid a loud noise. The crowd peered up. The pelicans peered down. The anthem finished, the people sat, and the birds flew out of sight.

·XLIV·

The Sioux had a term for whisky: "sacred water." To get their lips on it, the Sioux, Cree and other nations traded away horses and furs. Usually the merchants would cheat the Indians with a brew called "firewater." One recipe suggests that a quart of whisky be doctored with a quart of black molasses, handfuls of red pepper and root ginger, and a pound of rank tobacco. The brewer should boil up his mixture with water, strain it, bottle it, and make a handsome profit.

Other recipes are crueller. The traders who rode up to Canada may not have resorted to the Kansas practice of tossing a rattlesnake's head into the brew, but they sometimes mixed a drink containing painkilling medicine, red ink and even detergent. Indians often mistook the result for the delirium induced by liquor. The whisky traders flourished, if such is the word, in the decade after the U.S. Civil War when the international border was a legal fiction. Their activities helped to ruin the plains Indians and to create the North-West Mounted Police.

In the spring of 1873, a nomadic band of three hundred Assiniboines pitched their tents in a valley of the Cypress Hills. A dozen traders and sidekicks set up business within three miles of the camp — some of them dealing in firewater, others in blankets and knives. Near the main trading posts, which belonged to American merchants named Abe Farwell and Moses Solomon, a dozen wolfers also camped one day. These men earned their bread by poisoning wolves for a bounty; they and the Indians held each other in mutual contempt. That night, after hard hours of drinking, the wolfers received a call for help from George Hammond, a ne'er-do-well trader whose horse had disappeared. They were in an excellent mood to raise hell; and hell is what they raised. Even when an Indian gave back the missing horse, the wolfers were unappeased. A fight broke out and the white men, who possessed prime rifles, killed twenty or more Indians. In revenge for the one white death, they went on to rape Assiniboine women.

The following morning, perhaps remorseful and certainly worried, the wolfers, merchants and hangers-on burned the trading posts and left the area.

The incident caused little stir in the west. Over the next few years, courts in Montana and Winnipeg would decline to convict the wolfers of any crime. But in Ottawa, "the Cypress Hills Massacre" provoked fury. It demonstrated the vulnerability of an unpatrolled Canada. Soon the House of Commons passed a bill to create the North-West Mounted Police. And when Superintendent James Walsh ordered his men to build a fort in the hills two years after the massacre, he chose a site a mile and a half upstream from the ruins.

I drove southwest from Maple Creek to see Fort Walsh, which the government has rebuilt and proclaimed a National Historic Park. Its log buildings nestle inside a high palisade halfway up a green valley. From old photographs on display, I discovered that the moustachioed, curly-haired Walsh had looked very similar to the young Josef Stalin. A third of the entire NWMP was stationed under his command here in 1881. The first buildings had sod roofs—Walsh, an Irishman, must have felt at home—but only one of the reconstructions suffers that moist fate. Thin weeds were shooting from its sloping earth like exalted bean-sprouts.

I met Mrs. Friesen, an amiable grey-haired woman who cleans the fort. Her yellow cap had an inscription: IF DOLLY PARTON WAS A FARMER, SHE'D BE FLAT BUSTED TOO.

"Did you see the graveyard yet?" she asked.

"That one by the woods?"

"That's right. Well, some of us are real mad at Parks Canada."

"Why?"

"They won't allow any more burials. Even if your whole family's already inside. They say you can't be buried in a historic site."

The trouble with making history official is that you decree when it stops.

I hitched a ride in a Parks Canada van to a replica of Farwell's store. A kingbird teetered on a poplar's utmost twig. A student in period costume crossed Battle Creek to greet me.

"Once you walk over the bridge," she warned, "you're stepping back in time. We're here to make history come alive for you."

Oh.

"That means," she added hastily, "we don't really mean what we say. I mean, as people."

In its good nature, its incoherence and its urgent desire to avoid offence, it seemed a quintessentially Canadian remark.

I strolled into a cabin. "George Hammond" slid off a bunk and looked me over.

"So what are you doin' in these parts, stranger? Panning for gold?"

"Well, actually I'm travelling. I'm a writer by trade."

"A writer! Abe's the one you should talk to, then. He's got a Grade Three education."

I was waylaid by a lovely blond woman who was attempting, I think, to be Abe's Indian "wife."

"Travelling, you say? Where'd you leave your ox-cart?"

"Up the hill, beside the fort."

"What fort?"

"Abe Farwell" was posing in his warehouse, a room clogged with supplies.

"I don't see any whisky here," I said.

"You're making a mistake," he replied sadly.

"I am?"

"It's some of them other traders who deal in firewater. I'm an honest man, I don't want no trouble. But let me tell you something—" He leaned forward confidentially across a canvas bag labelled FLOUR. "You know what Moses Solomon adds to his firewater?"

"Red ink, maybe?"

"Worse! Strychnine!"

194

·XLV·

A twining backroad through the Cypress Hills hauled me the following morning into Alberta, the province where my childhood grew like a tame rose. Postcard scenery embraced the car; a sharp whiff of pine freshened its plush interior. The hills contain the highest land in Canada east of the Rocky Mountains, and their lush vegetation escapes the drought of the plains. I was growing accustomed again to the prospect of lakes and evergreen forests when the forest died, the water dried, and the Buffalo Trail began. I had emerged from the bushy topknot of southern Alberta onto its bare, neglected shoulder. A provocative sign reminded the wind and the grass:

NO SERVICE OR
RESIDENCES
NEXT 134 km

A ridge of hills quivered above the southwestern horizon: a blue, far promise: a beckoning.

There were no other drivers. There was no other road. The clouds played hide-and-seek with the sun. A stray fragment of memory fluttered up to consciousness: *Among themselves, American hobos call Canada "Big Lonely."* Framed in my contact lenses, the passing land looked delicate: sagebrush speckled the grasses, smudged with clover and golden bean . . . The frame is an illusion, its perspective a distortion. The land, enclosed by nothing, open to every atrocity of weather, survives far beyond delicacy.

I turned west along a gravel road, leaving the Buffalo Trail to push its unserviced, homeless track into Montana. Over the horizon's lip, the bruise of hills was growing tangible. The gravel and the barbed, unswerving wire had something of the melancholy dignity of a Roman or an Inca road: they offered linear proof that the human race had passed this way. Attempts to farm the region were abandoned early in the century, for even in the fat years after the Ar-

195

mistice, when most people on the prairies were relishing the Years of the Big Wheat, southeastern Alberta lay sick with drought. Its fields have returned to pasture, yet few ranchers thrive. That morning I saw as many pairs of antelope as herds of cattle. The rare ponds were already pillows of alkali. And I wondered, as I had in northern Manitoba, whether the advent of white civilization has not left parts of the west emptier than at any time since the last Ice Age.

Antelope, like buffalo, came close to extinction. Their numbers tumbled to fewer than twenty thousand after the ravages of settlement. But thanks to a fast fertility—and the co-operation of ranchers—more than thirty thousand antelope now graze in Canada, and many times that number in the U.S.A. I stopped near the crest of a gradual hill to watch a big male antelope standing indecisively in the middle of the road. The contrast between the animal's stout, muscular body and his needlelike front legs astonished me. He pawed the gravel, nervously shifted, and declined to budge until I drove within a few yards. Then he slipped into the dry ditch and scrambled without elegance under the barbed wire. I would have liked to see him run; pronghorn antelope are the quickest mammal on the continent. Donkeys, however, do not bray to order.

The hill led to, of all things, a village. I had a fine, unhurried view of Manyberries from above: a clump of vehicles and wooden buildings dwarfed by a turquoise elevator of the Alberta Wheat Pool, dwarfed in its turn by a city of fluffy clouds. The clouds outnumbered the houses; so, I eventually saw, did the discarded cars and trucks. "Manyengines" might be a more truthful name.

Drilling rigs from Home Oil and Shell dwindled in the grassy obscurity. A colony of cliff swallows dive-bombed the car. On a paved highway I trundled west beyond Orion, hunting fuel and lunch. The village of Etzikom had neither, nor did it have a Catholic church; one windy night in 1946, the church blew away.

The countryside flattened into rich farmland, some of its vast fields sown to barley, others green with the rising winter wheat. A town called Foremost had a resolute appearance and an empty, sleek Chinese café. The girl who served me was a prodigy of silence: without a word she handed me a menu, took my order, brought me food and tea, and presented a bill. I discovered when I paid that her lips were indeed capable of "Thank you." Starved of verbal stimulation, I was reduced to reading the printed envelope from the People's Republic that encased my jasmine tea bag:

AROMATIC FLAVOUR!	GREENISH INFUSION!
HOMELY REFRESHER!	VALUABLE GIFT!

Refreshed and doubtless homely, I continued westward through the wheat. For the first time in more than eighty springs, the farmers of southern Alberta had refused to plant a crop of sugar beets: a glut of cheap cane from abroad had so depressed the price of beets that every farmer in the region was reverting his fields to grain. As the little towns grew in the windshield—Legend, Skiff, Warner—and shrank in the rearview mirror, their first and last vestige was a grain elevator or two. The standard comparison likens an elevator to a sentinel, but I had decided, after thousands of miles and hundreds of grain elevators, that they resemble giant Monopoly hotels and act like medieval churches—dominating, identifying and justifying the villages in their dusty shade. That day another idea sprang to mind. In their brooding speechlessness, their solemnity above so many withered communities, the elevators are also Canada's towers of silence: its watchers of the prairie dead.

The land was rising. When I headed south, the highway gently breasted the watershed of the Milk River Ridge. Weary of driving, I parked at a glossy motel outside the little town of Milk River. My room contained, among other paraphernalia, four toothpicks wrapped individually in plastic.

I took an instant, irrational dislike to the town. Strolling round it for half an hour, I saw no other person on foot. The town's swank houses stand on streets devoid of sidewalks. What they do have, in grotesque abundance, are garden ornaments. In Milk River, flamingoes, gnomes and Bambis are only the beginning. I found plastic pheasants in front of one splay home, a plastic donkey in front of a second, and a large plastic frog in front of a third. Somewhere between the artificial chickens and the make-believe swans, I passed from disgust to bemusement; by the time I had also marched past a plastic owl and a few sitting ducks, I even felt a grudging respect. Milk River is, to say the least, unique.

Its ornery individuality gives the lie to one of the stranger claims that Heather Robertson made in her brilliant, much-hated book *Grass Roots*. "Prairie towns all look alike," she remarked: "identical grain elevators, identical banks, identical railway stations, a main street that is called Main Street and a road along the tracks called Railway Avenue: when you've seen one, as they say, you've seen 'em all."

Such is the raw form. But the cooking varies dramatically: all you need to do is approach the little communities with innocent eyes. Milk River looks no more like Gimli than a village on Galway Bay. Western towns have always differed in their main churches (bulbous Orthodox? trim Protestant? aspiring Catholic?) as well as their settings (a river? a hill? a lake?). Now that most of the towns no longer have active stations, they also differ in the fate of the station house. Some communities have torn it down or allowed it to rot; others have converted it to a museum or a home; in a few, the station houses a business. Even the businesses vary according to the local wealth and traditions. One town's video arcade will be another's Gospel Book Room.

Among the disintegrating villages, too, decay occurs in an assortment of ways and leaves a variety of racks behind. The process is, unfortunately, common enough to suggest that an unsettled emptiness might be the prairie's destiny. Heather Robertson's central argument—that economic forces, far more than natural ones, are transforming much of the plain into a wasteland—remains sound, however much the inhabitants of prairie cities have loathed her for saying it.

A big lonely sun sliced the horizon far beyond the motel's dining room. My dinner arrived on a platter large enough to hold a turkey. I nibbled for a while and went to bed. Nighttime brought a dense, unexpected rain. Come morning, I drove away with eagerness, basted by a certain fear.

·XLVI·

As a child in the early 1960s, I yearned to see the provincial park named Writing-on-Stone. My family lived in Lethbridge, seventy-five miles away, and occasionally my father drove to Waterton Lakes or Calgary or the Crowsnest Pass. But something always forestalled him from Writing-on-Stone: the bad roads, probably, or uncertain weather, or doubts about what he might find there. It remained a country we would forever see "next year." In my mind the place grew mythic. For some reason I thought of it as "Writing-on-the-Wall Park," and I associated it with Belshazzar and messages of ancient doom. Even in childhood, I guess, my imagination veered towards apocalypse.

We moved to Saskatoon when I was twelve, and Writing-on-Stone became a green triangle on a disused map. I was growing up; I had other discoveries to make. "You'll study law," I was instructed, or "You'll major in political science," or "You'll go through graduate school." I raised an inward eyebrow, faithful to my own suspicions, although they were yet too molten to cohere into hard plans. Lecture rooms and courtrooms and committee rooms—the smoky realm of offices and hard-bitten backs—held small appeal for me. I felt that to be a creator of messages, a teller of tales, would prove an honourable calling. An image of desire and loss flickered at the back of my mind. But I quit the prairies without finishing the dream.

Now that I was back in Alberta, the idea of the park made me strangely nervous. How could it match my yearning? I was nostalgic, perhaps, for the illusions of childhood, when the future was radiant with power and unlimited choice.

The future had come. I was driving through it on a paved, slippery road. The morning wind churned up puddles under a morose sky. "A miracle rain," the waitress had told me gladly in the pancake-scented motel, "the only thing that could stop the grasshoppers!" My car scudded past the wet fields of wheat. Listening to the Voice of Southern Alberta, I learned that the poisonous fogs against grasshoppers and cutworms were murdering the region's honey. A farmer north of Milk River had lost six million bees in a cloud. I was contemplating that glum total when the road switched to gravel and pulled me into the park.

Writing-on-Stone Park is small and dramatic. It exists where nature, as though bored at last with the great scraped mat of prairie, has humped herself to form cones, pinnacles and fallen arches: a serpentine Carnival slithering through a Lenten plain. Outcrops of sandstone, twisted by wind and water into bulging hoodoos, flanked the car. Capped by its hard deposits of ironstone, the sandstone has eroded into shapes that defy probability. I drove cautiously down through a city of tawny sculptures to the bushy valley of the Milk.

Some of the sandstone cliffs, scoured by centuries of blown dust, made an ideal screen on which to record a skirmish, a rite of passage, a flight of spirit. Usually the recorders carved or scratched their tale; occasionally they would paint it in ochre. The visual language of the messages was familiar to the many Indian bands—Shoshoni, Blackfoot, Sioux, Plains Cree and others—who roamed the prairies for food and took shelter among the Milk's cottonwoods and willows. The valley was no one's property; its gifts were gifts for all. It became a sacred place.

But the messages are growing more and more secret. Rubbed by cattle, defaced by vandals, eaten by rough weather and alkali salts from within, the images are approaching their final silence. "Here, take this map," a warden said that morning, handing me a crowded chart of stylized horses, tipis and men at war. He told me where to look for the battle in a virgin forest of stone. I climbed out of the groves and riverside glades, and strolled for twenty minutes across a high scrap of plain. A muscular wind began to clear the sky; the sun appeared in force. Scarlet mallow, blue flax and the first wild roses of summer shone in the grass. Droplets of the night's rain still clung onto stalks and petals. Below them, a good path fell to the outcrops.

It took me a long time to reach the battle scene, for I was dazzled by the grace of the park. It compressed so many landscapes into so little space. Its birds, refreshed by rain and sun, were exuberant:

200

rock wrens dappled the cliffs; towhees darted in the thickets; a patient heron fished from a sandbank at the river's curling edge. I grew bored waiting by a patch of musineon—the clustered flowers resembled lemon-coloured broccoli—for a snoozing doe to budge. She was lying, catlike, on a ledge beside the path, her chin resting on her outspread forelegs; catlike, she looked annoyed when I gave up waiting and clumped down the trail.

I found the battle scene and felt a fool. The chart disclosed what I might have been able to see: a complicated fight involving rifles, arrows, spears and a big axe. Horsemen were attacking a ring of tipis. The defence was strenuous, the outcome unsure. My eyes might have picked out dozens of warriors from the early nineteenth century as they struggled for glory and stolen horses. But all I could discern was a faint scattering of grooves and crosses on a pockmarked cliff. Does every vision quest collapse into a question of visibility?

Depressed, I clambered to a viewpoint and gazed across the river. And there, beckoning over a few grazed miles, were the blue-green buttes I had seen from the far-off Buffalo Trail. To a plains Indian, these Sweetgrass Hills and the Milk's sinuous valley form part of the same land. In my terms, unfortunately, the hills lie on private property just south of the 49th Parallel. I still imagined that somewhere on their firred, lithe slopes a message might await me. But if childhood means a longing for adult power, adulthood means an acceptance of power's borders. The Sweetgrass Hills rise beyond my personal territory. I may dream of them, and nothing more.

In the hills' shadow, the North-West Mounted Police created one of its most isolated posts. The policemen who lived there fought fires, guarded horses and relieved a famine or two; most of all, they were border patrolmen charged with keeping American cattle and liquor out of Canada. The latter task proved the harder. When the Canadian northwest was dry, smugglers hauled alcohol across the Medicine Line disguised in casks of flour and cartons of eggs, or even in the underwear of "pregnant" women who enjoyed miscarriages a mile out of Montana. Depression was common for the lonesome mounties, and temptation close at hand: in 1892, five of the six constables at Writing-on-Stone deserted to the wet U.S.A.

201

By 1918, when the outpost closed, the boundary was mostly fenced and the ranchland mostly docile. The annual Writing-on-Stone Stampede—still held in a wooden corral at the park's edge—had become a tradition. The first stampede, which celebrated the British king's birthday in 1910, included a race between a dog and a horse.

The dog won. I could imagine all that history; it was recorded in my own tongue. But with the other, foreign stories—the messages on stone—I needed help. I retreated to the warden's office and asked to see a fragment of the Archaeological Preserve in Eileen Hassett's company.

Eileen had a serious, efficient air; her directness of manner and the calmness of her voice bespoke a practical competence. But her warden's uniform camouflaged a romantic, even obsessive devotion to Writing-on-Stone. Her descriptions of the hoodoos under a tuque of snow or the moonstruck Milk on a summer night's canoe trip invested her eyes with love.

She drove a van into the preserve, which lies out of bounds for unescorted visitors, and we scrambled down a sharp hill to a pack of outcrops. Shrubs and slender trees stretched below the path to the water. By now the jagged, rumpled rocks seemed as natural to me as a field or a forest. The common adjective "weird" turns to a lie after the second glance.

"What do you see there?"

I squinted at some carved lines. They suggested a freehand drawing of a fish.

"No idea."

"Well, it's a fish," Eileen said. She pointed out adjacent images in the panel: a horse with a long lifeline, two men with pointed shoulders, and an odd humanoid figure with a semicircular head. The more she explained, the more I saw.

"So what could this be?" I asked.

In my enthusiasm I had pressed two fingers against the stone.

"Don't touch it!" Eileen said at once. "Please!—I'm not sure about that image. A man praying to the spirits, maybe?"

We moved slowly on, past a headless man and a phallic man and a buffalo. In one superb panel, a child was born beside a battle. Its

202

labouring mother stretched an arm backwards to the shielded warriors. Form was inseparable from content, gesture from emotion. The image's force was tense and raw.

"Will you look at this?"

I thought that Eileen must be pointing to a rare carving at ground level. But when I looked, I saw a cottontail rabbit cowering under a bush, trapped between four legs and a rock. Its ears had been pushed into the lustrous auburn fur of its back in an effort to hide. Above the rabbit stood a carving of a bugling elk. We stayed there talking for a few minutes, and the rabbit relaxed enough to resume a watchful nibbling.

"It's like learning a foreign language," Eileen said. "You have to work at it, and ask a lot of questions, and try not to get frustrated. Sooner or later, it all starts to make sense."

Yet the erosion and defacement are enough to ensure that the full story will never be known. Even to Eileen's eyes, the images retain a quality of mystery. Because of their inscrutable power, the carvings have attracted explanations far more contorted than the hoodoos. Back in 1952 Henriette Mertz suggested that the stones were inscribed by Chinese explorers in the twenty-third century B.C. Later dreamers have proposed that the lines and grooves are specimens of Ogham—a system of writing developed by the ancient Celts. Or if the Ogham theory fails to hold, perhaps the carvings could be Viking runes?

Certainly there is much about the ancient world that escapes understanding. Writing-on-Stone tantalizes: one of its hoodoos contains a carving of the three-legged wheel of life, a symbol that adorns Greek coins from Sicily and the heraldic emblem of the Isle of Man. But to my mind, the desire to prove an exotic influence at Writing-on-Stone—and other Indian sites across the continent— has a malign undertone. Whether they aim to show the range of Celtic or Norse exploration, the pervasiveness of Chinese or Polynesian culture, many writers erode the accomplishments of native people. They suggest that the art of the Indians depended on inspiration from beyond. Their dogged labours remind me of the discredited essays of Englishmen who denied that a performer from a small town, never blessed by a degree or a pedigree, could have composed *The Tempest* or *King Lear.* For decades scholars tried to prove that Sir Francis Bacon, or the Earl of Southampton, or some other appropriate gentleman had used the pen name "Shakespeare." Yet in truth, just as a provincial actor wrote *Lear,* so too did the plains Indians create the visual grammar and the graphic vocabulary of Writing-on-Stone.

"Do Indians ever come to the park?" I asked.

"Sure," Eileen said. "Some of them still leave a gift for the spirits."

"What kind of gift?"

"A wad of tobacco. Or a string of beads."

Halfway up a cottonwood sapling near the river, a porcupine had come to rest. The trunk looked too flimsy to support its fat, yellow-quilled body.

"I guess they don't tell you everything they know."

She nodded. "That's the problem. If it *is* a problem. One time I was showing the images to some people from the Peigan reserve, and an old woman suddenly turned away and walked down the trail till she was out of sight. We caught up with her when we moved on. I asked her why, and she finally told me: it was forbidden for her to look at that particular scene."

"You don't know why it was forbidden?"

"I could make a guess. That's all."

The images erode to silence yet, in some minds, the spirit remains. The powers be. They inscribe their ancient messages on our paper skins or our stone hearts in ways that we perhaps fail to recognize, let alone control. To the Indians who travelled through the Milk River valley, the rocks held out a vision of experience and a promise in the jaws of time. The rocks were oracles where a wanderer might glimpse, like a dream passing across the face of stone, the pattern written for his life.

"They believe," Eileen said, "that to even look at some of the images can be dangerous. The story goes that a hunter once camped here in a certain place alone. He disregarded all the warnings of the medicine men. And the next morning he was found stumbling across the prairie—blind."

I left the park. Beyond its sweet domain, the blue remembered hills stretched out like a resting body. Exhilaration and astonishment had given way in me to something approaching joy. Not to have made the pilgrimage would have been dangerous: a denial of my childhood; a rejection of its incomplete dream. The English name of the park had worked its power but I decided, in the end, that the Blackfoot word *aysin'eep* was more eloquent and more exact. Aysin'eep means: "is being written."

·XLVII·

A toothed shimmer of white on the southwestern horizon threatened to become the Rocky Mountains. I strained and double-took in case the teeth were merely clouds. Pressed between a blue sky and the green earth, they looked impossibly pale. But as the miles floated into the past, the peaks grew in my eyes, assuming depth and weight. Mountains should always be allowed to grow on you.

> It is the hour of highest privilege and duty.
> We are laying the foundations of empire in righteousness and truth. The heralds of the Cross must follow the adventurous pioneer to the remotest settlement of the Saskatchewan, the Qu'Appelle and the Peace River and the vast regions beyond.

The General Conference of the Methodist Church reported so in 1883. A spirit of fervent duty would inspire the rooting of the white man's culture on the prairies through the next generation. Yet when the first adventurous Methodists reached a remote tributary of the Saskatchewan River with the name of Lee Creek, they found a claim had been staked already. Rising in the mountains' jagged shadow, a settlement flourished in the highest righteousness. It was a colony of American Mormons.

They built on a hill. I came down it from the north, parked and looked. Cardston's streets were immaculate. The shops looked prosperous. Between a confectionery and a hardware store, Charles Card's home, a log cabin with white-painted windows, still graces Main Street. Card, who was married to one of Brigham Young's forty-seven children, trekked north from the salt lake with a few dozen followers and founded the community in 1887. He entitled his list of followers "Names of Missionaries for the Land Desolation."

Cardston's temple, the only one in Canada, was dedicated in 1923. By then the town's most unlikely daughter was cutting a swath in Hollywood. Vina F. Wray appeared at sixteen in *Gasoline Love* and went on to suffer seductively in *The Street of Sin*, *The Legion of the Condemned*, *The Mystery of the Wax Museum* and other chillers. Her ability to scream with luscious terror lifted her, at the height of the Depression, to the apex of her career: King Kong's arms.

It was all downhill from there, despite her almond eyes. In 1963 Fay Wray returned to Cardston and dedicated a fountain.

I walked past it along a street of virtue. A bookstore contained, to my regret, nothing but Mormon material. I checked into the Cahoon Hotel. An old, tall building with shuddering corridors and extravagant green lintels, it deserves a swing-door saloon. This is, however, Cardston. Not only is the town dry, it also forbids the display of cigarettes for sale. At the front desk, where most hotels proffer Black Cats and Camels, the Cahoon holds *The Book of Mormon.*

"Guess you'll be going up to the temple," the manager said with pride.

But I decided to wait until my stomach was appeased. When I stepped into the lukewarm afternoon, I saw the definition of Canada's multiculturalism (or is it national schizophrenia?): two Blood Indians in the doorway of "Tibetan Pizza" watching a Hutterite woman stroll through a Mormon town.

206

Fresh & Special
Tibetan Desh
Style
called Shabali
means, meat pie
each 75 ¢
Thank, you

Well, why not? I walked to the front counter, where a stocky man in a grey T-shirt was talking to a black-capped Blood, and asked for two shabalis.

The request created a sensation.

"Are you sure?" the man in the T-shirt asked. "I'm on my own. It'll take me some time to prepare."

"That's okay," I said. I was feeling unusually brazen. "You don't have tsampa, by any chance?"

"*Tsampa?*" He looked as incredulous as I expected. "No, sorry. There's not much demand for it in Cardston."

"So I'll just have a coffee."

The man was unwilling to see me turn and sit. "Have you been to Tibet?" he asked.

"No, I got as far as the border, but I didn't have a visa to go beyond. I've looked across a river into Tibet, that's all."

He dug out copies of *Tibetan Monthly* for me to read while I waited. Tibetan Pizza appeared to consist of four bare tables, each of them encompassed by a few hard chairs. When I had chosen a table, the man brought me a place mat, a bowl of sugar and some serviettes.

"My name's Namgyal," he said. "Are you *sure* you want to wait for shabali?"

"I'm sure."

The only visible customers, aside from me, were two middle-aged Indians lingering over coffee. Their reserve, which touches on Cardston, was once Buffalo Child Long Lance's adopted home. But as I glanced through the resigned or outraged pages about the Chinese rape of Tibet, I began to realize how Namgyal scrapes a living. Tibetan Pizza is a divided room: behind a thin partition stand a juke box and a selection of video games. Electric yips and buzzes, and rare clatters of metal, emerged from the restaurant's eastern sector. Every few minutes an Indian girl or boy would appear at the front counter and interrupt Namgyal's labour in the kitchen by exchanging paper money for coins.

"I can't drink cold water no more." The black-capped Indian was standing at my table, pain on his face and apology in his voice. "It's got to be boiled. Cold water gives me diarrhoea bad."

"That's tough," I replied, wondering what I had done to deserve this confession.

He leaned across my coffee and removed a handful of serviettes.

"In this place," he said, "you got to take your toilet with you!"

Even after I had drunk a refill, my lunch was nowhere in sight. I was reading about the education of refugees when a white man with dark glasses and thin, unkempt hair entered the restaurant. He paced up and down for a minute, dragging on a cigarette through a wispy beard, and made a futile attempt at a phone call from a machine behind the counter. Sitting at the next table, he gave me a cool stare.

"You're not from Cardston, are you?"

"No," I said. "I just arrived today."

He lit a fresh cigarette from the butt.

"You're lucky," he said. "I grew up here. It's a goddamn awful town."

"Why don't you leave, if that's how you feel?"

"I left! I've got a place up in the Peace River country. Work on oil rigs up there. That's where the next boom is going to happen, did you know that? But my father still lives here."

"You're not a Mormon, eh?"

He grimaced. "I was."

The man got up and made a brief, anxious foray out to the street, as though the café were a small fort and the town were hostile territory. In Cardston the Bloods, the Mormons and the white non-Mormons coexist in a state of mutual distrust. A lot of small towns in the west affect a show of unity, even unanimity; Cardston does not pretend.

208

My shabalis arrived with ketchup and tasted like undercooked meat pies. The indeterminate ground flesh was red.

"How are they?" Namgyal asked anxiously. "Are they good?"

"Excellent," I lied.

He looked uncertain. His eyebrows might have climbed towards his black swooping hair, but Namgyal had no visible eyebrows. He smiled shyly. A front tooth flashed metal.

"Have you lived in Cardston for a long time?"

His story poured out then, with no further encouragement. Namgyal fled his homeland as a boy in 1959, crossing the snow peaks to India, and moved to the U.S.A. in the Woodstock generation. He married a Tibetan woman and came to Cardston when the local hospital hired her as a physiotherapist. But the couple are separated; Namgyal lives and works alone. Having lost his country, language and community, he has now lost his wife as well.

A short, irate woman of about thirty-five marched in to retrieve her son. She vanished behind the partition and scolded at length: "You must have heard the honking! I've been sitting out there for ten minutes. Just who do you think you are?"

He emerged two steps behind her, looking sheepish: a boy of sixteen or seventeen, more than six feet tall. A few generations ago, he would have been a warrior.

Namgyal grinned at me and shook his head.

"Do you ever have any—trouble?" I asked.

"Sometimes I get taken for an Indian. And then there's the RCMP. A couple of officers have been harassing me." His face was cloudy. "This can be a hard town."

His refuge is financial fantasy. His dreams have become commercial. If he could gather sufficient capital, or if he made some choice investments, or if a venture by his brother-in-law turned a handsome profit . . . Despair takes hold of a man through such dreams. Deprived of a culture of his own, Namgyal was fighting to master the dominion of money.

"There must be other Tibetans up at Calgary."

"Oh sure. But I don't want to have too much to do with them, you know?"

I was not sure I knew anything. Only when Namgyal spoke

about his daughter did I see his face uncrease. Her photograph, black hair tumbling to a red dress, hangs framed above the front counter, some inches from a Coca-Cola clock. The girl lives with her mother. But perhaps her image and her intermittent presence rescue Namgyal from total materialism.

"Why don't you move somewhere more—" I wasn't sure what adjective to use.

"Civilized?"

"Well," I fumbled, "I didn't mean . . ."

"No, it's okay," he said. "I know what you mean. This isn't a very civilized town. I may go somewhere else, I'm not sure. But my daughter's here. And I have this restaurant . . ."

It was four o'clock when I left. Namgyal's dis-location, his dis-orientation, had depressed me. Only one precious thing was left to him—a daughter—and because of her, he refused to leave a place that was corroding him, eating his spirit.

·XLVIII·

Wearily, I climbed a couple of leafy streets to the focal point of Cardston: the green knoll that supports the Alberta Temple of the Church of Jesus Christ of Latter-Day Saints. A pair of stone walls protects it from the secular world. I remember glimpsing the temple as a boy; but memory had tricked me by turning its granite into a shining, paper-white marble. As a result I was vaguely disappointed by the building's greyness. Most of the octagonal complex was beyond limits to me: unbelievers are allowed no farther than the little Visitor Center. The Mormons have an absolute right, of course, to keep the temple private; they have good reason to save it from the synthetic fate of a mere tourist attraction. Nonetheless, I felt slight annoyance that their concept of a sacred place should exclude all outsiders.

If you go back far enough, are *secret* and *sacred* brothers?

The porch of the Visitor Center offered me a choice: left for photographs and pamphlets; right for videos. I turned left and found a short woman in a mild brown dress, her curly hair dusted with grey, her big glasses minimizing bright blue eyes. A nameplate on the dress identified her: SISTER COLMAN. Heavy ELDER COLMAN was escorting a middle-aged couple towards the videos. They did not reappear.

Sister Colman greeted me thoughtfully and led me around the room, pausing to interpret the pictures that filled the walls. Photographs of the temple and happy families rubbed against "artists' depictions" of Biblical scenes.

"Our church," she informed me, "is founded entirely and utterly on the gospel of the Lord Jesus Christ." She was standing beside the fishermen at the Sea of Galilee; Peter resembled Abraham Lincoln. "We believe He is literally the Son of God."

What I *heard* was: "literally the Sun o' God." I assumed that American accents had endured through the decades in Card's town until Sister Colman announced she was a missionary up from Idaho.

We moved on to a picture of Christ in glory, sporting a white robe and enveloped by cheerleading angels. Jesus wears a beard but, aside from that aberration, suggests an all-American hunk: a first baseman; a tight end. The skins in all the images are white.

The colour is of more than aesthetic interest. I picked up *Christ in America,* a pamphlet that announces: "The Great White God of ancient America still lives!" Quetzalcoatl—whom Henriette Mertz identified as a Chinese Buddhist—Mormons believe to be Jesus. After His experiences in the Middle East, they claim that Jesus arrived in America and ministered in a land called Bountiful. "What did he look like, this Great White God? He was frequently described as a tall white man, bearded and with blue eyes."

"Do you do any work among the Blood Indians?" I asked.

"Elder Colman and I don't go in there," she said, "but some of the younger elders perform missionary work on the reservation. You know, I guess it's kind of hard for those people to give up their traditional way of life, such as drinking liquor and not having proper marriages."

Beside a photograph of marble oxen, a blond family grinned at the camera. Temples are the sites where Mormons bind their families for eternity and baptize every ancestor they can trace. "I can't imagine," Sister Colman admitted, "what heavenly glory will be like except with my children and grandchildren around me."

Recently the church has built temples across the world: Guatemala City, London, Santiago: all the places where American influence is potent. Showing me a magazine with photographs of the buildings, Sister Colman pointed to West Jordan.

"Oh," I said, "the Holy Land."

"No," she answered tartly. "West Jordan is in Utah. We don't have a temple in the Holy Land. The Jews will build a righteous temple for themselves when the time comes."

Perhaps she repented the sharpness of her tone. Bidding me farewell, Sister Colman seemed nearly apologetic. "You should see the Visitor Center at Salt Lake," she said. "It has very modern presentations. With live mannequins."

I retired to the Cahoon and found I was the only guest.

"Indians," the hotel manager said with scorn next morning. "Always feeling sorry for themselves and always making trouble for us. Been ruined by all the government handouts. And alcohol. You find a lot of bootleggers up there . . ."

Yet the pastures and wheat fields looked affluent enough to me, and except for some dingy houses on the edge of Cardston the homes bore a sleek appearance. Nearly six thousand people live on the Blood reserve—the most spacious in Canada. The government has tried and tried to shrink it; each time the Indians have held firm. In twenty miles I passed only two wrecked cars. But the drive stirred a memory. This was the road on which, when I was shy and seven, I heard my parents' friend announce: "Dirty people. They almost wiped out the buffalo, you know. They just left 'em to rot in the wilderness."

The closer I drove towards Lethbridge, the nearer I approached my boyhood. In a pasture off the highway, a covered wagon stood in

212

the wind. The wooden cart wore a fading coat of green, but the wagon wheels were red. The style, called "western," means nostalgia. As the grey clouds descended, the snow peaks disappeared.

·XLIX·

I grew up in a painting by Norman Rockwell. My family lived in a stucco house on a crescent near a verdant park. I swam and read and played road hockey and, for a year, attended Sunday School at the big church where my father worked as organist-choirmaster. There were strains in the canvas, cracks that threatened to split it open, but the image was one of smiling harmony. The faces of the citizens looked as sleek as a catalogue's models. My Lethbridge was a dream of security floating on a prairie sea. I worked to drown my differences—especially my British accent—out of a hunger to fit the contours of the dream. That may help, I guess, to explain why I remembered the place unwell.

I grew up ignorant of the little city; I grew up hardly knowing where I was. Many of my parents' friends were newcomers too, from Britain or British Columbia, Saskatchewan or Europe. During the Second World War Lethbridge had (though I never knew this as a child) been the prison of twelve thousand Axis soldiers, some of whom chose to stay. Perhaps it was a former prisoner—a cultivated man who directed a chamber orchestra—who once told my father that although Herr Hitler had made mistakes, he had been wise with regard to Jews.

My schooling taught me nothing about the place. I could hardly have expected my teachers to mention that in the 1920s, Lethbridge contained one of the largest brothels on the prairies; but they might at least have talked about Fort Whoop-Up. For me, as for Wallace Stegner in the Eastend of 1918, "Knowledge of place, knowledge of the past, meant . . . knowledge of the far and foreign." I remember studying in painful detail the geography of the Hudson Bay Lowlands; I remember compiling a scrapbook about New Zealand; but I recall no lessons about southern Alberta. Its literature, its history, even its sundry landscapes remained a closed book. The scraps of information and folk wisdom that I happened to pick up about Lethbridge never cohered into a pattern. I understood none of the ideas that would make sense of the tranquil dream. "Books didn't enlarge me," Stegner saw; "they dispersed me." Because I knew so little, I could leave the place without dismay.

When I drove into the city on a warm Friday in early June, I had no desire to rustle up schoolmates unseen for eighteen years in the hope of attaining a glow of artificial nostalgia. I wanted to look, and I wanted to look alone. I began where Lethbridge began: in the deep valley of the Oldman River, where a forest of cottonwoods and wild roses proliferates near the quick water. Above the path, a downy woodpecker was battering dead bark with its beak, twisting its neck after each loud foray as though it were practising yoga.

The city stands (I never knew this, of course) beside the Old North Trail, travelled for centuries by the Blackfoot Confederacy. In the years when the Hudson's Bay Company was relinquishing the west to the new dominion of Canada, American traders built thirty or more posts north of the line. Abe Farwell and Moses Solomon were part of a sad pattern. The first and worst fort arose in 1869 at the confluence of the Oldman and St. Mary rivers, on a site where so many Bloods had fallen from smallpox that it was called *Akaisakoyi:* "many dead." Approval for the fort was given—not that it was his to give—by Montana's Superintendent of Indian Affairs, General Alfred Sully, a man who considered Indians "red-skinned cannibals." The enterprise flew its private flag: reminiscent from a distance of the American emblem, but with a double-barred cross instead of stars.

It was a firewater fort, of course. Somewhere in its brief history it

214

acquired the name Whoop-Up. The stories are sufficiently pictur-esque: one trader is said to have written to a friend, "Dear Friend, Bill Geary got to putting on airs and I shot him and he is dead. My potatoes are looking fine." In fact, Fort Whoop-Up served to con-tinue a process—the spiritual and physical weakening of the In-dians—which the epidemics had begun and the extermination of the buffalo would complete. In a single year at Whoop-Up, about ninety Blackfoot died in drunken brawls. The mounties closed the fort in October 1874, but by then its work was done: for better or worse, white settlement of the region would encounter little resis-tance.

Perhaps, in that sense, Lethbridge has cause to celebrate the fort. A cleanly reconstruction stands in the valley below Scenic Drive; every August, Whoop-Up Days occur in Whoop-Up Park across the river from Whoop-Up Drive. The past is distant enough to spruce up and falsify. Exploitation of the cute name has replaced the shame and silence that still held sway when I was a boy.

If the city has made Fort Whoop-Up respectable, it remains un-certain how to market Indian Battle Park. The year after the fort opened its corrupting gates, the Cree and Blackfoot fought a vicious battle a couple of miles downstream. Hundreds died. I knew about the battle as a child, not that anyone explained its causes. The war-riors seemed as remote from me as Medes or Trojans. Their strife had left no ruins, no trenches, no white-crossed cemeteries for the victims.

A town grew above the battle site thanks to the discovery of coal. In the 1880s, indeed, the settlement was called Coal Banks. With the devotion to foreign investment that still characterizes the region, it finally took the name of an English businessman, Wil-liam Lethbridge, who governed the mining cartel. The first houses stood in the valley, close to the seams; wandering among the poplars and chokecherries, I was also wandering past the feral asparagus and phlox of the town's first gardens. A flood drove the residents up onto the plain, but their plants endured. Miners still foraged under the brink of Lethbridge when I was a boy; trains car-ried their coal west to the Pacific over the miraculous black stilts of the Oldman valley bridge.

215

I lived at the other end of town, near the swimming pool and the golf course at Henderson Lake. (No one ever told me its first name: Slaughterhouse Slough.) Having turned its back on the whisky-trading, coal-mining past, the city was swelling across the irrigated plain. Its past was mean and hilly; its future, genteel and flat.

We left, and things changed. In 1969 a University of Lethbridge began to rise on the far side of the Oldman. Its main building nestles against the willowy contours of the valley; a rich constellation of new homes twinkles above and beyond. At sixty thousand, the city has nearly doubled its population since I was a boy. Thanks to the university, Lethbridge has a new awareness of the river. Its past has become part of its future.

Climbing out of the valley through a field of cactus and buffalo berry, I walked slowly eastward towards my own past. Some elements of the central core surprised me: as a child I had never noticed the old brick building with painted signs that read CHINESE NATIONAL LEAGUE and KUO MIN TANG. A brewery founded by a certain Fritz Sick, and known for decades under the evocative name Sick's Brewery, had become the mere Lethbridge Brewery. The stone, ornate post office, crowned by a Belgian clock, and the settled fragrance of honeysuckle and lilac were not things I knew I had remembered; yet at once they seemed familiar. In my memory, Lethbridge was a place to trust. I was content to see a vegetable garden set in a small front lawn without any fence to shelter its lettuces from light-fingered passers-by an arm's length away.

In my memory, too, nobody transgressed the rules. The city—at least, the fragment I knew—lived by a code of appearances. It was large enough to devour eccentricity, but small enough to expect conformity. I was unsurprised to suffer a verbal attack when I stepped onto a lush ribbon of turf between a paved sidewalk and the street. My feet were aching; the grass looked tempting. But eyes were watching me behind plate glass. After I had taken three or four steps, a householder—bare-chested, glowering, young—opened his front door and barked: "Could you walk on the sidewalk!" It was a command, not a request, and I obeyed. Lethbridge was his world, not mine. Norman Rockwell held no further appeal; I could glimpse what his charm concealed.

When I walked past an old friend's house, a familiar school, I felt strangely inert. My memories arrived like dry flakes: I lost them again without regret, like the cottonwood fluff that a warm breeze brushed across the city's nape. My childhood home had grown an extension. The sight meant nothing, though I grieved a little that the "waste patch" behind the house—a relic of prairie, where the kingbirds hunted dragonflies and our cats procured the odd vole— had turned into Normandy Road. The whole district, I suddenly realized, was named for war. For years I had played road hockey in a gathering twilight along Dieppe Boulevard, and never had I thought about its name.

I stopped finally at the Nikka Yuko Gardens. In 1967 Lethbridge showed the courage to confront and surmount its history: a city that, a generation earlier, had persecuted and abused its Japanese residents opened a traditional Japanese garden on the banks of Henderson Lake. I took off my shoes in the pavilion and watched the calligraphy of light. The sun poured like pale wine over the stones of meditation, spilling nothing. But there was, in truth, no serenity that day, no refuge from disorder, for the city was in the process of "improving" the green park beyond.

The "improvements" had turned a corner of the park into a mountain of débris. The swimming pool was empty and so, to my amazement, was the lake: it had become the rummage ground of a dozen sandpipers, pecking for dinner on the mudflats. Coke cans and cigarette cartons studded a chewed-up mess.

I had never seen the park looking so ugly. The sight was a shock to me: a fine, necessary shock. For I understood that I was doing to the past exactly what Lethbridge had done to the park: broken it, torn it apart, ransacked a green space. No secret meanings awaited me in the downy city, no battered traumas lurked in the playgrounds. My memories are not so rich and sensuous as those of many writers; but memory is not a competitive sport. I can recall enough to live in peace. To come back in the hope of some kind of revelation was an ailment born of restlessness, my rootlessness, my homelessness.

Lethbridge was never "my" place, as Saskatoon would so quickly become. Only my idea of it mattered: the serenity, the absence of pace and blight, and the comfort that enabled me to grow into my dispersed self. The facts I had lately discovered about the city — its mines, its university, its riverine history — were foreign to the bored heart. I began to feel impatient to leave, and a little annoyed with myself for wanting to vandalize the past.

Lethbridge, in the end, vandalized me. I strode into a parking lot after breakfast on a meek Sunday morning and thought to myself: "That's strange. Why did I leave a window wide open?" Then I saw the smashed glass on the gravel. Sometime in the night, the window had been broken and my binoculars removed. The car must have disappointed the thief, for he/she/they had stolen nothing else. The uninteresting contents of a plastic garbage bag were strewn across the floor. It was the first vandalism, the first theft of the journey.

So I stayed in the city for two extra days while I waited for an appropriate window to arrive from Calgary. I visited the library, I rested, I brooded. I saw at last — the shattered window was proof — that "my" Lethbridge was a sentimental illusion. On weekend evenings the city centre has its little dangers, and no doubt it always had; I wouldn't have known, for I was always safe watching "Hockey Night in Canada" in the stucco suburb. Lethbridge is not a place to trust; nowhere can be trusted entirely; trust is a necessary fiction, a creation of the longing mind. It was too late for me to invent another meaning for Lethbridge: I was a child there and I went away.

The mechanics installed a fresh window, and I could go away at last. There were still a few discoveries I hoped to make in the west, places that would stand apart from the complications of memory. Lethbridge and I are at peace: we have nothing to make war about. It is nowhere I resent, nowhere I love.

·L·

The treasure which you think not worth taking trouble and pains to find, this alone is the real treasure you are longing for all your life.
—epigraph to *The Treasure of the Sierra Madre* by "B. Traven"

Northwest of Lethbridge lies a realm of forests, streams and rising meadows that the Stoney Indians called "Paradise." Some of its white residents agree. The common name—foothills—implies that the region is but a low appendage to the sky-slicing Rockies; and while this may hold a grain of geological truth, it has kept the Stoneys' Paradise little visited and little known. The area has a rarer name: the Porcupine Hills. Sitting in a Lethbridge café one afternoon, I heard of a guest lodge in the hills that promises rustic accommodation. Within twenty minutes I booked a room.

Far to the west, the mountains shone. Climbing the sharp, confusing roads, I thought the hills and tucked-in valleys had the turbulent energy of Welsh and Scottish uplands. The scale of the land was larger here, but the rough, green grace was similar. Only when I stepped out of the car did I notice the essential differences: the absence of salt in the air and of clamouring sheep on the land. The odd, disconcerting thing was that Skyline Ridge Lodge had the exact feel of a British home.

It arose during the First World War, a vintage that makes it "rustic" in Alberta. The kitchen, which was dominated by a well-thumbed table, contained a tea towel of Caernarvonshire, a kettle on the semipermanent boil and a plate with an inlaid recipe for Banbury tart. Wartime volumes from the Readers' Union rubbed the jackets of bloodless thrillers in the living room's bookcases. The lodge's manager, Peggy Owen, was a trim, white-haired Englishwoman. During the war she had studied at Oxford University, guarding the Bodleian Library from firebombs and singing in the Bach Choir. All appearances to the contrary, she had become a militant Albertan.

219

"This is the most beautiful countryside in the world!"

I raised an eyebrow.

"Well, it is!"

I decided to play devil's advocate.

"But you're seven hundred miles away from the sea."

Peggy looked annoyed.

"You can't always dwell on what you *don't* have," she said. "England doesn't have the Rockies, does it?"

She then cooked a dinner that could have emerged straight from the kitchens of an Oxford college: thin soup; beef with boiled cauliflower and mashed potatoes; rhubarb tart.

Next morning Peggy had business elsewhere, and I went trail-riding with her assistant. Jane rode a robust quarter horse in heat. I chose a chubby, twenty-two-year-old gelding with the inappropriate name of Cheetah. Every few steps Cheetah bent his yellow head and attempted to snatch a meal of forget-me-nots or mountain shooting-stars. I tolerated his guzzling for the sake of his loose-reined equanimity.

We climbed through a chain of meadows and a cool pair of woods to Skyline Ridge. Cloud-shadows shimmered on land that dropped away in three directions. Half the world seemed visible.

"Just think of 'em all," Jane said with pity, "down there on the flats."

She had the accent as well as the prejudices of the hill country: *bears,* on her lips, rhymed with *players.*

The Porcupine breeze—a far better insect repellent than Deep Woods Off—tugged about my head. The horses dozed, finding little to chew on the ridge, and swished their tails above a faint petroglyph on an exposed erratic boulder. Arms outspread, a human figure danced in the stone. At least, I think he danced. I think he existed. "All memories are fallible," the anthropologist Selwyn Dewdney once observed, "and, not least, pictographs, like fish, are where you find them."

"If you ride up here at night," Jane said, "you can see the glow of Calgary over the horizon."

She sounded suddenly unhappy.

We arrived back at the lodge in the late afternoon—the prospect

220

of hay inspired Cheetah to a portly, eccentric gallop—and I brewed a potful of tea. I glanced up from the floral cups and saucers to see, in the field beyond the big corral, a young moose. The horses across the fence showed no fear of the gawky apparition: a blotched, grey-brown animal with spindly legs and an outsize head. The moose examined the horses, and the horses examined the moose. After a few minutes he lay down and nuzzled their salt lick.

"Probably it's the same calf who came round here in the winter," Peggy remarked over a dinner of ham and boiled potatoes. "With his mother. And now she must be pregnant again, so she's packed this fellow off to fend for himself."

I remembered that when the Earl of Southesk and his bevy of retainers reached the foothills in 1859, they dined on moosemeat: "excellent though rather tough: the fat delicious." Southesk had fallen behind schedule, and the privations of the journey were vexing him: "How one longs for a good larder and an educated cook!" Yet he continued westward into the Rockies, naming fragments of them after himself, reading *Titus Andronicus* and devouring "great meals of mountain mutton."

Our plates were empty. I waited for Peggy to fulfil her promise of a folk tale about the hills. "She tells it," Jane had said, "like she made it up herself."

"No, not yet. I mean to say, look how bright it is outside!"

So we made polite conversation while the colours leached from the light. The debonair singing of the white-crowned sparrows faded to a silence fractured by rare calls of alarm.

"Peggy," Jane said at last. 'It's pretty dark out there."

"Well. You're sure you wouldn't like another cup of tea?"

"We're sure."

"All right then. Now remember, this is a true story. It happened a long time ago, not very far from where we're sitting now.

"Back in 1870 or so, there were two prospectors living near a fort in Montana, and their names were Blackjack and Lemon. Americans. One year they came north, all the way to Rocky Mountain House, and then they spent weeks working their way down the eastern slope of the Rockies. At first they didn't find anything of interest. But they knew that no other white men had travelled that particular route, and so they persevered."

"How did they know?" I asked.

"Please don't interrupt like that," Peggy said severely. "They knew they were the first. The whole region is just a maze of creeks and springs and hills. It's terribly difficult to find one's way around. So. Where was I?"

"Nothing of interest," Jane prompted.

"That's right. But they persevered. And one day, early in the fall, just before the leaves were starting to turn, they came upon nuggets of gold. By following the stream up towards the mountains, they reached the mother lode. It was beside the headwaters of the Oldman, perhaps, or else the Highwood. The gold was remarkably pure. It was worth a fortune."

"That was the trouble," Jane suggested.

"Exactly. That was the trouble. Blackjack and Lemon loaded up their horses with samples of the gold, and they decided, of course, to come back in the spring. Together. They were going to divide the wealth in two."

"There's a *but* on its way," I said.

"But that very night, they had an argument. And when Blackjack had fallen fast asleep, Lemon crept over with an axe and murdered him. He wanted to keep the gold for himself. And he suspected that if he didn't get rid of Blackjack, Blackjack would be more than happy to get rid of him.

"So. There were the remains of poor Blackjack, mouldering away in the creek. Lemon believed he was alone. But little did he know that all this time, ever since the two of them had found the mother lode, they were being watched! Now who do you think was watching?"

"Indians?" I suggested.

"Very astute. Two young braves of the Stoney tribe had been out hunting in the mountains, which they knew, of course, like the back of their hands, and they happened to hear the white men. They watched the treacherous murder and they were *not* impressed. So for the rest of the night, they kept up a strange kind of wailing. Like a banshee, perhaps, or a dervish. By the time dawn broke over the hills, Lemon was half-insane with guilt and fear."

222

The tale was starting to remind me of something but, for the moment, memory eluded me.

"Lemon climbed onto his horse and rode away just as fast as he could. And by the time he arrived in Montana, he was delirious. He confessed his crime to a priest at the fort, and he showed off a sample of the gold. Well, that got everyone's attention! But the winter was closing in, and so Lemon was more or less immobile.

"Meanwhile, back in the Porcupine Hills, the Americans had left quite a commotion. And when the two young braves went to the chief of the Stoneys and described what they had seen, he told them to hurry back and destroy all the evidence of the mine. He told them to move the boulders and cut a new trail and tear down some of the bushes and, above all, to hide any proof that white men had passed that way. The chief also made the young braves swear that they would never, never reveal the secret. You see, to the Indians the gold was lying in a sacred place. The last thing they wanted was a gold rush!"

It was too dark for me to see Peggy's face. Her pale blouse glimmered in the night.

"Well, the next year Lemon and the priest and a number of other men came north once more. But Lemon was still unbalanced. And when he approached the area where he'd committed his terrible crime, it all became too much for him. He lost his reason. He went berserk. Some say he was under an Indian curse. But his descriptions of the mother lode didn't quite fit anywhere the men could find. Oh, they tried. For years and years they tried. But Lemon was beyond hope, and the Stoney Indians were the only ones who knew the real location of the Lost Lemon Mine. Perhaps, who knows, someone in the tribe could tell the truth even now!"

Silence fell. After a quantity of seconds Jane switched on a lamp, and we all blinked and grinned.

"That's a true story, mind," Peggy said.

"Oh, sure."

"I remember on one occasion I was just getting to the part about the Indians wailing when a pack of coyotes up in the hills began the most unearthly shrieking. The visitors were frightfully impressed."

An hour later I climbed the steep, creaking stairs past an ancient

223

Salmon calendar of Worcestershire into a cold room. The walls and bedspreads were a delicate pink. I was holding a booklet about the Lemon mine, published by the Alberta Frontier Society, which Peggy had lent me as I said good night "in case you don't want to sleep for a while."

There is a more prosaic version of the story, I was unsurprised to find. On the western slope of the Rockies, a prospector by the name of Frank Lemmon once found a creek with showings of gold. Lemmon's partner (who was not called Blackjack) died. Out of such scanty raw material, a bogus priest had perhaps manufactured the legend. The demystification of the tale had a certain interest; but I was still puzzling out the myth. Lying on the high, deep bed, listening to the cries of a monotonous owl and the rare whinny of a horse in the darkness, I finally realized why Peggy's story had seemed so familiar and so powerful.

Its action takes place in a distant range of mountains that conceals a treasure. The main characters are American prospectors, adventurers in a foreign land. They set out from a dingy frontier town, they trek up into the hills, and after considerable effort they discover the marvellous lode. But they quarrel. One of the men commits murder. Fabulous wealth brings him no joy; instead, he is tormented by anxiety. He starts to lose his mind. The region has other inhabitants: Indians, who maintain a traditional culture and who are troubled by the Americans' work. They know more than they admit to strangers. In the end the lust for gold destroys the murderer, whose mine is lost. The Indians and the mountains reclaim their secret.

Until that evening I had never heard of the Lost Lemon Mine. Yet the story's basic elements—all the details of the paragraph above—were known to me from John Huston's film *The Treasure of the Sierra Madre*. When Peggy was evoking Lemon's dementia, my mind's eye had unconsciously been watching the face of Humphrey Bogart.

At first, elated, I assumed that a direct connection must exist between the two stories. Such a bond is conceivable, for Huston based his film on a novel by one of the most mysterious authors of the century, B. Traven. A resident of rural Mexico who wrote in German,

224

Traven was almost certainly the same man as Ret Marut, a Munich actor, editor and novelist. (He perhaps knew Felix Paul Greve.) In 1919 Marut served on the Propaganda Committee of the short-lived Bavarian Soviet Republic. After the republic was crushed, he vanished; a few years later the fiction of Traven started to emerge. *Der Schatz der Sierra Madre* was published in 1927, eight years before its English translation and more than twenty years before the movie. By the time Bogart loured at the cameras, Blackjack and Lemon had appeared several times in print. It is possible, though unlikely, that Traven's novel influenced early versions of the Alberta folk tale; a further possibility is that the folk tale inspired the book.

Traven's movements are, after all, obscure, and Ret Marut's early life is unknown. He need not have visited Canada to hear about Lemon's gold, for the story is known in parts of the American west. Moreover, Traven may have elaborated some of his novels and stories from raw material — legends — given him in Mexico by wanderers unknown. The writing of *Der Schatz der Sierra Madre,* like the plot it unfolds, may even have been an uneasy partnership.

I devoted time and energy to finding a firm connection between Lemon and the mountains of Mexico before it dawned on me that the less glamorous possibility — that the two stories are unrelated — is, in fact, equally suggestive. It points to a subconscious pattern that informs many goldseeking narratives: a pattern of obsession, guilt and murder. The same themes appear in El Dorado films as different as Charlie Chaplin's *Gold Rush* and Werner Herzog's *Aguirre, Wrath of God.*

The model pioneers of the New World, from Virginia west to Utah and north to Alberta, were farmers. And the opposite of a farming pioneer is a goldseeker: while the one man digs to give and build, the other digs to take and exploit. Men who engage in a gold rush live and die by chance: they can make a fortune in an hour, or gain nothing from a year's hard work. The discoverer of the Klondike gold fields, Robert Henderson, trudged out of the Yukon with little more than a thousand dollars — and he was robbed even of that sum on the boat down the Pacific coast.

Like the earlier quest for a holy grail, the quest for El Dorado exemplifies a striving for perfection. It adapts and perverts the religious search for salvation, with the lust to find a pure vein supplanting the desire to attain a pure heart. Gold is the ultimate sacrament for those who worship the material world. To find it and lose it is secular damnation.

Perhaps, too, men who abandon their motherland are especially tempted to search for a mother lode by way of compensation. It is as though the white man's invasions of Indian country have left psychic wounds, which the creators of gold-rush stories have tried to cauterize. Their treatments are warnings: that a ravishing of the land can also ravish the spirit. That nature occasionally takes revenge for acts of plunder. And that the love of gold provokes a romance with madness and conceives a child called shame.

Even black gold. Even now.

·LI·

I headed down from Skyline Ridge towards the flats. The mustard-speckled hills were shining in a sun-dogged light. Cirrus clouds drifted through the sky's ring like pale spirits of the air.

A gust rattled the car's new window as I turned a gravel corner. The Porcupine Hills lie in the grasp of the Chinook, a warm, unpredictable wind that chops and whittles a southern Alberta winter. Indians described the Chinook as the south wind's small, blind daughter. White legends make up by extravagance what they lack in poetry.

"Why, I remember one time when the warm air hit the cold air right down the middle of Second Street!"

I was listening to the proprietor of a café in the old ranching town of High River. A Hollywood studio found the place ideal as Smallville, the setting of Superman's boyhood. Joe Clark was a boy here too.

"On one side of the road, people were walkin' around in their shirt-sleeves and moppin' the sweat off their brows. On the other, snow was comin' down!"

The man took my doubt as an insult.

It was only a short drive then until the oil-fired sprawl of Calgary began. The narrator of Graham Greene's story "Dear Dr. Falkenheim" lives on the edge of Calgary in a bungalow called Kosy Nuick; outside a suburban mall he watches the blades of a helicopter decapitate Santa Claus. I drove somewhat nervously down the organized chaos of a typical strip—fast-food joints, gas stations, motels, car lots, shopping malls, all advertising their wares with the spangled brilliance of neon—gave up, checked in, and dived for a sauna. The fever and commotion of a fast city were foreign to me after so many weeks on the road. I needed time to adjust to the pace, the visual and emotional barrage.

"You live in Montreal, eh?" the girl at the reception desk inquired.

"That's right."

She shook her head in sympathy.

"I wouldn't want to live in a big city."

But a big city is precisely what Calgary has become. In the past couple of decades, and despite a traumatic recession, it has outstripped Winnipeg to rival Edmonton as the largest city in the prairie west. More people inhabit Calgary—about 620,000—than all of rural Saskatchewan. They have arrived from most of the countries in the world and from every nook of the prairies, swelling the city as though its burgeoning concrete hid the key to unlock their dreams: striking it rich, sometimes; moving on, in many other cases, as a fragment of the astonishing, unending migration of our times; or staying put, perhaps finding compensations for their lack of instant wealth. Calgary imagines itself the vanguard of a luminous future.

It purports to be a Midas city, and many of its citizens crave the Midas touch. It's a metropolis on golden wheels: restless, occasionally reckless.

One result of its rapid-fire development has been a parochial, narrow-minded approach towards the outside world. "Distant Ontario is perhaps small business of ours," a columnist in the day's *Herald* announced, "unless our own interests are involved." Such ingrown attitudes—foreign to the traditions of Saskatchewan and Manitoba—repelled me. I disliked the unanimity of belief that enabled one of Calgary's Conservative politicians to gather more than 53,000 votes in the last federal election while her nearest opponent collected fewer than 8,000. I loathed the smug self-satisfaction that could produce, during the energy shortages of the 1970s, a mob of bumper-stickers that read: "Let the eastern bastards freeze in the dark!" Yet behind the glib selfishness stands a grievance: that Alberta's immense resources have created more benefit for eastern Canadians than for the citizens of Alberta.

"It's like they say about the States," a young executive remarked. I was eating dinner at his split-level home in the Ranchland development of northwestern Calgary. The trees for miles were saplings. "We always use the image of Canada as a mosaic, right? Calgary isn't like that. Calgary's a melting pot. The only people who talk about their origins are the ones who want to leave. Everyone else becomes—a Calgarian."

"So people can create a new identity for themselves."

"That's right! If you want, you can give up the past completely. We moved here in the late '70s, towards the end of the Boom, and it seemed like everybody in town expected to get rich. It wasn't just a dream they shared, it was an anticipation."

From the Ranchland hills, or from a westerly bridge across the Bow River, or from its island full of life-size dinosaurs, Calgary's business core can look almost noble. Rather than attempting to blend the old with the new, the city has gone all-out for novelty. Its glass and concrete towers in blue, black and white glitter like a man-made range of mountains. They are the phallic symbols of modern architecture; Calgary's specimens are very tall and very macho.

The office towers offer vertical, dizzying proof of Calgary's passage from an Anglo-Saxon provincial town (no more than a hundred thousand people lived here in the Second World War) to a centre of cosmopolitan business. Buffalo Child Long Lance would hardly recognize his former home. Yet the downtown streets retain their old narrowness. Wind tunnels and claustrophobia are the result. Because of the city's faith in unrestricted enterprise, its developers have enjoyed a clear hand to destroy historic buildings and open spaces. Sometimes the "development" has been mere vandalism. The stone fabric of Hull's Opera House—a heart of culture at the turn of the century—was demolished in 1963 to make way for a parking lot. The site remains vacant even now.

Although Calgary's wealth derives from petroleum, and although the vast majority of its residents have no more connection with ranching than they do with marmalade, the city likes to maintain its image as "Cowtown." The myth allows an illusion of continuity with the rural past. Even now, the strip roads that straggle out of Calgary go by the comforting name of "trail." The city has built up a kind of back-patting history—as a haven of rugged entrepreneurs and cow-punching individualists—that stands somewhat at odds with the truth. In fact the federal government created the place, and its first name was French: Brisebois. (Colonel Macleod of the mounted police rechristened it "Calgary," a Gaelic word for pasture, after Inspector Brisebois had fallen from his grace.) The annual Stampede, modestly promoted as "the Greatest Outdoor Show on Earth," was organized by a vaudeville performer from Wyoming in a calculated effort to bolster Alberta's economy. He succeeded beyond anyone's dreams.

One evening I decided to bolster the audience for Handel's oratorio *Judas Maccabaeus.* The performance took place in the Anglican cathedral, one of the few buildings to survive from Calgary's sandstone era. I emerged from the spanking Convention Centre—a hand-dryer in the men's room bore the strange inscription SANITATION FOR THE NATION / SALUBRITÉ UNIVERSELLE—onto an empty downtown street. Traffic lights shimmered on the wet pavement. A siren called in the distance near T. Lobsang Rampa's final home. I turned a corner to see a pale figure hurrying

229

down the sidewalk. A young man with a sandy moustache was gaping after him, motionless despite a quick squall of rain.

"Did you see that guy?"

"I didn't get a good look, no. Why, what happened?"

"He walked up to me and called me a racist. Then he called me an asshole!"

"Was he drunk?"

"I don't think he was drunk, I think he was scrambled."

A common brand of incident in Toronto or New York, but still a novelty in Calgary. The citizens seem unwilling to face the consequences of size and wealth. They want glamour without glamour's underside: the glory of free enterprise without the casualties, the stress, the distress. They hope against hope that a sophisticated metropolis can remain affable ol' Cowtown.

The music, full of pious orgies and conquering heroes, managed to be both righteous and militaristic. It went down very well.

·LII·

I took my leave of Calgary by driving west along the old highway to the mountains. So near, so intimate, so powerful—yet they constitute another region, another state of mind. It is part of the prairie consciousness to look towards the Rockies, squinting against the dusty light, with a kind of hunger and a kind of awe. From the plains, they seem a border as extreme as salt water; only the accidents of history make the land beyond them a province in the same country. I decided to leave the mountains for some unknowable future. Whatever other havoc man creates on the earth, the mountains will be there when I feel ready.

Briefly I stopped at Cochrane, a town that snuggles into Big Hill's foot with a tranquil ease. Wealthy, polo-playing Englishmen occupied "Big Hill Country" a century ago. One flamboyant couple failed at ranching, at mining, at brick-making, at lumber-producing and at Conservative politics; after fifteen years of failure they sailed back to England with their honour, if not their bank account, intact. The town's narrow, scissor-beamed Anglican church contains an unsigned painting: a pallid Last Supper, with blue hills that glimmer behind the diners in a manner oddly suitable for Cochrane. Local legends ascribe the painting to a daughter of Queen Victoria.

A miserable highway carried me northward past the villages of Dogpound and Westward Ho. To my left, the pale ramparts of rock gradually ebbed. A mule deer peered at me, anxious, unmoving, on the edge of a pasture ten yards from the onrushing car. Earlier in the spring I might have skidded to a halt. Now I made a curt mental note—mule deer in field—and drove on.

I stayed a night in the town of Rocky Mountain House, which rises far from the Rockies at the junction of the Clearwater and North Saskatchewan rivers. Rival fur-trading posts were established here in 1799. The park above their remnants offers "interpretive displays . . . slide programs . . . locations equipped with illustrations and recorded messages . . . animation programs dealing with life in bygone days." Thanks, but no thanks. I preferred to walk along the banks of the adolescent Saskatchewan—already burly and powerful, proud of its speed and its steep valley, but lacking the poise it acquires downstream.

Modern streets slope towards the river by its far, eastern shore. In the evening the town reclined in a magic realist light: a sharp, calm, cool blueness in which even the villas above the road glittered like the architecture of a dream. The scent of lilacs fondled the scent of pines; bottled air from Rocky Mountain House would sell out in the cities of the east. But in a back alley, a teenager wearing a green-and-white jacket pitched a stone at a black cat. The stone clattered against a wooden fence. The cat leaped over the fence and disappeared from my life. Two hours before midnight, I could read by the sky.

I slept, woke and drove east towards Alhambra. The hills flattened into rich farmland, flecked with woods that bent to resist the morning's agitated wind. I crossed the Medicine River a few miles downstream from Eckville, a town whose mayor—a churchgoing history teacher—inculcated a generation of students with his belief that the Holocaust was a fraud and that Jews were scheming to take over the world. Abandoning the highway for a chain of minor roads, I crept back to the gentle Medicine and the village of Markerville. It was, I suppose, a drive of homage. For nearly forty years, a wooden farmhouse near Markerville was the home of one of Canada's finest poets: Stephan G. Stephansson.

When I was growing up I never heard a word about him. But perhaps, for once, the ignorance can be excused. Stephansson wrote little in English. He was an Icelander whose poems renewed his country's literature with a hardheaded Romanticism, capable of political anger as well as descriptive grace. His sharp eye for folly, his tenderness and curiosity were at the service of a stalwart will.

He needed it. He passed through hard places and hard times. An unschooled farmboy, he sailed away from his ash-strewn country in 1873. His family settled in Wisconsin, then in North Dakota where an Icelandic colony grew. Yet drought, debt and dust storms obliged Stephansson to mortgage his Dakota homestead, and in the wake of a bruising quarrel with the Lutheran church he moved again, pioneering after 1889 in Alberta. Stephansson—a slender man who wore a thick moustache and, in most of the photographs, a dour, taut expression—stayed here until his death in 1927. Neighbours knew him as a leader of the village and an adaptable, forward-looking farmer. He and his sons raised wheat, sheep, rye and other produce, and they sold milk to the local creamery.

Things were never easy, though, on the farm or off it. His refusal to accept church dogma made him some enemies; his hatred of the First World War made him more. Stephansson poured public contempt on the war at a time when hundreds of young Icelandic Cana-

232

dians were hurrying to the oblivion of trench warfare. Though he was called a traitor, he refused to trim his convictions to fit a majority's opinion. He was tough, a little cranky, unafraid.

His house shocked me. Even though its elaborate, unsymmetrical design—embellished by a bay window, a gable and a pillared veranda—bore some resemblance to turn-of-the-century homes I had seen elsewhere, its flamingo colour did not. The buildings had once been painted pink and green, and I like to imagine that Stephansson changed his mind. Posterity, in the form of Alberta's Ministry of Culture, has restored the pink for good.

The garden, full of picnic tables and antique machinery, was overrun by touring schoolchildren and harassed guides in 1920s costume. I learned from a guide in a long mottled dress that the house was Stephansson's handiwork; it had expanded piecemeal over the years, triumphantly disguising its origin as a log cabin. "In the family's first winter," she announced, "there were eight people living in the cabin!"

Thirty children groaned as one.

I walked into the house. Its rooms were numerous but small, by Canadian standards at least. The walls of the pantry were lined with replicas of period newspapers: the Icelandic-Canadian *Heimskringla* and the Montreal *Daily Herald.* Advertisements in the *Herald* promised cures for boils in women and weakness in men. In the living room the children, who suffered from neither ailment, were baffled by a darning egg.

"What does your mother do," the guide asked brightly, "when your socks get holes in them?"

"Chuck them out!"

"The pioneers had to be willing to tackle all kinds of work," another guide said. (The house was providing him with a black suit and a summer job to support his studies in Creative Writing.) "Stephansson would go on survey crews sometimes, or he'd work for the railway. He used to shear sheep, too. You know how much money he'd make for shearing a hundred sheep in a twelve-hour day?"

"Twenty-five dollars, maybe?" a boy piped up.

233

"One dollar fifty!" the guide answered.

"What a rip-off," the boy said with scorn. His opinion of Stephansson had tumbled.

The room that interested the children least—the poet's study—intrigued me the most. It was more than twice the size of the adjoining bedroom, which had space for little except a double bed. Fortunately, neither Stephansson nor his wife Helga Jonsdottir cared much about the domestic pretensions. They had a good marriage, although (or because) she appears in few of his poems. Helga owned property in her own name, a rare phenomenon in pioneer Alberta.

Stephansson composed so many of his verses in the small hours that his collected volumes bear the title *Andvökur:* "wakeful nights." The books he owned, an eclectic throng in English and Icelandic, still occupy a tall, glass-fronted case. A translation of Schiller's *Poems* leans against a dog-eared *National Geographic.* The study window used to overlook the Rocky Mountains, but Stephansson's gardening has succeeded too well: his spruce trees and caraganas hide the peaks. Like a sightless mind, the house is closed in on itself.

Its builder never relinquished the intricate culture of Iceland. Yet he took a brisk interest in the affairs of his adopted country, the land that would become his children's only home. Stephansson struggled to gain a double vision. Some of his best poems weigh his consciousness of his two worlds.

Though he lost his fatherland, he kept his mother tongue. He made his own peace. He was strong enough to accept the prairies on his own demanding terms.

The homage that the man deserves is, in part, a function of his sheer perseverance. He perfected his craft with sleepless love. Poetry was an inner need for Stephansson, most of it written without hope of reward. Private, often tense, intense, he had much to surmount. Early hardships trained him in the concealment of emotions. His isolation from other poets scarred him. Yet he gave in to nothing and nobody, wrestling a living from the soil and making, in the wakeful nights of his homemade study, a homeless beauty that outlives him.

The children had left in a bus; more were expected soon. The guides were in need of a rest. I stepped out the kitchen door, opened a gate in the fence and knocked at the new farmhouse beyond. The poet's grandson, Edwin Stephansson, lives there: a big man with a firm handclasp and a shock of grey-brown hair. Guarded on the subject of his grandfather, who died when Edwin was a child, he was content to talk about farming: "It's good country here. Mostly beef and grain. No, not many farmers have got dairy herds anymore. The creameries in Eckville and Markerville were shut down, eh? So the milk's got to go into Red Deer."

We sat around the kitchen table. A window overlooks the old farm. Near the ceiling a canary improvised in the language of caged birds. "My son's a steam engineer in Red Deer," Edwin said. "Oh sure, I hoped he might take over the farm. But he married a girl from town, and she said no way was she going to live all the way out here. Then when I see the money he makes, I figure he made the right decision."

I remembered that Edwin's grandfather, at the end of a loving "Toast to Alberta," had warned this most richly endowed of provinces to "lock your embrace / with glacier steel / against the trenchboots / of a capitalist."

"You know, not to gamble against nature every year."

But his voice was doubtful.

Edwin's wife handed me a mug of coffee. "I'm not an Icelander," she said. "I don't speak the language."

"I can still talk Icelandic some," Edwin said heavily. "But there's no one to talk to."

235

·LIII·

The mown suburbs of Red Deer contain a building that did much to reconcile me to Alberta, even to suburbs. St. Mary's Roman Catholic church arose in the late 1960s from a field of barley on the margin of town. Red Deer grew up around the church, enfolding it at a cautious distance with station wagons and barbecues, bicycles and marigolds. The church among them has a quality of permanence matched by its austere serenity. It makes the houses look flimsy and provisional—a makeshift encampment of bystanders, huddled into rows for convenience, ready to blow at the wind's whim.

The church's architect had attended a convent school in town during the Second World War. His father, a game warden, was half-Blackfoot. When the young man began to study architecture, the University of British Columbia asked him to leave because his designs were radical and his Métis background "inappropriate." The man left Canada for Mexico, then spent six years at the University of Texas. Douglas Cardinal returned to the Canadian west only when he knew he was strong enough to resist its prejudices and its linear aesthetics. St. Mary's was among his earliest commissions. Within fifteen years, Cardinal would be asked to design the National Museum of Man.

For the church, as for many of his later buildings, he selected a rich, copper-coloured brickwork. Stark, almost windowless, the walls defy the prairie elements to fling their worst. Yet the brickwork curves and ripples with remarkable fluidity. From some lights or angles the church resembles a beached whale. Inside, stones from an ancient ocean bond the building with the sea. The font and the altar derive from a Manitoba quarry that was lapped once by salt water. Shells and a fossil lizard appear on the font. Embedded in the altar is a fish.

As you pass through the curled, protected entranceway, you leave the city's light behind. You desert the artifice of right angles, the grid of western streets, in favour of a body's curves. You slip into the belly of the whale. A swooping roof, strengthened with concrete, pulls your attention down to the altar. The bare floor slopes to the same destination. No pillars or columns, no ornaments or memorials divert your eyes from the table of cut rock. The church's stillness is the stillness of an inner drama. St. Mary's is nowhere for Jehovah, the sky god: the eyes don't raise in awe. The lord of the starfields can be worshipped elsewhere. This place is sacred to the lord of the prairies, the god of the rolling earth.

A heavy concrete funnel hangs over the altar, hurling light downwards from the roof's obscurity. Smaller cobs illuminate the confessionals. Radical, intense, the effect has little in common with the shimmering play of radiance and shadow in a Gothic church, where the clerestory and the stained windows flood high walls with the Light of the World. In Red Deer the roof resists the sky. Standing in his circle of light, a priest appears to mediate between the private selves of his congregation, wrapped by the dark, undulating brickwork, and some great spirit of the plains.

On the day I saw the church, the baptistry held green plants around its red-brown walls. Even bodies who are baptized by water belong to the earth. St. Mary's, I thought, is the right dedication, for this is a church of the mother: the earth mother: the womb of life.

The building and the land make sense of each other. Cardinal's acceptance of the good earth suggested to me a peace that erases damnation, nullifying the terror of hell with the rootedness of love. I felt as though the cataclysmic mural that William Kurelek had painted in Saskatoon had its answer here. The building seems to heal deep stress. I valued it for another reason too: its mingling of white and Indian civilizations, states of spirit, approaches to transcendence. It embraces worshippers in something of the way that a sweat lodge embraces a warrior. Each of its bricks has been tried by fire.

St. Mary's is a body. Its structure, its proportions are organic and humane. It stands on a patch of prairie earth as though it were the prairie's dream made manifest, embodied in a sacred arc. Without

237

nostalgia or sentimentality, open to the cultures of the world but embedded in Alberta soil, St. Mary's bodies forth the pride, the aspirations, the latent power of the west.

It strengthened me for the trials ahead. I would call the church to mind in the days to come, when my faith in prairie culture was under siege.

·LIV·

What do you lack? What do you buy, pretty mistress? a fine hobby-horse, to make your son a tilter? a drum to make a soldier? a fiddle to make him a reveller? What is't you lack? Little dogs for your daughters? or babies, male or female?

—Ben Jonson, *Bartholomew Fair*

"Downtowns die," the driver told me with a shrug. "Once you lose that traditional Saturday shopper to the suburban plazas, it's hard to keep the downtown stores alive."

The man spends forty hours a week shuttling a white van between hotels and "The World's Largest Fashion and Fun Centre": the apogee of suburban plazas: the West Edmonton Mall. When his work is over, he drives back there for fun.

We approached the mall along roads that would, a few decades ago, have been prairie capillaries; a few years ago, veins of a tranquil suburb. Nowadays the roads flow to the shopping heart of western Canada. The mall is more than a civic resource; it is a regional phenomenon, the advance guard of the New West. From Saskatoon and

238

Yellowknife, Regina and Vancouver, chartered planes haul the affluent to wonder and consume. A quarter of the retail trade of Edmonton occurs within the mall's pale brick walls. Its main concourse of shops is more than a mile long.

"Doesn't look like much from here," I said.

"That's the way they want it," the driver answered. "No use in people standing outside, is there?"

Beyond the walls, life is uncontrollable. Storms and cold snaps flourish; terrorists maim and kill; unhappiness is epidemic; darkness ends the day. But in the mellow sanctuary of the mall, the world is under control. Entrances and exits are subdued, discreet; windows onto the city are nonexistent. Once inside the West Edmonton Mall, nobody is meant to look out, still less to think out.

In the engorged claims of its own publicity, the mall is "The Eighth Wonder of the World. Much more than a shopping centre, its [sic] a totally new experience in fashion, fun, and fantasy for the whole family!!!" Behind the ridiculous rhetoric lies a grain of truth: the four Ghermezian brothers, who conceived and created this dreamlike folly, have yoked together a shopping centre and an amusement park. Their gamble is that the glossy multitude of distractions will, in the end, magnify sales in the eight hundred stores. In the mall's terms, consumption and existence are synonymous: to be unable or unwilling to buy is to have no reason to live. Glazed with the joys of acquisition, buyers hand away their earnings with delight. They spend; therefore they are.

The brave new wealth of the complex is designed to dazzle. Devoid of litter and graffiti, West Edmonton Mall has nothing of the casual shoddiness of so many suburban plazas. The floors of its upper level don't just resemble marble; they *are* marble. If a fountain looks familiar, so it should: it replicates a water-spring that plays in front of the Sun King's palace at Versailles. The mall is a giant stage-set for the dramas of the dollar bill. Its unrootedness, its unearthly glamour suggest a system that might as well be functioning on Jupiter. The mall has conquered nature.

As proof, it gluts the eyes with birds. They live in glass-fronted aviaries the length and breadth of the building. The Ghermezians own three kinds of Asian pheasants (all of them in danger of extinc-

239

tion), breeding ibises, crowned cranes, flamingoes and a magnificent white peacock, his tail stretching out for yards behind his back. Whistles of macaws puncture the Muzak for a dozen stores around.

The birds restore to the mall a breath of wilderness. In an environment where everything else is artificial, they satisfy urban man's craving for a lost natural grace. The tropical fish perform the same task. Blue-faced angelfish, barred squirrelfish, the offensively named giant jewfish (a fat predator with protruding eyes, fond of lurking around wrecks)—these and many other shining specimens enliven the broad aisles between the Japan Camera Centre and the Filipino Gift Shop, Casablanca and the High Road to China. I was smitten by the tomato clownfish, which looks like a floating bowl of soup embellished by a blob of sour cream.

The fish and birds are all spectacular. West Edmonton Mall would have no interest in exhibiting dowdy creatures, small brown specimens of anything. The wild lives, like the fountains and the palm trees, exist here as a symbol of man's supreme authority and as a technicolour embodiment of his fantasies. "Permanent residents," the official brochure shrieks, "include . . . SHARKS!" The mall has a patronizing word for its captives: "Wempets."

The irony is that the same commercial lusts and pressures that nourish vast shopping centres are also destroying the natural habitat of ibises, flamingoes and giant jewfish. As Brazil uproots its Amazon forests—the lungs of the planet—to insert coffee plantations, the buyers of Brazilian coffee glance at the country's bright, diminishing birdlife behind a wall of glass. The mall embodies a culture of acquisition in which the end results of acquisition are concealed. Its shoppers use a never-ending present tense, devoid of prior causes and aftereffects. Even the mall's profit is less important than its image; or, more exactly, the profit depends on the image for its growth.

The secret of the mall's vast appeal is power: the power of man to subject the earth to his own desires. Those who lack power at home or work are especially fond of the place, for it allows them to exert an authority limited only by their bank balance and imagination. The Ghermezians understand the physical allure of spending. An impulsive purchase, like a shot of whisky or cocaine, brings instant gratification. The mall enfolds its visitors in a world that promises continual pleasure, a world where no one gives and everyone gets: a world, in short, that magnifies and justifies the illusions of early childhood.

Its colours are gaudy, its music jaunty. It offers nourishment and relaxation, stimulation and security. It releases its guests from the burdens of adult life. "Come spend," it says. "Come play. Have fun. Come buy." Strictly speaking, "Fantasyland" refers only to the organized amusements for the young. But in truth, the mall itself is a giant fantasy, an idyll of the credit card.

Adrift in such a world, you purchase happiness at will. A store with a red, glowing sign has the telltale name L'Amour. Not that it proffers sexual trinkets (superficially, the mall is sexless; its preferred mental age is about nine): L'Amour sells cards, mugs and tacky gifts. Other shops are called Fantasia, Enchanted Forest, Hollywood West.

I visited the mall a few months before its expansion into "Phase III," when the number of cinemas increased from eleven to thirty-four and Fantasyland inflated like a hot-air balloon. Even before the expansion, the mall boasted thirty gift shops and thirteen jewellers. Yet it contained only two drugstores and a single supermarket. The price of beans makes a poor partner for that rosy commodity, romance. West Edmonton Mall is a peddler of dreams, and until you walk away to the bus stop or the parking lot, your little life might never be rounded by hard facts.

What's the price of dreams on the Futures Exchange?

I wandered into Fantasyland. Its style suggests an updated Sergeant Pepper: a flashing fairground, fast and noisy, mingling archaism with high modernity. Most of its effects are simulated, most of its experiences unreal. The barrage of lights, noise and music does little to provoke a child's imagination; it aims to overwhelm. On the faces of the children at Fantasyland—playing pinball, emerging from the ferris wheel, stroking Wempets—I could detect no real joy. They betrayed instead a greed for more and more amusement, a hunger to be glutted by sensation. I have seen a similar expression on adults examining cheesecakes.

241

For a few minutes I stopped at Alladin's [*sic*] Amusement Arcade, a glittering array of video games. I glanced at M.A.C.H. 3 —the initials stand for Military Air Command Hunter—a machine that simulates the invasion of a foreign land. It promises three lives for two coins. A nearby teenager was absorbed in Missile Command, which turns nuclear war into a game. Launching his missiles from Omega Base, the boy gained points for intercepting bombers, missiles and killer satellites. The instructions said: "Defend the cities—play until all cities are gone."

All the cities went. The boy put his hands into his leather pockets and walked into Fantasyland. "And adults wonder," I thought, "why their kids don't believe in a future?"

A minute's stroll away lies Gourmet World, where I had a fast, cheap lunch. The cuisines of the planet compete here on a basis of microwaved equality: China Court, David's Deli, Taco Time and other alliterative bazaars. There is even a Korean Bar-B-Q for those who prefer Seoul food. It was apt, I thought, that Gourmet World should exist in the mall, for the man who invented the concept of the global village—Marshall McLuhan—was a native of Edmonton. (His father dealt in real estate.) At West Edmonton the global village has become a smorgasbord for the pleasure of North America.

I almost wrote: "America." In the mall it is sometimes hard to tell what region, even what country you are in. A bronze statue of oilmen is the sole reminder of productive labour among the toucans and boutiques; it also gives one of the few hints that the mall spreads across the Canadian west. Even the caged wildlife comes from somewhere, anywhere else. The publicity material alludes to Canada with a sneer: "Who has more submarines than the Canadian Navy? WEST EDMONTON MALL, of course." The press releases about Phase III are unequivocal about the mall's particular mimicry, the sources of its power: "you will be able to visit Disneyland, Malibu Beach, Epcot Park, the Houston Space Centre, Bourbon Street in New Orleans, Rodeo Drive, the Pebble Beach Golf Course, California's Sea World, the San Diego Zoo, and the Grand Canyon's white water raft rides." It seems untypically modest, not to say honest, that the publicity fails to promise the Grand Canyon. The language, like the mall, bullies; it seeks to pummel doubt into an abashed submission.

If the building reflects local desire, then part of that desire is to forget where life is taking place. West Edmonton is a homage to the American dream, the American way of spending. Perhaps it takes a family of immigrants (the Ghermezians come from Iran) to compile so devoted an image of America's fortune.

The mall's confidence is brazen, imperial. It is also the antithesis of prairie co-operation. Shoppers here rarely speak to one another. In the men's wear department of Sears I made a nonchalant remark to a stranger; he looked at me with dismay and bafflement, and quickly moved elsewhere. The crowds in the marble aisles form no real community. They share nothing but a drive to experience and (if possible) acquire for themselves. What you are, in the mall, is immaterial. All that matters is what you have, and what you desire to have.

Only once did I feel a glimmering of fellowship: in front of a glass cage that contained a pair of young Siberian tigers. Three and a half months old, weighing little more than cats, the tigers bounced and scrambled with a kittenish mischief. They had lived at the mall for less than two weeks. The young, the old and the middle-aged watched the mock fights and fierce caresses with evident wonder. Their eyes were innocent. The tigers were not for sale.

Just beyond the cage was an ice rink. Heedless of the tigers and the professional shoppers, a skater in a brown sweater glided and span. The Edmonton Oilers were nowhere in evidence; nor, to my relief, was the two-year-old chimpanzee who had fallen into the mall's tender mercies. He was doomed to spend the summer learning to skate and stickhandle, so that by the fall's training camp he could face off against Wayne Gretzky. "Watch for the WEMPETS soon to be introduced at West Edmonton Mall."

By rights, Edmonton is too small a city to support so grand a folly. When the Earl of Southesk passed this way in 1859, it consisted of little more than a fort by the North Saskatchewan River. The fort no longer exists, nor do most of the city's other historic buildings. Although in the oil boom of the 1970s Edmonton's pop-

243

ulation caromed to more than 600,000, its citizens still appear to suffer the old prairie fear of insignificance. Many feel that the development has "put the city on the map." So what if the central core has withered?

There are other reasons for the mall's popularity. For one thing, it offers a climate-controlled respite from Edmonton's March blizzards or deep-frozen Octobers. No matter what the weather, the province's traditions are those of free enterprise, which the mall glorifies. It has provided Albertans not only with something to enjoy; it has given them something to believe in. In addition to its many other functions, the West Edmonton Mall is a shrine.

I discovered an exit and took the shuttle van back to my hotel.

"So what did you think of the place?" the driver asked.

"Amazing," I replied truthfully.

"Isn't it great?" he said.

I let that one pass without comment. Next morning I drove into downtown Edmonton, an area that should and still could be beautiful. I parked below an office tower and took an elevator to the capital of the strange empire: the head offices of Triple Five Corporation.

"The boys live and breathe the business," explained Triple Five's director of public affairs, Deane Eldredge. Her office, stuffed with orchids, overlooks the Alberta Legislature. "The boys are not responsible to any board of directors. One day they make a decision and the next, it's implemented."

The jargon of business schools—"a fast-track company," "the bottom line," "a hands-on organization"—clogged her tongue.

"Do the Ghermezians intend to expand the mall even further?"

"Well," she confided, "the boys are talking about Phase IV. But they're very secretive about what it will be."

The mall is not the brothers' only development in Alberta. They also control hotels, office towers, an arena, a nightclub, apartment blocks, two shopping malls of normal dimensions, and some fifteen thousand acres of Calgary and Edmonton. Rumours abound of their desire to change the face of British Columbia, Minnesota, Illinois, Ontario, New York and Quebec.

"Are there plans for developments elsewhere?" I asked.

244

"Yes, there are. But the boys don't like to talk about that. You remember in Burnaby, there was so much local resistance that we pulled out. We've learned to be a little quieter now until our projects are well advanced. Then, even if there is public opposition, it can't affect our plans."

Her scarlet lipstick beamed. I remembered a couple of sentences from Edward Abbey's *Desert Solitaire:* "Growth for the sake of growth is a cancerous madness . . . an economic system which can only expand or expire must be false to all that is human."

"There has been a lot of interest in the mall," she added, "all the way from Japan and Europe."

"Why?"

"Because there's nothing else! The nearest man-made attraction is Vancouver, and we're becoming a sidetrip for tourists to Vancouver. East of the Pacific, there's no competition: we *are* the attraction."

So much, I thought, for a century of white civilization across the prairie west.

"We're the first mall in the world, both in gross space and gross leasable space."

I rose to go. On my way out, I bumped into an unobtrusive, middle-aged man with a small moustache and sparse dark hair. He bore an odd similarity to Groucho Marx.

"Oh, Nader," Deane Eldredge called from behind me. "This is Mr. Abley. Mr. Abley, meet Nader Ghermezian."

Could this really be the man who had informed the *Globe and Mail* that the West Edmonton Mall was "the world's largest and most complete tourist attraction in the universe"?

"Pleased to meet you," I said.

"Mr. Abley," Deane Eldredge hurriedly explained, "is writing a book about the west and its financial institutions."

I looked surprised. Nader said: "Good, good," and ducked into the nearest office.

245

·LV·

I fled. I manoeuvred through the suburbs, found the Yellowhead Highway and rode it eastward towards Saskatchewan. I was in a kind of grief: that the prairies should have come to this! "Even if there is public opposition, it can't affect our plans." For the first time in my life I passed through a national park not only failing to stop in it but also failing to look at it. I halted for lunch at an old hotel in Vegreville, a sweet town watched over by an aluminum Easter egg. The Ukrainian meal was delicious; the Ukrainian language rolled gently from a table where middle-aged couples gossipped; but when a young mother arrived with a child who was dressed in a white embroidered blouse, a flowered skirt and a red scarf, her costume looked unreal.

It was too soon after West Edmonton. My mind needed time to recover. Such was the seductive force of the mall that the girl's costume seemed a prize exhibit in some ethnic boutique. *What do you lack? What do you buy, pretty mistress?* I regained the driver's seat and drove some more.

The road passed through a green, rounded countryside with no abruptness of mountains or vista of great horizons. Spidery black-and-red machines pumped oil from a few of the fields. After an hour I felt tired again. My eyes had grown debauched: after so much experience they were demanding something miraculous, a landscape bursting with sensation, to make them see afresh. I pulled in at the Vermilion Provincial Park and rested my eyes. When I opened them, three black butterflies skimmed above the picnic tables in a gathering wind. But the notice-boards were plastered with invitations: "Come and share the riches of days gone by as we meet Vera and Vernon Vermilion out on the veranda." It was enough to impel me away.

I stopped for the night at Lloydminster, an unattractive little city bisected by the meridian of longitude that acts as the provincial border. The big green elevator of the Alberta Pool rises west of the meridian, and a pair of white Saskatchewan elevators stand just east

246

of the line. My hotel leaned a few steps into Alberta. By taking a deep breath inside my room, rushing down the stairs and over the road, I could make it to Saskatchewan before I breathed again. The meridian acquires the name 50th Avenue in Lloydminster, where the Yellowhead Highway becomes 44th Street. But 1st Avenue and 1st Street do not exist. Red Deer, Rocky Mountain House and many other Alberta communities share that affectation: that fear of being small. It is as though the incongruous numbers of the streets provide a reassurance, a mathematical comfort that the place will not fly away in a wind or dwindle to a glade of ghosts.

Friday night, and the boys were out in their pickup trucks and their souped-up cars. The oil-rig workers and the Indians had come to town, hoping for fun. As I strolled down a side road, the wind produced a torrent of dust and the sky emitted a trickle of heavy water. Only on the prairies do you have to battle the dust and the rain at once. The driver of a black station wagon hit the accelerator when a Chevrolet turned across his path, coming within a quarter-second of a thrilling accident. Cars cruised the streets, there being nowhere else for them to cruise. No doubt some of the drivers were dreaming of West Edmonton. I was expecting a nightmare. But instead, I dreamt of home.

·LVI·

Rain dripped again on the following morning while I visited the Fuchs Wildlife Display and the Imhoff Art Gallery, which rub shoulders in a civic park on the Saskatchewan edge of town. I walked quickly round the conventional trophies that Nick Fuchs had assembled over the decades. Fuchs was an American who came to Saskatchewan as a boy and worked in the north as a trapper, hunter and big-game guide for forty years. He taught himself taxidermy by correspondence, gaining just enough skill to turn his private passion for stuffed animals into a public exhibition. What drew my reluctant gaze were his unconventional items: the animal freaks.

The Siamese calves, balancing uncertainly on two front legs and four hind limbs. The double-headed calf, whose four-eyed faces gape out of a wall. The monstrously deformed calf, born without a nose and with a single Cyclops eye above its distorted mouth. There were other young animals so misshapen, so hurt, that I looked away in fear.

What is it in the human mind that makes it treasure such pain? But Fuchs was not only the collector of deformity; he was also the creator of Bunnyland. Its taste, its sensibility are so atrocious that they verge on the sublime.

In front of a painted backdrop of gnomes, four rabbits in coloured waistcoats are playing cards at a tiny table. One of them holds a cigarette, another has a little mug of beer. A rabbit in a purple dress, meanwhile, parades below a florid parasol. She is, no doubt, the wife of the big white rabbit with a bow tie and pipe who pushes a wicker basket on wheels; inside the basket, a baby rabbit clutches a milk bottle. Easter must be coming, for an old Ukrainian rabbit in pink spectacles is decorating eggs.

And the band plays on. A white rabbit holds a toy trumpet; his brown cousin plays an accordion. In the centre of Bunnyland, spellbound by the heavenly music, two white rabbits are up on their hind legs, dancing cheek to cheek, naked as the day they were born. Their nudity seems obscurely shocking.

A stuffed monkey on a swing surveys the melancholy scene. For some unfathomable reason, an ostrich egg lies at the front of the display. And the thought hit me: *It ain't the West Edmonton Mall!* A second thought was more worrying: *Is this what I was missing at the mall—a display of the raw west? A lovingly chosen gallery of grotesques, where the taxidermist and the doll-maker join forces to couple the "cute" with the "weird"?*

248

Then there was Berthold von Imhoff. I began by feeling amused. Nick Fuchs had done well to choose the German count for his father-in-law, as the two men shared a delight in perished wildlife. A pamphlet about the count describes the building in Lloydminster as "one of North America's most unique Art Galleries." It goes on to praise the beauty of Imhoff's native Rhineland and the solemnity of "the master" 's work. Nowhere does it so much as hint that Imhoff was an artist of abysmal, grisly quality. If there have been painters as terrible, none has been so prolific. If there have been painters as prolific, none has been so terrible.

Partly it is his complete lack of originality: many of the canvases that cram these rooms from ceiling to floor are (more or less inept) copies of European work from the past. Partly it is his appalling sense of colour: in one canvas of Yellowstone Park, salmon-pink mountains jostle a lemon sky as though they belong together in some jellied salad. Partly it is his shaky grasp of form and perspective: the way that in almost every landscape the painter felt a need to fill the foreground with a moose loitering in water. And partly, too, it is his inability to evoke movement. Nothing breathes in an Imhoff canvas, whether or not it is meant to be dead.

The man had a terrifying persistence. His gallery displays, side by side, four attempts at the same hunting scene: a bouquet of dead rabbits, dead ducks, dead sandpipers and dead vegetation. From canvas to canvas there are minor changes, but no improvements. The paintings hang by their hundreds in oily profusion and no apparent order, so that a portrait of a moose might be flanked on one side by a yearning Virgin and on the other by "The Victory of Prince Eugen Over the Turks, 1686." Of all Imhoff's subjects, only the Mona Lisa and a Prussian general's horse have smiles on their faces.

His life fell into three periods: twenty-four years in Germany, twenty-two in the eastern U.S.A., and the final twenty-five in Saskatchewan. Yet unlike Stephan G. Stephansson, he made no effort to reconcile the Old and New Worlds. Were it not for some Rocky Mountain extravaganzas and his much-loved moose, Imhoff could have been painting in Europe. There, of course, his art would not have won such praise, and his murals would not have adorned so many churches. In Saskatchewan the count failed to attract the articulate, responsible criticism that might have spurred him into competence.

I began by feeling amused at his massive, inert art, and I ended by feeling horrified. Imhoff's work does not disgust an onlooker, as do the slaughtered victims of his son-in-law, but to my mind it is more subtly, more deeply offensive. Imhoff lost feeling on the prairies; he lost touch. His proud gallery is a defeat, a humiliation: the pathetic record of a man who squandered his early promise on a crowd-pleasing visual rhetoric that bore no relation to real imagination.

But the crowds were pleased. They still are. Imhoff's department-store brand of landscape (mountains and forests, water and an antlered animal) no doubt delights more spectators than the work of contemporary painters who have developed artful, original ways of interpreting western land and sky. With Imhoff, you know exactly what to expect. Though he fed on the naiveté of prairie dwellers, the count never allowed the prairie to enter his state of mind.

I am being unfair, of course. I have to be unfair. Imhoff represents everything I was escaping when I left the west, just as Fuchs perhaps represents much of what my home had been a refuge from: the stupidity that slides so easily into cruelty, the pretension that can puff itself to blindness. The worst of Europe and the worst of America, marrying to make a big complacent family, with their work cherished as "one of the outstanding tourist attractions of Saskatchewan's northwest."

I was still recovering from the shock of the mall. But my dislike of West Edmonton's vicious glamour afforded no good reason to sentimentalize an older west. Imhoff's art deserves to be condemned; he was a prisoner of a dated vision and a paralyzed style, and he battened on their proceeds. If I had seen his gallery ten years ago, I would probably have called it typical. Never having searched out the places or the people of imagination in the prairie west, I feared that its culture was, by definition, derivative.

I knew better now, at last. I had seen alternatives. I had tried to open my eyes.

250

·LVII·

Southeast of Lloydminster the wind began to cry. Yelping, whistling, treacherously murmuring, it toyed with the car. The weather's dangerous moodiness suited me. I had spent so much time on the road that I was starting to feel on the run. Travel books seldom mention the traveller's occupational hazards: anxiety, loneliness, fatigue. I was suffering from them all. Near the end of any long journey, the land in view and the place to come both start to seem unreal. The circle was closing. I was only two days from Saskatoon, the end of all my driving, and three days from Montreal. It was growing hard for me to look at the west without glimpsing other images that coalesced into a screen between my optic nerve and the road.

The summer grass, grown tall in the ditches, lunged against the wind like a free animal. My wandering attention scurried back; the screen of fantasies and memories dissolved. I passed seven bay horses in a field, one of them dipping his head to drink from a rippling slough in the sun. As the land smoothed out, the sky hesitated between rich blue and a richer, menacing blue-black. Near the valley of the North Saskatchewan the rising, unfenced wheat made an ocean of prairie waves combed by the air.

In travelling, everything depends on the mood of the beholder. When he first saw the river, the Earl of Southesk loved it: its banks reminded him of a British park, "luxuriantly clothed with wood, disposed by nature in groups and gladed masses." Then his men tried to row him down the river in *The Golden Era*. An early freeze-up stranded the party east of Edmonton, and Southesk promptly found the landscape dreary. The gladed masses turned to bruises. Waiting to be rescued, he plodded through Shakespeare's *Henry VI* and meditated on the duty of poets to keep their facts straight: for "where one man reads history a hundred read poetry."

This is still true, rumour has it, in Somalia and Iraq. It is not the case in North Battleford, where I checked into an unpoetic motel and took a long shower. My room overlooked a chokecherry bush and a confederation of weeds. When I was dry and dressed again, I phoned. "Nope, you won't find Negroes round here anymore," a woman had told me in Lloydminster. "Talk to Murray Mayes in North Battleford."

"Sure," he said, "come on over."

He was living in an anonymous, low apartment building on the outskirts of town: a balding man near the far limits of middle age, wearing spotless overalls.

"There's the ball," he said, gesturing at his coffee table. Sunlight glinted off his metal-rimmed glasses.

"?"

"When Rueben broke the record."

"?"

"The national record for yards gained!"

It took a minute to clear the misunderstanding. Murray thought I wanted to discuss the exploits of his son, a football hero at an American university. But I was hoping to hear about his forebears —some of the most unlikely settlers in the entire Canadian west.

Murray's grandparents were slaves. They settled freely in Oklahoma after the Civil War. But when the territory at last became a state, black people endured a chain of fresh humiliations. Many of them elected to leave their homes in search of a new promised land. Some tried their luck in Mexico; others took up the offer of virgin soil in Canada's west. In all, more than a thousand Oklahoma blacks gained shelter in the young provinces of Saskatchewan and Alberta.

Their welcome was far from unanimous. The Boards of Trade in Edmonton, Calgary, Saskatoon and Winnipeg demanded an end to the migration. In the House of Commons a Conservative MP asked whether it would not be desirable for the government "to preserve for the sons of Canada the lands they propose to give to niggers." Finally the government agreed.

By then, however, Mattie Mayes and her husband Joe—a Baptist preacher as well as a farmer—had led a party of forty-two families from Tulsa to North Battleford. They homesteaded on plots of land between Big Gully and the North Saskatchewan River. Soon they built a log church and called it Shiloh: a holy city in Judea and a

252

battle in the Civil War. They became the Shiloh people.

But the land was poor: light, bushy, stony. The poverty was extreme. Shiloh brought its people peace and respect; it took the Second World War to bring them money. The allure of steady jobs with the railway, the army or the factories made most of the blacks leave. Their church fell into disuse. In 1953 Mattie Mayes, who had toiled as a slave, died in an Edmonton hospital at the age of 104. Murray, one of her many grandchildren, was already a mechanic in North Battleford. He acquired a body shop.

A few years ago the shop fell into debt, and his Ontario bank pounced. "Sometimes," Murray confided, "a man will make his plans. And it's like there's another hand that's guiding him. Now I recall the story of Job. Perhaps you know it? He was the wealthiest man in the East and he lost everything in a day. A single day! At the end of the story, it says that he gained back all his property twice over. So where he started with five hundred camels, after all his troubles he had a thousand.

"Now I'm not looking to double my assets. But I know—I know! —that I'll regain everything I had. The way I look at it, I haven't lost *nothing*."

A photograph of Rueben clutching a trophy furnished an otherwise naked wall. As the late sunlight poured into the room, the athlete basked in a stripe of light. Yet despite his son's fortune south of the border, Murray Mayes felt rooted in Saskatchewan: "An atomic bomb's the only thing that'll make me move!" If he was free of nostalgia for a golden era, he was free of bitterness too.

The next day dawned wild and changeable. Puddles in the motel parking lot reflected clouds on the move above. A crow flapped slowly over the North Saskatchewan as I shivered out of town. The quirks of prairie weather had made June colder than May. Oblivious to rain, a line of big-wheeled tractors and harvesters confronted the road. Dwarfing the dealer's shed, they looked as mean as tanks. A battalion might control Saskatchewan, if anybody could afford to buy them.

I drove west for the last time to the little town of Maidstone. The railway line was even quieter than the adjacent highway. I coincided with the hailstones at a gas pump.

253

"Shiloh, eh?" the young attendant said. "In this weather? Why don't you look up Carl Schmidt first?"

I found him in a bright house in Maidstone: a grey, paunched man examining the instructions on a package of herbicide.

"Hell," he said with satisfaction. I was standing on the mat inside his back door, shaking myself dry. "I guess I used this stuff all wrong. Didn't get round to reading the label till now."

"What's it supposed to do for you?"

"Get rid of the wild oats. Maybe it'll get rid of my rapeseed too!"

He chortled with delight.

I should have waited in the car two minutes longer, for the rattle of hail died away in a sudden armistice and the sun poured over the town. Carl's lawn glistened in moist light.

"So how do I get to Shiloh?"

Instead of answering, he shook his head.

"I used to go into that church sometimes just to hear those coloured girls sing!"

"I guess they didn't have a lot of money."

"Sure, they were poor. But that didn't stop their dancing. Negro folks would come all the way from Edmonton just to get to one of their dances."

"And now there's nobody left."

"That's Saskatchewan for you!"

Then he told me the exact directions. A rainbow was binding Maidstone to the sky as I closed Carl's door. He lumbered after me to sniff the air.

"Look out for the big spruces," he said through the driver's window. "I can remember Mrs. Bailey coming past our farm with the trees in her cart. They're a memorial to her husband, eh? She went all the way to the river to get them."

Even though I followed his instructions to the letter, I almost drove past the church. Paradise Hill shines to the northwest, Livelong lies over a horizon, but Shiloh huddles into low brushland beside a rock-strewn field. I unlatched the gate.

And the men arose, and went away: and Joshua charged them that went to describe the land, saying, Go and walk through the land,

254

and describe it, and come again to me, that I may here cast lots for you before the Lord in Shiloh.

The church has no paint, no ornament. Its plain glass windows tilt. Cracks in the dovetailed logs allow the wind to hiss. The pulpit and the bell have vanished. All that lingers are two rows of benches, a table at the front and a small, framed photograph of Mattie Mayes.

Shiloh faces west, not the traditional east. West in the teeth of the prevailing wind: west towards the falling sun: west for the people's long migration in quest of home and land.

I stepped out through the western door into the grassy cemetery. Fifty bodies lie buried underneath the wild roses and the larkspur. In the 1920s and '30s the Shiloh people, unable to buy headstones, marked the graves by Ice Age boulders. The fieldstones are visitants from another epoch, another space of time. Like petroglyphs, they preserve a memory. Above the boulders in a corner of the cemetery, two spruces scrape the sky.

The grass, in need of mowing, soaked my shoes and socks. Barn swallows skimmed and wheeled above Julius Caesar Lane, Anderson Cotton, Honey Robinson and the others. And I remembered the words of Murray Mayes: "I grew up in a sod house. When it rained, the roof would leak for days. I tell you, until I was twenty-five I was afraid of rain! We was too poor to even own a horse. And yet—" his voice glowing "—we owned the land. The land was ours."

"Freedom" is too easy a word for what Murray's people gained on the prairies. At Shiloh they were never free from destitution and disease. But they found an opportunity to make their peace with the past, and they took the chance to contrive a future. In that sense, the land fulfilled its promise. It let the people go.

Their history of struggle made these worn logs, wet flowers and spruce trees sweet to my eyes. Unlike my first Shilo of the plains, they suggested a reconciliation. For if Imhoff's gallery was the little west I had scorned years ago, Shiloh was the larger west I never knew: a place of dignity and human grace. A site of bitter love.

And the whole congregation of the children of Israel assembled together at Shiloh, and set up the tabernacle of the congregation there. And the land was subdued before them.

Perhaps the only west I could fit wore the contours of silence. No matter: the land clung to my mind. I knew now: it was writing me.

Aysin'eep

Index

257

258

DATE DUE

BRODART

Cat. No. 23-221

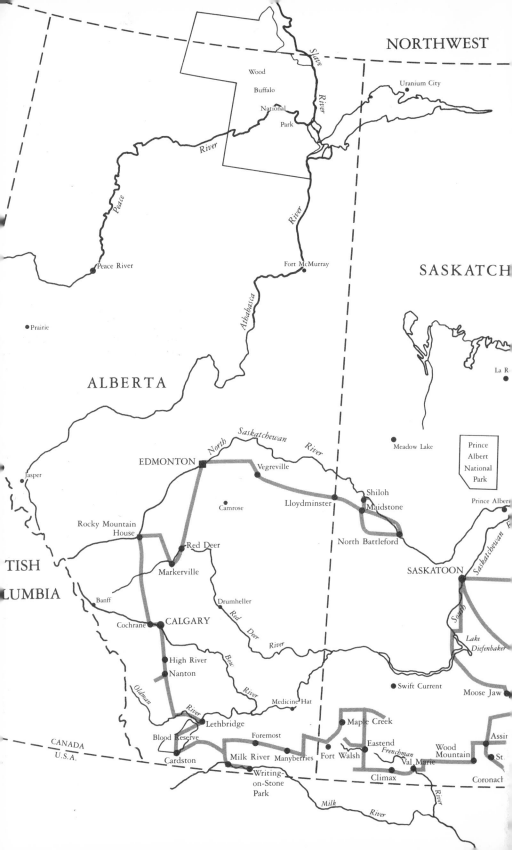